ma River

WILCOX COUNTY

Mobile

Gulf Shores

A T L A N T I C   O C E A N

Panama City

Apalachicola

Tallahassee

St. Marks

Aucilla R.

Perry

Steinhatchee R.

Steinhatchee

Crystal River

Tarpon Springs

Tampa

Sarasota

Fort Myers

Marco Island

Goodland

Miami

M E X I C O

DRY TORTUGAS

MARQUESAS

Key West

Islamorada

Tavernier

ALONG
THE EDGE OF
AMERICA

Other Books by Peter Jenkins

A Walk Across America
The Walk West
The Road Unseen
The Tennessee Sampler (with friends)
Across China
Close Friends

Peter Jenkins

ALONG THE EDGE OF AMERICA

RUTLEDGE HILL PRESS

Nashville, Tennessee

Published in Nashville, Tennessee, by Rutledge Hill Press, 211 Seventh Avenue North, Nashville, Tennessee 37219.

Typography by D&T/Bailey Typography, Nashville, Tennessee.

Library of Congress Cataloging-in-Publication Data

Jenkins, Peter, 1951–
    Along the edge of America / Peter Jenkins.
      p.   cm.
    ISBN 1-55853-327-3
    1. Gulf Coast (U.S.)—Description and travel. 2. Boats and boating—Gulf Coast (U.S.) 3. Jenkins, Peter, 1951– —Journeys—Gulf Coast (U.S.) I. Title.
F296.J46   1995
917.6'00946—dc20

                                                    95-2676
                                                     CIP

Printed in the United States of America.

1 2 3 4 5 6 7 8 9—99 98 97 96 95

To Rita

CONTENTS

ACKNOWLEDGMENTS

There are certain times during the varied cycles of life when family and friends mean even more than ever. For me these times are during the hard times and the great times.

I express my love and deepest appreciation to my great family. Thanks for everything, Frederick Jenkins (Dad), Mary Jenkins (Mom), Winky and Randy Rice, Scott and Bonnie Jenkins, Fred and Colleen Jenkins, Betsy Jenkins, and Abby Jenkins. (You too, Brendan.) Plus Alex, Jesse, and Tyler Rice; Isaiah, Andrew, Seathan, and Katrina Jenkins; Molly, Sarah, Derick, and Colin Jenkins; and Rhoda Jenkins.

And the same goes to my extra-fine in-laws, Jerry Jorgensen (Dad), Dorothy Jorgensen (Mom), Val and Kevin Karikomi, Le and Mike Turner, Eric Jorgensen (you too, Michelle), Aaron Jorgensen, and Chris Jorgensen. Plus Matthew, Michael, David, and Daniel Karikomi; John, Michael, and Scott Turner; Tami, Kari, Rachel Coates-Jorgensen, and Derik Jorgensen; Gena, Julie, JJ, Cory Bo Jorgensen; and Inez Keith.

During my hard times I found out just who my true friends are, and I'd like to pay tribute to them here. Thanks to Skip Yowell, Pat Golbitz, David Andrews, Bill and Mary Lucy Fuqua, Sam and Lucy Kuykendall, Craig McAllister, Jess and Mary Lou Morton, Paul Uhrig and Diana Rae, Gary and Jean Wysocki, Steve Boyle, Lamar and Honey Alexander, Ernie and Betty Pennell, John and Patti Thompson, and Robert and Evelyn George. A special, special thanks to Glenda Andrews, who not only worked for me faithfully for several years, but who gives the word *friend* special meaning.

I give credit to two talented editors who worked on this book with me. Thank you very much, Pat Golbitz. Thank you very much, Anne Buchanan. Also thanks to Barbara Morgan for her insightful advice.

Thank you, Paul Breeden, for your fine illustrated maps. We've been working together for twenty years, and I appreciate your friendship and your gifts.

Special appreciation to Tom Smith, who was my mentor while I walked across America. What you taught me then means even more now.

[9]

Thanks for the party of destiny, friends Dave and Janet Thomas, where we met Jackson and Rosemary Brown.

I'm glad to have Rutledge Hill Press as my new publisher. It is the kind of place that understands and appreciates the people and places I write about, and it is also the type of place where everyone rolls up their sleeves and gets the job done and done well. I would like to thank the following: head man Larry Stone, a special thanks to you and to Ron Pitkin, Tracey Menges, Julie Jayne, Bryan Curtis, Natasha Mink, Bill Jayne, Jennifer Greenstein, Adrian Booy, Kath Hansen, Linda Adams, Alice Ewing, Jack Moore, Christine Taylor, Amy Wilson, Mary Ann McNeese, Orval Grieser, Sabrina Cashwell, Whitney Wells, Dabney Hopkirk, Jaime Bernardez, Albert Lebouef, Heather Pomfret, Julie Dupree, Rena Conley, Melissa Gray, Tracy Ford, Julie Pitkin, Norwanda Prince, James Newsom, Ed Curtis, Keri Downing, Gay Sparks, Lisa Adams, Michelle Vahldiek, Valerie Jackson, Jonah Calcutt, Wes McBride, Ken Russell, Larry Bilbrey, Eddie Saverance, and Detrick Smith.

When I take a trip like this, there are so many people who offer their assistance and deserve my thanks. I have to list them by state and I wish I could add each generous, compassionate thing they did.

Florida: Bill and Allison Fahrer, Larry Dukehart, Kenny Hildebrant, Denver and Joyce Fleming, Ideal Fish Camp, Tony and Colleen Hammon, especially Trent, Gary Weeks, Jess VanDyke, Mona Ives, Gene and Sue Killinger.

Alabama: Guy McCullough, Judy Anthony, Harriet Norville, Tom Mason, Melissa Bowden, Leo Hollinger, Jennifer Robinson, James Bonner, Laura Furman, John Furman, Jandy Hanks.

Louisiana: My Louisiana family: George, Jackie, and Jimmy Dantin; the Crescent River Pilots Association; the Bar Pilots Association; Doug Lipka; Jerry Wise; Charlie Hebert.

Texas: My Texas home: Joe and Annette Whitehead, Bernice Whitehead, Kathy Yarborough, Tom Martin.

Special thanks to the advance readers and critics of this book: Carol Hester and Jennifer Roark.

Special thanks to my team of B.A. students and teacher, who gave me some good feedback: Calvert Gentry, Helen Andrews, Nicole Marston, David Bowers, Michele Haggard, and Brenda Evans.

Dick and Lynn Estell, a big thanks for the hand-held compass. It saved us!

Especially grateful thanks to those who assisted me with the tools I needed to survive this long adventure, especially my main man, Frank Longino of Grady-White Boats, and Eddie Smith of Grady-White also.

Thanks to Yamaha Outboards; Mike Mitchell and Raytheon Electronics; Mack and Bee McKinney, Mike and Lee McKinney, and Randy Rice and askSam Systems; Russ Setzekorn and Compaq Computers; Skip Yowell and Paul Delorey and JanSport; Shimano; and Achilles Boats.

To our dear friend in Germany, Sabine Rachowka. To the great church we go to, Christ Community Church, which did much to restore my faith. Thank you, Scotty and Darlene Smith, Scott Roley, and Mike Smith. Thanks to our good neighbors: Ray, Cindy, and Tiffany Williams; Buzz, June, and Billy Morton; and Bess Luther.

And special appreciation goes to other people from all over the United States. Thanks, Rusty and Nona Jones, Bill and Camille Morris, Harold McIlwain, Betty Sain, Jerry Kennedy, Lucinda Dyer, Kathy Gangwisch, Winne Kingsberry, and Jill Hamilton.

To Rita, the deepest and most appreciated thanks for your real love. It is a challenging but rewarding job to blend a family together that has six intelligent, talented, and very individualistic children. I want to tell all of you that I love you and, as time passes, I enjoy each of you and all of us together more and more. God continue to bless each of you, Julianne, Luke, Jed, Rebekah, Brooke, and Aaron. May each of you find your own exciting and special way through our great world with much happiness and as little pain as possible.

ALONG THE EDGE OF AMERICA

Blasting into the Darkness

A hundred miles of traveling on the water, and I was ready for rest.

Apparently my teacher was, too. With the calm I had come to respect and rely on, Warren Norville steered the *Cooper* into the end of a peaceful-looking bay.

It surprised me that two men, Warren and I, could live together in a space that before I would have considered suffocating, like a prison cell. But on my boat the views were almost always wide and free of clutter. Right now the sun had entered the sea and was tinting the bay a clear pink. The beautiful sand of the barrier island that shielded us from the rowdy waves of the Gulf beyond was a tranquilizing deep yellow-pink. The wind was sweet and heavy—unbelievably warm for January. I looked south to see pelicans gliding to the places they spent the night. It was that caressing time between daytime and nighttime, and every living thing seemed to be preparing for rest.

After a few days with Warren on this boat, I was beginning to know the drill. It was that time of day to find a still, protected place to throw out our anchor. Warren would circle this little bay as slowly as the *Cooper* would go, feeling the winds, deciding when to tell me to drop the anchor. Then the day would be over and the evening would begin.

Warren had promised to fire up the boat's tiny alcohol-powered stove and make a gourmet meal of fresh shrimp, heavy spice, and rice. Warren would have his nightly wine, and we'd tell stories. And then it would be time for deep sleep. I thought about how good it would feel to lie in my V-shaped bunk down below, filled with Warren's food, covered only with the blue sheets I had brought from home. The darkness was deepening, and I looked forward already to the soothing night breezes that would create small waves and rock me to sleep.

The voice on the marine radio droned monotonously as I moved toward the bow where the anchor was stored. Warren liked to keep an ear out to the weather reports. As I passed the cabin, I could see him cock his head toward the radio to hear better, then reach over to turn it up. His sailor's beard was white and neatly trimmed at a natty slant, projecting both wisdom and daring. His unlined face caught the last purple-pink light of our soon-to-be-tranquil night. Had he not chosen to marry and have three children, this was the sort of man who could have spent his life circling the globe in an oceangoing sailboat. Now Warren sped up a bit, stopped circling, and appeared to be heading for a channel between two islands. All right, I whispered to myself, he knows a more protected place to anchor. But we need to stop soon; I can barely see a thing.

And then, with no warning, Warren let loose a howl, a growl of glee as he pushed down the chrome lever that sent fuel to the two huge engines behind us. With a startling roar the *Cooper* blasted across the quiet bay waters, between the islands, and out into the endless dark of the Gulf.

What's wrong with you? I wanted to shout over the engine noise and Warren's shriek of joy.

I should have asked myself the same question.

Warren Norville, retired naval commander, author of celestial navigation books, husband of "what's-her-name," sailboat fanatic, and my "Boating 101" teacher.

CHAPTER 1

When the
Dancing
Stopped

I 'd been feeling invincible for so
many years that a crash was
inevitable.

I'd been strutting here and there and all over, and it seemed that
everything was going right for me.

Maybe that's why it hit me so hard when things went desperately
wrong.

I had been a late bloomer. The normal period for the cool-guy strut—high
school—passed me by. I was potently insecure in high school—my skin was
bad, we lived in a federal housing project, I wasn't an athlete or a brainiac.
Sure, I could dance better than any other white boy in my hometown, but
how many dances could there be? Besides, I sweated when I danced, and
how many girls would want to get close to sweat-soaked me? I was also
pretty quick with flippant comebacks, but that was more a self-defense
mechanism than anything else. Being witty didn't make me confident, at
least not in high school.

College was where my self-assurance started to bloom. As an art student I found I could get positive attention from my professors. I seemed to
have a talent for sculpture, an ability to create objects that had some origi-
nality to them.

I still had no money, but in the small town where my college was,
nobody seemed to have much more money than me. If they did, they
didn't reveal it. The fashion and politics of the time helped me out, too. In

the late sixties and early seventies, cheap was in. Everybody I knew dressed in frayed jeans, farmer's overalls, flannel shirts, and hiking boots. My two-hundred-dollar '64 Chevy Impala was considered cool. No college kid even imagined driving a BMW or other high-priced new car then. It would have been decadent, connected to the industrialist elites. They, the rich, were supposed to be the enemy.

In college people called me P.J. instead of Peter. I guess I wanted to change my identity some, begin again. I stood alone at college. It was just me that people saw, not all six of the Jenkins kids and my parents. I loved it. And I could still dance better than anybody I knew.

Then I stretched way out. Instead of going off to graduate school—and, a shock to me, I found I could have gone to some really good ones—I decided to walk across America. Alone on the walk with my beloved dog, Cooper, I gained an inner strength, a confidence that I could survive on my own anywhere—in the woods, blinded by a brutal blizzard, confronted by a violent, escaped convict. I was exposed to different—radically different—people that at one time I would have mocked, feared, run from. But I learned so much from these unlikely people, and many became my friends.

As word of my walk spread, people began asking my opinions, asking me to speak to them from my "acquired wisdom." I was asked to write for famous magazines, then offered huge amounts of money to write for famous New York publishers. Then the articles became widely known, the books became bestsellers, and famous television shows invited me to share my experiences onscreen.

And then came the strut, the confidence, the newfound wealth. If I wanted something I bought it. Having grown up poor and having always been turned off to "outrageous" materialism—and absolutely hating to shop—I didn't buy all that much. But I never worried about paying my bills; the money was always there. I'd pay off my credit cards every month, no matter how much the total. In fact, I hired people to take care of all the distasteful stuff—paying bills, filing my taxes, answering phones, dealing with interruptions. Slowly I became more and more cut off.

I was married to Barbara then, and most people assumed we had a great relationship. We had three beautiful, spunky, each-so-different children, and we lived on a 190-acre farm with green hills that rolled like dark green silk blowing in the wind. Our home, more like a mansion, had taken more than a year to build, with its massive oak beams, its twelve-foot, custom stained-glass window, its walnut floors and cherry paneling and state-of-the-art appliances—even a trash compacter. (That trash thing seemed especially decadent to me.) I drove a turbocharged, off-white Volvo; Barbara tooled around in a big white station wagon with simulated wood siding. We were invited to the governor's mansion for parties.

Down in my truth center, I knew something was wrong. I was eating too much. I was concocting reasons to stay out late. But I never really stopped to notice what I was doing until my world ripped apart in 1987. It happened while I was on a media tour, doing television shows, newspaper interviews, and autograph sessions for my latest book, *Across China*. This new book was high on the bestseller lists, as high as any of my books had ever been. Yet as I walked off the plane after two weeks on the road, returning home to what should have been a triumph, I was greeted by my friend Bob.

I knew from his face that something was really wrong. Some part of me probably knew what he had to say—but it still came as a shock. Bob handed me the keys to my car and said there were some clothes in it. Then he gave me a letter from Barbara. I just stood there, staring at the unopened envelope.

I knew there were reasons. I knew I hadn't dealt with compelling problems in my relationship with Barbara. But divorce was something I had never expected.

I felt like I was being pressed to the ground by a cold, gray slab of steel. I felt I might strangle. I had no fast comeback. I had almost nothing left and little to say. I made it to the parking lot, but I barely had the strength to steer the car. I was in a city and on roads I'd driven hundreds of times, but I felt lost. Somehow I made it to a motel near the airport.

I read Barbara's letter. The kids would stay with her until we could work out a custody arrangement. Her new lawyer would be talking to our old lawyer.

Still in shock, I sat on the edge of the bed. I couldn't call anyone. I couldn't think. Finally, after hours of staring into space, I slept. I felt like a vase that had been smashed into a thousand tiny pieces, too many to ever put back together.

I'm not yet sure what happened over the next several years. It was as if part of me fell asleep, or was in shock, or died.

There would be long periods of rage, then guilt, then that crushing gray slab pressed down on me again until I could do almost nothing. That live wire that was me before, that man who had strutted through the last ten years and had danced on the mountaintops, now found it a major challenge to get out of bed.

What hurt most, and it all hurt like I was a raw cut dipped in salt, was not being with my kids every day, every night. My spirit was also bothered by what I had let myself become. I was haunted by the untruths I had allowed to be part of my life, by the way I'd let myself get loaded down with so many things, temptations, and diversions. Where I had once been blatantly open and honest, I let myself become dulled. I was living off the past with the riches gained from doing the right thing before. One of my true friends from high school, Craig, told me later that he knew something was bad-wrong with me when I wouldn't dance anymore.

For a while I became a recluse. I did not want to go anywhere—just holed up on my farm and tried to gain back my strength. Then I got a little better. My kids came to stay with me on the weekends. I spent time with friends, found therapy in working on the farm, got counseling.

And I met a wonderful woman named Rita and began to consider the impossible—that I might marry again. She was a farmer's daughter, and her quiet strength helped me move a little closer toward healing. After more than a year of deciding, then changing my mind, then deciding again, I married Rita.

But it was not enough.

Even Rita was not enough. No person could fix me. Only I could take the responsibility to attempt—with all kinds of help and assistance—to get that job going.

I had lost some part of me that I needed to find again if I was ever going to be whole.

What I needed to do to get myself back came to me one chilled fall afternoon. I was out walking on the farm, as I did almost every day. The setting sun coated selected objects with its golden light, but it could not light me up then, even if it did touch me. Looking around listlessly, I spotted two whitetail does at the edge of my back hayfield, twenty feet away from the darkest woods on the property. Behind my woods, over the rusted barbed-wire fence, was a neighbor's even wilder, denser woods. The neighbor's land fell into a hollow that was overgrown with thorny vines and booby-trapped with wet-weather springs. Dead leaves there never blow away; they just rot.

I lay down on the ground, as I often did, almost trying to hold on to the earth for security. The dry ground felt so strong and held me well. Then I sensed movement in the woods. Just a last leaf falling to the ground? No. It was a buck, his antlers high and curved. He would not come out. I don't think he saw me. I was more than two hundred yards from him, partly hidden by a fence between us. There was nothing around to harm him. But still he held back, motionless, refusing to come out into the open.

How could such a powerful, perfect being be so timid? Why would he not stride potently first into the open field to lead the way for the does? I thought I knew the answer. He was haunted by the ever-present fear of letting himself be seen. If he opened up his body from any angle, there might be someone out there who was waiting, camouflaged, ready to shoot him. If he stepped out into the open, he sensed that someone might be waiting to put a bullet in his heart or through his neck, snapping his spine.

I knew how the buck felt. For so long I had lived out in the open. I had thought I was invincible. But for the past few years I did not want to step into the lighted places anymore. Even when I ventured off to church, surely a safe place, I would begin to sweat profusely before I ever got inside. All through the service I would sit, sweating through my shirts, hoping no one saw, knowing they did.

I just lay there in my field, my body finding the best way to fit the ground's contours. There was a time when I was on the walk across America that I much preferred sleeping on the ground to any kind of bed. There was a time when the right things, things that were based in purity and truth and discipline and fresh air and genuine people and stretching my mind and the adventure of who or what might be around the next corner or at the end of the next straightaway, were my motivation. What happened? Could I find that motivation again?

The buck would not hide forever. He would wait until dark, when it was safer, and then he would join the does in the hayfield. And it was now time for me to venture out again, to discover once more who I was and who I could be. I needed to go somewhere I could be healed, cleansed. But where?

My thoughts started drifting . . . to the one place on this earth that had always made me the happiest, the most pure, that had healed me most. It was the place where the ocean met the sand. The surging waves had always thrilled me in such a righteous way. I could swim in them for hours, almost believing that if I could stay in a bit longer I would be able to breathe underwater, join the other creatures I saw diving and darting in the water. My teenaged skin, sometimes trashed by zits, had cleared up when I spent time there—the only time that ever happened. My body had become more elastic, felt more powerful in the dancing waves.

A little surge of hope stirred as I remembered those adolescent days on the beach. Maybe that's what I needed—to return to the sea. Should my next search, my next adventure I so longed for yet was so afraid to undertake in my present state of weakness, be a journey along the ocean's edge?

Quickly the possibilities began to play out in my imagination. I saw myself tramping along a beach, cooking fresh-caught redfish over a fire of gray driftwood. Would I be walking again—perhaps along the Atlantic shoreline or the Pacific Coast? Or maybe . . . what about a boat? If I really wanted to experience the ocean, surely that would be the best way to do it.

I knew next to nothing about boats. But then I'd known next to nothing about living on the road until I set out to walk across America. I could learn.

The idea of a boat allowed all sorts of other possibilities. Maybe I could sail around Australia. The thought was enticing. But no chance. Surely a voyage down under would require a big boat—and more skill than I could pick up in a reasonable time. I needed to choose a voyage that I could handle alone, for the most part at least.

I could float down the Mississippi River from its headwaters in Minnesota to Louisiana. No. I needed the saltwater, the sand, the deep seas, and the coastal islands. Rivers would be good to travel up when I needed a change, but they would not be the whole trip.

So what about the Atlantic coast, where so many of my roots are? What about the Pacific Coast? Alaska? The Gulf Coast?

The Gulf Coast!

Ever since seeing small bits of the Gulf on my walk across America, I'd been drawn to places I'd passed through in Louisiana and Alabama like Dulac, New Orleans, Lake Charles, and Gulf Shores. I'd been intrigued by the exoticness of the region, by the hardy, joyous individuality of its natives. And the waters of the Gulf of Mexico touched on so many places I'd always wanted to know. The Florida Keys. The Everglades. I'd heard there were endless narrow waterways lacing the Everglades. The Mississippi River flowed into the Gulf of Mexico. The Gulf Coast had smugglers, the King Ranch, Cajuns (especially Cajun food!). Best of all, I knew there would be countless lesser-known places that would earn a place in my heart.

If I did the Gulf, if I began in the Keys, say in winter, when it's supposed to be perfect there, then I could be swimming, diving, eating right, losing weight, getting healthy again. By the time I made it halfway along on my Gulf voyage, to Louisiana, I would be trim and hard and ready to pig out on the Cajun food, which I think is the greatest American food. I might even get well and be happy again. And then, once there, I could let the good times roll.

There would be much to do if these swirling passionate thoughts ever became a real journey. I had enough experience now to know that I could take a thought like this and make it a reality. I knew it would take a lot for me to prepare for something so radical as being alone, in a boat, along at least fifteen hundred miles of ocean. But all my other journeys had begun with growing thoughts that lived long enough for me to make them happen.

It was dark now, time to go on home. I loved walking on this land in the dark. I knew it better than I'd ever known any piece of the earth.

As I slowly got to my feet, I wished I could see if the buck had stepped out into the open.

I had a feeling he was there.

CHAPTER 2

Another
Cooper

Y ou've never seen anything like a really big boat show—the kind they hold in Chicago or New York or Miami. At least, *I'd* never seen anything close to the acres and acres of boats, navigational systems, and nautical accessories that crowded into the Miami Convention Center. Everything from rubber rafts to million-dollar yachts. And I was trying to choose a boat I could trust my life to on my voyage along the southern edge of America.

But it had taken me awhile to get here. Even after I'd made the initial decision to go to the Gulf, it had taken me months to begin sorting out the possibilities.

If I were still twenty-two, I might have chosen a different way to explore the edge of America. At twenty-two I would have wanted to take an oceangoing kayak. Even now, at almost forty, I was intrigued by the possibility. But at twenty-two I did not have a home, children, or knees that crunched when I walked. Then I could easily have gone off for six months to some small coastal town to train. I would have had plenty of time to learn how to venture out and lose sight of the coastline, to handle the capsizing seas. I could have become accustomed to traveling in the kayak with almost no equipment except my cameras, my diving mask and flippers, at least one fishing pole, some clothes.

Surely I would need few clothes. I'd be wet a lot of the time and in a state close to perpetual summer. But with my fair, freckled complexion, I would have had to stay coated in sunscreen. A dermatologist in New Orleans had once told me I did not have the kind of complexion for full-time living on the Gulf Coast; he said I needed to be farther from the equator. And now I seemed to be hearing more and more about the dangers of skin cancer. So as much as I enjoyed thinking of this daring and exposed way to travel, I could not get lost in the imagining for long.

And as much as I like to think otherwise, I am not really all that close to being twenty-two years old anymore. I still feel the inexhaustible spirit of that age, but I feel other stuff, too, like body parts I used to take for granted, brain cells that don't react as quickly, bits of me that are bigger or flabbier or hairier than they used to be. I've never liked mirrors, but I like them much less now. When I brush my teeth, I stand to the side of the mirror. If I'm naked, I don't want to get even a flesh-toned blur looking back at me.

Now, too, I have a blended family that depends on me—and I depend on them, too. It used to be my friends that I relied on; now more and more it's my wife and my kids that I put my heart, my being, and my time toward. I now want to live as long as I can so that I can be with my family, so I can watch them, take part in their development. Even though I probably could make this trip in an oceangoing kayak—given the right amount of training, time, and sunscreen—my time for that type of risk and that commitment of time has probably passed.

As much as I rebelled against what I think is an excessive creature-comfort addiction in our country, I would need a more seaworthy and comfortable boat than a kayak. A boat that offered more protection, that required less of my energy. And I would have to live somewhere on this trip when people I met along the way could not offer me a place to lay my head. The main requirement would be that the boat's sleeping compartment kept out mosquitoes. I did not even want to imagine the dark clouds of mosquitoes that hung over the waters of the Everglades. They were bad enough in the Louisiana marshes.

No matter what kind of vessel I decided on, this trip would be risk enough. Taking on sixteen-hundred-plus miles of coastline with no boating experience would be plenty. And that estimate didn't include the miles I might explore going around islands, poking around swamps, going across bays and lakes. I even thought I might take a break every now and then and head up some rivers along the way. How could I not go up the Mississippi?

I did not plan on getting lost, but how would I find my way in a sea that had no identification but thousands of empty miles of blue green? If I were going in the wrong direction, how would I know? When I was walking across America, I found that the best way to get from one place to another was to talk to the people along the way; they knew shortcuts and unused, quiet dirt roads. That obviously wouldn't work on the open Gulf too often. Mackerel don't speak English.

The more I thought of this trip by boat, the more overwhelmed I became by my ignorance. My fears seemed to be taking full advantage of my radical lack of boating experience. Should I not be more responsible now, at age forty? Should I not be wiser about the risks before me? Maybe I should call this trip off, I thought hundreds of times. Wasn't one major trip in a lifetime enough? And why was I doing this anyway?

Back when I was walking across America, many people had asked me that question. Why was I wasting my time on the back roads when I could be in graduate school, climbing the ladder at some company, making something of myself? Some had asked me what I was running from. But I hadn't looked at it that way. I had felt I was walking *toward* firsthand knowledge of myself, my country, my place in the world.

Now I was needing, wanting to do it again—to gain knowledge, to discover, to test myself and see what I was capable of. Something in me needed the challenge of making it down a road I'd never seen before or finding my way through a narrow pass into a sun-brightened bay and meeting strangers I could never have imagined. There was so much in the world that I needed to find out about.

The word *gone* has always had such a potent impact on me. And there was a part of me that still craved being gone. But this time, as I pondered being away from my family for long months at a time, I realized the word *home* also had a powerful pull on me. I wanted to be with Rita, my stepchildren, Brooke and Aaron, and our baby daughter, Julianne. And, very importantly, I had Rebekah (age thirteen), Jed (ten), and Luke (eight) for visitation every other weekend and on certain holidays, I cherished my time with them.

I determined that this trip would have to be different from the trips I had taken before. This time I would come home from time to time, and I would bring home to me. I would make visits back to our place, to the Middle Tennessee farm where I was planted. Maybe that's the subconscious reason I chose the Gulf for this new journey rather than, say, New Zealand, Alaska, the West Coast, Wales. Even at the southern end of Florida and the southern end of Texas I would not be impossibly far from the ridges, woodlands, and open pastures of the land where my center was.

And maybe it was time to start bringing my family with me on certain chunks of the journey. There would be no way for me to really make the connections I needed to make with people and places if someone was with me all the time, but I could bring Rita and the kids with me for parts of the journey. I'd be coming home to them, and they'd be coming down to me, to my home away from home, the vessel that I would choose to travel along our little-known Gulf Coast.

The more I thought about this, the more I liked the idea. One of things I didn't like about being one of six children was that I rarely had time alone with my mother or father. When I did, it was usually because I was in trouble with the principal or some other authority figure. That was never a lighthearted time, certainly not fun or adventuresome. This trip would give me the chance to do differently with my own children. I would make plans for each child to visit separately, so we could have a time when it was just me and them. For that matter, I might ask my father or mother to come along and enjoy the kind of one-on-one time we never had.

Already, in talking with just a couple of friends, I was realizing that I might have more trouble finding "alone" time on this voyage than I would have finding company. There had never been such a response from people wanting to come with me. No one had volunteered to walk across America with me.

As with all my adventures, this one was taking on its own life and separating itself from my best-laid plans as it grew. Would I still be able to float and flow, to follow the subtle leads that came as I asked questions in strange places to strangers? Could I still hear what the people and places I discovered had to say without injecting myself, my prejudices?

I wouldn't know for sure until I became immersed in this journey. And I could not do that until I chose my boat.

If the kayak was out, I needed to investigate other kinds of vessels. Sailboats had always been appealing to me. I had no doubt that for me the purity of the complex language of the wind would be superior to engines, outboards, inboards, diesels. And sailboats have long been the vessel of choice for adventurers. I'd read articles about people who had sailed around the world alone—Robin Lee Graham had even begun his circumnavigation at age sixteen.

Sailing would be perfect for crossing the Gulf, say from Tampa to Tampico, Mexico. On this trip, though, I wanted to go up rivers, not the easiest place to maneuver a big sailboat. I would need to go under low bridges that might block a high mast. And certainly I'd be exploring areas of shallow water around sandbars, up close to islands, in and around coral reefs, inside swamps. The keel of an oceangoing sailboat required too much depth for this.

I supposed I could carry a kayak or inflatable with me, lashed to the sailboat. But that still left the biggest problem of all: learning to sail! All that knot tying, rope pulling, sail raising, wind-direction figuring—I doubted I could pick up the skills I needed for a solo journey in the time I had available.

The next kind of vessel I thought about was an aluminum flatboat—wide open, no cabin, with a large outboard motor and maybe a windshield. I'd watched a television special about a couple of English guys who had gone up some river—the Amazon, I think—in a boat like that. They kept talking about how that boat allowed them to get into very shallow waters, yet carry enough equipment. They had medicines, movie cameras, tripods for their cameras, canisters of film, extra battery packs, food to last a month or more. One of the guys said a few times that they could run into things, like partially submerged logs, and usually not tear holes in the boat. That appealed to me because I felt sure I would hit some stuff.

But then I remembered back to early high school and the flatboat that a friend, John Lockhart, and I used to travel around in Long Island Sound. My major recollection of that was the outrageous pounding we took as it hit any kind of wave. My memory dealt up a comparative recollection that riding in that boat in waters that never got real rough, but choppy, was like being hung from a rope by my feet from the top of a tall building and being smashed continuously for hours against my backbone, all the time being surrounded by noise worse than the loudest dentist's drill.

No flatboat for me. The Gulf was no river, and I was not going to subject myself to a year or more of a brutal pounding and smashing noises.

I really needed a boat that I could live aboard—something that had a cabin big enough to sleep two adults or one adult and a child or two. Surely there were all kinds of possibilities. But living inland like I do, an eight-hour drive from the nearest saltwater, I was limited in the amount of investigation I could do.

A doctor friend of mine had suggested my going to a boat show. There, he said, I would be able to check out just about every kind of boat and boat-related equipment imaginable.

But the shows in the local convention center were almost exclusively concerned with bass-fishing boats, water-skiing boats, and perhaps a few river cruisers. One of the boat show organizers I spoke to recommended the Miami show, which was less than a month away. So before long I was headed to Florida for a scouting trip.

The first day of the boat show left me stunned and bewildered—not only by the array, but by the prices! I quickly realized that buying the kind of boat I wanted would be almost like buying a home. Where I live, a person can still buy a pleasant three-bedroom brick house for seventy-five thousand dollars. But a person could buy a short street of those Tennessee brick homes for the price of one yacht I saw—a million and a half dollars.

I was not interested in a yacht, even if I could afford it. One of those floating mansions would keep me too isolated from the sea, too isolated from the people I normally was interested in. All I needed was a place big enough to sleep, out of the weather and the blood-sucking insects. But I was quickly learning that even that would cost me more than I had planned to spend.

One salesman told me that no matter what kind of boat I chose, I would need air conditioning. His company made add-on units with their own generators that I could have for about ten thousand dollars. Ten thousand *just* for air conditioning! In my state of maritime ignorance, I had planned to spend about that for the whole boat.

After looking around at the Miami boat show for less than an hour, I could see that I was going to have to revise my budget. Maybe the cost of this trip would cancel it before it began. One thing was for sure; for an ocean journey I needed a lot more than the backpack and sleeping bag that had been my equipment on my walk across America. One point of savings: It probably never got cold enough along the Gulf for a sleeping bag. A sheet would probably do.

All around the ever-spreading convention center were boats, full-sized. Aluminum masts shot up from the most refined manufacturers in sailboating, attracting visitors to admire the fine, oil-rubbed teak. Near them were low-slung speedboats that reminded me of Corvettes. They had pointy fronts that bulged too far forward, were painted with ostentatious colors, and were fitted with engines loud enough to mask a hurricane's howl. These kinds of boats screamed to be noticed. But they were not for me.

There were boats here in Miami for every kind of ego, to suit just about any need. And as I went from exhibit to exhibit and asked questions, I begin to get a better sense of what my needs were. One exhibitor, after my tenth question, asked me if I'd ever owned a boat. He was being polite; my ignorance was obvious. He asked me if I realized how much maintenance a boat required. Had I thought about just how corrosive the water and the salt could be, not to mention the beating of the sun? No, I hadn't thought much about it. In my part of Tennessee it rarely snows; we didn't even deal with salt on the roads in winter. He told me that the best boats (like the ones he sold) used surgical-grade stainless steel for railing and important metal parts that would be exposed. Their boats started at nearly two hundred thousand dollars.

I gazed in awe at Bertrams, Blackfins, Vikings, Tiarras. Some of these were in the cruiser class, some in the sportsfisherman, some in something called motoryacht, and some in performance cruiser. There was one boat called a Bayfisherman 32 that the brochure said was designed in the down-east style, like some of the old-time Maine fishing and lobster boats I'd seen along the coast of Maine.

Finally, after many questions, someone suggested that I should find the Grady-White display. I went the way they pointed—no Grady-White. I backtracked a bit and started down a crowded, narrow aisle I hadn't seen before. And then I saw a boat that seemed to draw me to it.

It wasn't very long, but it wasn't squatty either. It wasn't too pointy or too showy. The hull was constructed of low-maintenance fiberglass, a creamy white color with narrow blue stripes. The name of the manufacturer was lettered on the side. It was a Grady-White.

I walked over to inspect the boat more closely. Two metallic blue Yamaha outboard motors were mounted to the back of it—no, to the stern. It seemed strange for a boat that big, at least twenty-five feet long, to have outboard motors.

I walked up a showroom staircase onto the back deck, up into the area where the console and steering wheel were. To my left, a small door about half my height led down a few steps into a tiny cabin.

This would do. This was what I needed. The boat was manufactured in eastern North Carolina and intended mostly for fishing the rugged waters of the Atlantic, Pacific, Gulf, and beyond; it was what the industry called a sport-fishing boat. It seemed sturdily built, even slightly elegant. I knew nothing about boats, but I thought as I walked away from the Grady-White that I did know quality when I saw it.

I spent the rest of my two-day stay at the boat show trying to find a better boat for me. I never did.

I flew home to Nashville with the Grady-White catalog in hand and my mind more or less made up. They made models ranging from nineteen feet to twenty-eight feet long, but I wanted the twenty-five-foot-long Sailfish. It was big enough for me to be forty, maybe fifty miles offshore, yet the outboard motors could be raised almost out of the water so I could idle in water as shallow as three feet. I also decided that I would carry a rubber inflatable boat like the ones I'd seen on Jacques Cousteau's specials. They could have a small outboard or just be rowed, and they would be great for getting into very shallow water, rocky places, or waters that were overhung with jungle.

Going to the show was the best thing I could have done. Now I knew the kind of boat I would like to use; I just had to work out the details of buying it (and coming up with the money to buy it).

There was one more thing that I decided on the trip back to Nashville. When I got my boat, I was going to name it after my first companion on the walk across America, the big half-malamute dog who shared my tent and my dinners. The good friend who had saved my life, just as I hoped this boat might.

My Grady-White was going to be christened the *Cooper*.

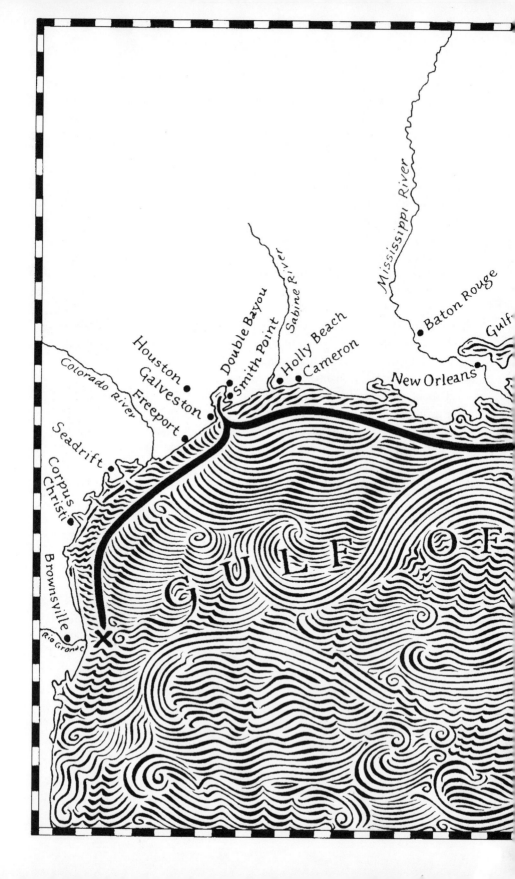

CHAPTER 3

Shakedown

This was supposed to be my shake-down cruise, but at the moment I was just shook up.

The way Warren Norville was acting, blasting off at full throttle into the night, was enough to make me doubt his sanity. We were lifting off in a NASA rocket, except it was a night launch, and this spacecraft was a Grady-White fishing boat shooting across the Gulf of Mexico.

There seemed to be no advantage to having a windshield. Ours looked as if it had been taped over with black tape. We were going thirty-five miles per hour into the darkness, popping over wave crest after wave crest, salt spray blowing past us as our bow parted the waters. Warren was hollering again.

And I didn't have a clue what we were doing or why.

Warren finally explained, after he gulped in some more salt air, that a front of bad weather was coming in from the west; that's what he'd just heard on the radio. If we didn't make it to the mouth of the Steinhatchee River tonight, we might have to wait a few days.

My choice seemed to be either risk my life out here in space with Captain Warren or spend two or three days cooling my heels (or soaking them) in Apalachicola Bay.

If there is anything I hate to do, it is wait.

Apparently, Warren felt that way, too.

Warren Norville had come into my life exactly when I needed him.

I've been blessed in my twenty years of wandering to have made a lot of lifelong friends and become part of several very different families. One of my first adoptions was into Mary Elizabeth's family down in Smokey Hollow in North Carolina. There have been lots of others. The Waldos and the M. C. Jenkinses in Alabama, the Dantins and Heberts in Louisiana, the Williamses in Idaho, the Frankes in Oregon—they all own a spot in my heart. But Warren has a special place all his own. He is my mentor on the water, the one who taught me to handle a boat. I love this man.

Warren lives with his wife, Harriet, whom he lovingly calls, "What's-Her-Name," in Mobile, Alabama. But Warren is ready anytime to sail around the world, dance till dawn, drink the best wine, and especially to feel the wild wind in his face.

Warren was sixty-seven when we met.

He'd seen a small blurb about my upcoming trip in the *Mobile Press-Register,* his hometown newspaper. Warren had read one or two of my books, and on a whim he had written me a letter. His white stationery bore the name of his forty-three-foot sailboat in such a way as to appear the most important bit of information on it. I was impressed. Anyone who would name his boat *Zubenelgenubi,* after the brightest and most dominant star in the constellation Libra, had to be my kind of person.

Warren wrote that he was a retired naval commander and that he too had written a few books, one on celestial navigation. He said that shipyards and ship brokers hired him to deliver boats they'd sold to places like Nigeria or Brazil. Captain Norville—even his name sounded nautical to me.

The last sentence of Warren's letter said to call if I needed any help or advice on my trip. I called.

After much conversation back and forth between my farm in Tennessee and his place in Alabama, Warren left it up to me to decide on the best way he could help me.

How about if he and I took a little trip in my boat, a shakedown cruise? I asked him one afternoon in late December.

Warren said it needed to be more than a little cruise. He drew a comparison: "For you to try and operate this boat without ever having operated a boat before would be like starting to drive an eighteen-wheeler without ever having driven a car."

Warren taught commercial boat captains' courses, but his students already knew a lot. I was ignorant enough to really worry him. But he never mentioned it then or for the first year of my journey, when I'd check in with him periodically and tell him of my latest progress or near disaster.

I decided that if Warren was willing to help me, then I should have my boat delivered from the factory in North Carolina to the closest Grady-

Peter and the Cooper, *stuck on a sandbar*

White dealer near Warren. That turned out to be Killinger Marine in Pensacola. Warren and I decided to do what he did for other boat owners; we would deliver my boat to the Florida Keys, where I would officially start my journey. This shakedown cruise would allow me to learn the basics of navigation and also to test the boat and equipment. My Yamaha motors needed to be broken in just right to avoid damage. Warren figured it might take us a week to ten days, depending on the weather, to make the journey to the Keys. The trip was about 650 miles. Navigating those miles in a boat is like driving back and forth across America.

The first day we'd gotten a late start and only made it from Pensacola to Destin, less than fifty miles. But the second day we'd already zoomed more than a hundred and had just fueled up in Apalachicola. Warren had taught me much so far.

Warren had told me right off he would not allow me to use any of my navigational electronics until I learned to read navigational charts, learned how to "dead reckon." First we'd find the mouth of a river we wanted to hit. ("Hit" is not a good word to use, Warren, I thought. Neither is "dead." I was just a bit uptight.) I would choose a target to head for (that was a better word choice) and then figure out the heading on my compass. It sounded too much like math; I wanted adventure. But Warren said being lost on an endless expanse of sea with no landmarks and no knowledge of navigation would be more adventure than I wanted.

So far we had been traveling along the Intracoastal Waterway and had done no real navigation. The Intracoastal Waterway is just what it says—a route of protected waters, some of it man-made, some going through bays, all of it dredged to make navigation easier. The Gulf portion stretches from Carrabelle, Florida, to Brownsville, Texas. (There is also an Atlantic Intracoastal that runs from Boston to the Keys.) Barges use the Intracoastal mostly, but it is also a safe place for a novice to learn. And there was plenty for me to learn, even in those protected waters. Some babies take their first step in a playpen; my playpen was the Intracoastal Waterway.

We had gone through some big bays, but there had always been marker buoys to show us where the channel was. (Before, I didn't even know there *were* channels that boats had to follow.) Sailors heading east, as we were, needed to keep the green buoys to the right and the red buoys to the left.

Everything about piloting a boat was absolutely new to me. I'd been a passenger before, but I'd never been responsible for anything except my own fishing rod. Now I was learning that almost every operation involved some kind of special procedure, such as getting the boat under the bridges along our way. The charts showed the clearance for each bridge. If the

Cooper could not fit under them, then I had to call the bridge tender on the marine radio. I would identify myself, give the name of my boat and its identifying numbers, and ask them nicely to open it. (The low-slung bridges either lifted up or swung open on a pivot.) Warren warned that some bridge tenders could be a bit hostile, and they could leave me idling there for who knows how long.

Warren also explained that I would have to pay close attention even to bridges that appeared to be high enough, because the antennas for my radio and loran were higher than the rest of the boat. Both antennas could be lowered, but I had to climb outside the cabin and do each one manually.

I felt alone in a country where I only understood twenty words. I probably would have sunk by now if it hadn't been for Warren.

We had only a bit more than a hundred miles to go over that black water. Warren said that he felt the seas would be mild this evening and that we'd have the winds to our stern. ("Stern"—now there was a word I *did* know!) But he warned that we needed to miss Deadman's Bay, just south of the mouth of the Steinhatchee River.

I could not catch hold of Warren's soaring mood and join him in his elation. What if we hit a waterlogged pole and it punctured our hull? What if we sank and couldn't hold on to whatever was left floating? Hadn't I heard that sharks are far more active at night? My mind wanted to imagine floating in the Gulf, held up only by a life preserver, my legs dangling down in the water like big worms on a hook . . . stop it!

"Warren, how do you know where we're going, anyway?" I asked, trying to break my terrible train of thought.

"You remember when I was looking at the charts back when we got gas?"

"Yeah."

"You'll see. All we've got to do is hold our course at 87 degrees. If the compass on this boat is accurate, we should hit the mouth of the river in about three hours."

"What if it isn't accurate?" This was something new to worry about.

"We'll find out, won't we?"

"Yes, Warren," my voice trailed off with resignation, although I tried to make it sound unconcerned. I am not the kind of person who likes to put this much of my life in someone else's hands. But that was what I was doing now. Surely my instincts about Warren were right. He was not the kind of man who thrills at stressing people out. Or was he?

We were heading out into the darkness—a darkness that was thrilling and comforting to Warren but unfathomable to me. Yet I had always been excited by the prospect of striking out into the unknown. Maybe someday I, too, would want to shout with passion as I entered unknown waters in the dark.

Just as Warren promised, about three hours and fifteen minutes later I saw some tiny white lights in front of us. They had to be on the west coast of Florida. Just as he'd said, we came to a marker that rose out of the water, Marker 1. There, the charts told us, began the narrow channel we needed to follow to avoid the oyster bars and rocks that lay in wait for the ignorant or unlucky.

We had to pull out my portable spotlight to light our way in, but we arrived triumphant. I felt like we'd made it to the top of Mount Everest.

This small success held a great lesson for me and charged me with confidence. Warren and I had blasted forth into the darkness together, me gray and dismal with doubt and fear, Warren bursting with faith and confidence. I had trusted him, mostly, and he had proven my faith in him.

I had once, a few years ago, been a man who had much faith in myself and the world around me. In those days, I never even doubted that God would watch over me. He had been and would always be there to save me if I really needed it. How had I become so negative, so pessimistic, a man of so little faith? It was time for a little faith building. Faith in other people, faith in myself, faith again in God. I needed to shed the anger, the cynicism that influenced me too much these days.

As Warren and I entered the river's mouth and searched for a place to anchor, I felt something familiar, something almost forgotten. That thrill of a challenge overcome, that rush of arrival as a stranger in an unknown world, that hunger to find out what was around the next corner—all these feelings seemed to be smoldering within again.

Surely that was what I was feeling right now.

Surely.

CHAPTER 4

Passive
Panic

I f we're lucky on our way to the Keys,"
Warren had said, "we will experience several different kinds of weather systems.
Definitely we will have several kinds of navigational problems. Maybe we'll
even get pulled over by the Coast Guard."

Well, the Coast Guard never caught us. But the weather got so bad
above Cedar Key, right below the Big Bend where the Florida Peninsula
turns south, that we were blown into port and forced to stay a couple of
days. We did more navigating in the dark, still a nerve-jittering experience
for me. We fueled up many times, filled the oil reservoirs, and docked over
and over again. I learned how to pass a sailboat, an intracoastal cruiser, a
string of barges. I also learned not to give up my place in the water. Bigger
boats will run you aground, swamp you with their wakes, even sink you if
you're small enough, sometimes just for laughs.

Warren taught me how to read the charts. At first they were as per-
plexing to me as a novel in Russian. There were hundreds of symbols referring to bridges, water depths, exact locations. To comprehend water travel, I
would have to learn them all.

Warren also filled my head with marvelous sea stories and fascinating sea lore. His tales helped me begin to understand what it means to
love the sea, yet fear it, too. I think he was serious when he suggested that
I might want to carry a duck with me. "They make great guard dogs at
sea," he said without a smile. He also thought I might want to take after
the Polynesians and carry a pig. If early Polynesian sailors ever got disoriented at sea, they'd throw the pig in the water, and it would always swim
toward land. The Polynesians also carried vials of shark blood, because

when the barometric pressure dropped (an indication of a coming storm), the blood would get cloudy.

Warren often tried to explain to me the way the earth is laid out and organized in mathematical systems. That caused me to wish for an oxygen tank to increase my mental clarity. Take this explanation (please) that I was to understand about the earth: "There's 21,600 miles in diameter at the equator. There are 360 degrees in a circle. In a circle there are 60 minutes of arc, and in a minute there are 60 seconds of arc. If you take 21,600 miles and divide them by 60, you come up with 360 degrees. A great circle in geometry is a great circle, the center which intercepts the sphere it's drawn on."

I didn't ask too many questions when Warren got into stuff that made that explanation sound as simple as the ABC's. But I asked a lot of questions about everything else. There was so much I had to learn.

Docking, one of the most elementary skills, was really freaky for me at first. Warren taught that I would have to know which direction the current was moving in relation to the dock before I pulled in. Then I'd have to gauge the wind's velocity and direction. My boat, with its high sides and relative light weight because of its fiberglass hull, was very easily affected by most winds.

And then I'd have to take into account a million other things, which I struggled to keep in my head. Sailboats, for instance, always have the right of way. Kids might be goofing around in small boats. (Wouldn't it be possible for me to have a big sign hanging from the side of my boat: DANGER! GIVE THIS MAN LOTS OF ROOM!) There would be the wakes made by other boats. There would also be gas pumps, set well back from the edge but vulnerable if a novice captain panicked or if the accelerator got stuck. There would be times when million-dollar yachts would demand their way. There were ropes to be tied to the dock and knots to be learned. Why didn't I pay more attention when we learned knot tying in Boy Scouts?

No matter how much attention I paid to Warren's every word, I felt that I would never learn all that I would need to know in the week or so that he and I would be together. I wished he could stay with me longer, but that would not be possible. Warren was a busy man, and he needed to get back home. But I dreaded his leaving, and the pressure of limited time seemed to make all the new stuff more difficult to learn. I would never really know what I knew until he left. But would I know enough by then to keep myself out of serious trouble?

The place where we were headed, Plantation Key, was right at the base of Florida's thumbnail.

If you picture the tip of Florida as the fat end of a giant thumb, then the 170-mile string of reefs and islands known as the Florida Keys can be thought of as a very long fingernail curving around toward the southwest. About two-thirds of the way to the end of this alien-shaped fingernail is Key West, the last inhabited key. At the very end, far out in the sea, is the group of uninhabited keys called the Dry Tortugas. But Plantation Key is much closer to the mainland, just southwest of Key Largo. Between Plantation Key and Everglades National Park in southern Florida lie the beautifully green and sometimes treacherous waters of Florida Bay.

Warren, of course, had no difficulty getting us down Florida's west coast, around the Everglades, across Florida Bay, and into our slip at a dock on Plantation Key. But even after ten days at sea, I still felt like a total novice.

The Plantation Key dock was filled with million-dollar yachts on which very financially relaxed retired people spent their winters. These craft had mahogany-paneled formal dining rooms, extra boats for fishing the flats, potted plants, power—everything. No one seemed to mind our being amongst them—as long as Warren was with me. But Warren caught a bus for the Miami airport the day after we arrived, and once he was gone I sensed a change in attitude among the financially secure yacht owners.

I'm pretty sure it started when I brought my boat back alone from a brief training session out in the bay. I had been letting the wind grab hold of the *Cooper* while it was in neutral, then using my motors to make the boat go where I wanted it to. My practice session—far away from any expensive craft to run into—went very well indeed. I learned how to put one motor in reverse, the other in forward, and turn the boat around in neat little circles.

But as I eased into the marina everything closed in on me. I felt pan-icky. There's no room! The wind's too high! How am I going to control the boat and not hit something? I've got to get out of here, but there's no place to turn around!

My slip was next to a gorgeous, overly polished, million-dollar yacht registered in Michigan. I tried once to tuck the *Cooper* in beside it but had to back away. (Well, that was something. I backed away without hitting any-thing!) I felt so ridiculous. All I was trying to do was park this thing. People were watching me.

I tried again. By this time the yacht's owner, a suntanned man in tight white shorts and hair too black for his aged face, was watching me from his deck. I went in as slowly as my boat would go. I turned very nicely and managed to elude the wind. I was headed perfectly into the slip. But I relaxed too soon and BOOM! I had hit the seawall at the end of my slip. I had forgotten to put the *Cooper* into reverse to stop my forward motion.

Now my boat had its first scar, a dent in the fiberglass with a bit of the blue striping scraped off. And the suntanned man had been a witness to it all. A few hours later the harbormaster told me I would have to move to the very outside spot in the marina, the one farthest away from the other boats. He said another boat had reserved this slip. Yeah, sure.

No boat ever did take that space.

It was a few days later that I moved to a dock on Windley Key owned by Allison and Bill Fahrer. Docking at Allison and Bill's felt like trying to land the space shuttle on a helicopter pad: there were boats on my every side. In fact, when I came in to dock I had to inch my bow forward and actually touch a boat gently with mine before backing into my narrow space. To do this without hitting a dock or another boat, I had to put one of my two-hundred-horsepower motors in forward and the other in reverse. Why do I get myself into these situations? I asked almost daily.

Even after three months, I never felt comfortable about coming in to dock. But at least the few charter captains who docked here were understanding of megarookie me.

Practically every boat captain I met, after looking over my boat, said, "Oh, great, your motors have counterrotation. You can do anything you want with that boat. You can turn it in circles, even cut a ninety-degree turn without going forward." Maybe *they* could.

The first half-dozen times I came in here, I would begin sweating profusely before I ever started into the terribly narrow channel. There were always people around watching, even shouting out commands.

"OK, keep coming."

"Reverse, turn your wheel . . ."

One of the charter captains (I forget his name, but he drank Irish whiskey for breakfast) actually got on the boat with me one time and helped. "Look. This boat is nothing but a tool. These motors are not to be feared. You must be in control of them. You cannot be afraid of this boat. The only way you're going to learn is just to take control of this thing yourself. In a few months, you should be able to do anything you want with the boat."

I wasn't very encouraged. What would I do for the *next* few months— and what is a few anyway? Two, four, five?

He was right; I *was* afraid of the boat. I was afraid of what I would hit, what I might break, where I would get stuck. It had been a long time since I'd been afraid of something. So much of this boat trip was overwhelming to me. Operating the boat, docking it, docking it with strong winds at my bow, my side, my stern. Docking it with powerful currents pushing at it.

Docking so it would stay up against the pier and I could get my bowline tied onto it without the stern floating away from the dock. And the Florida Keys, where space was so tight, was the worse possible place to start learning.

Nothing on a boat this size, alone, was simple for me. When I got into stressful, overburdened situations I was prone to panic, passive panic. I'd never heard that phrase till my scuba instructor taught me that passive panic is not doing something when action is sorely needed.

CHAPTER 5

A
Deteriorating
Condition

Would 197 gallons of fuel take us straight there and straight back? The rougher the seas and the stronger the winds, the more we'd burn. Would there be any allowance for getting lost?

Once you're in the Dry Tortugas, it is a far journey across the wild gulf to *anywhere*—the next closest human habitation is Cuba. We had to take along absolutely everything we would possibly need: food, spices, coffee, fishing equipment, diving gear, ice, fuel, oil (my motors burned a gas-and-oil mixture), clothes, navigational equipment, lifesaving equipment, electronics, marine charts, music, drinking water, everything, everything.

What would happen if there was an electrical short, if the wires melted and we could not repair them? Or if both batteries were somehow drained of their power? If we lost power, nothing would work—not the electronic navigation system, not our marine radio, not even the starter for my outboard motors. We would not be able to call for help; we would have to be seen. And there were few boats where we were going. My guide, Scott Bannerot, said that he'd be surprised if we saw four or five once we got past Key West. Tankers avoided the wilderness keys of the Marquesas and the Tortugas, where we were going. There were too many shallow reefs.

We would be so alone in the keys beyond Key West, the ones that few ever see. Even Scott said that he'd never been there before. If we made it, we'd be in a place as isolated as anywhere in America. And I was going there with a near stranger, a man I'd first set eyes on just a week before.

[45]

I'd met Scott at Larry Dukehart's house, a lonely little bungalow that the sun hardly ever touched. Green mold grew on the siding and the roof, and leaves from two palm trees curved down, forming a gloomy archway to Larry's door. The aura of the house and the grounds was not inviting and I would have turned back. But inside was this young man, an "extraordinary" sea captain Larry had invited me to meet. Larry, a famous charter captain, had sold his charter fishing boat, the *Man o' War,* to Scott Bannerot two years before. He said that Scott was the man I needed to teach me about the Keys.

I didn't know exactly what to expect, although by now I had heard a lot about Scott Bannerot. People who thought they knew Scott said that he was a mixture of wild Caribbean-style free bird, fiercely competitive charter fishing captain, reggae music fanatic, and ocean-roaming sailor. A few knew that Scott Bannerot also held a Ph.D. in marine biology. No one claimed to really know the man.

I decided to reserve judgment. I'd already learned that the Keys attract a lot of gifted people who don't fit in elsewhere in America. They also attract a lot of impostors. Who knew about Scott Bannerot?

That night Larry answered the door quickly. The man who rose from the sofa looked to be in his early thirties. His handshake was strong. His long hair was still wet from a recent shower. He was shorter than I expected, maybe five-foot-eight. The beard, the wet blond hair, the old flannel shirt and cutoff shorts, and the combination of deeply tanned skin and contrasting light blue eyes made him look more like a high-seas outlaw than a deep-sea scholar. But then he spent the first half-hour calmly answering my questions about sharks, Gulf currents, how to live on a boat. After a couple of hours of conversation I felt convinced that Scott Bannerot was both a brilliant marine biologist and an accomplished mariner.

But what drew me to Scott was something beyond that. He seemed to give off a force field of energy. He had the assurance of a man who did not doubt himself, and I sensed he would be one to court danger, adventure. Was he the one to teach me what I must know to survive on my Gulf voyage? I was sure there were safer people to travel with, but my instincts shoved me toward Scott Bannerot.

Scott and I planned to start out from Windley Key, where Scott docked the *Man o' War* and where I'd been docking the *Cooper.* We were heading for the Dry Tortugas, an isolated grouping of desolate keys far southwest of Key West—the southernmost point in the continental United States. They are reachable only by float plane or boat—in this case the heavily loaded *Cooper.* Scott had told me what to bring and had assured me that with these provisions we could survive even if we did get stranded.

Highly skilled charter fishing captain Scott Bannerot stands among a day's catch of blackfin tuna, red snapper, and sailfish. Also caught that day were bull dolphin, yellowtail snapper, and amberjack. We ate the blackfin that night as my first sushi. Scott, who holds a Ph.D. in marine biology, allowed me to join him on his charters for several weeks. The two of us journeyed to the Dry Tortugas together.

Once out of the dock, we headed west-southwest. The morning sky looked threatening—gray in chunks, black in others. The winds roared through the mangroves lining Snake Creek at twenty-five miles an hour. Scott said something about "a deteriorating condition." He held his face into the cooling wind and seemed to love what he felt. I had a lot of thoughts about not wanting to leave.

With the rough weather, there was no way we could head south on the ocean side of the islands, so we decided to make an inside run, across Florida Bay. But this raised some new problems. The problem with Florida Bay is that it's quite shallow—four to six feet in many places—and big hunks of coral wait to tear off the bottoms of outboard motors, or worse, tear gaping holes in the hull. When this happens, it is traditionally a time to sink. There is little that is more destructive to a boat than to hit a coral head while running at thirty miles per hour.

There was a pounding chop on the surface of the bay, and rain began about twenty minutes out. This was not good. The wind was blowing us off course, which had to be precise.

Fortunately Scott knew the area by long-time experience. Shell Key was to our south, hiding behind high fences of gray rain. To make it to Marker 93, we'd have to weave a taut course through chancy waters. We were looking for Bowlegs Cut, a narrow passage through Peterson Key Bank. Fifty feet off course either to the north or south, and we'd have every chance of destroying my boat.

Scott said again, "Our conditions are deteriorating." And again he seemed thrilled, like an extreme-conditions surfer excited by hurricane-induced waves.

Scott said something about the bay's being "whipped into a froth." The water was an opaque jade green and was filling with sediment as the wind churned it up. This sediment contributed to our deteriorating condition because in the Keys you navigate a lot by the color of the water. The color lets you know whether to proceed without worry, go ahead carefully, or stop your boat as fast as you can. Deep violet-blue means deep, deep water—relax, no problem. Coffee brown means very shallow water—do not get anywhere near. But now all the water was all the same murky green. Bad.

The wind mashed against us harder. I could hear the clear vinyl curtains that enclosed the cabin make pop-pop-popping sounds as they slapped against the fiberglass. The sky to the west was not dark gray but black—a rare shade of black that means terrible weather on land, much worse on the sea. On land, I could feel when weather was moving toward me, getting ready to smash and trash. I did not know if my land knowledge could transfer to the sea. I felt a lot more insecure on the water, with its massive mood swings.

I asked Scott what he thought we should do. He said that we were directly north of Seven Mile Bridge, a stretch of the Overseas Highway that crosses the water between Vaca Key and Bahia Honda. He thought maybe we could slip around this rapidly deteriorating condition, with its vision-obliterating rain, and make it south of Bahia Honda to Big Pine Key. As he spoke, an electric crunch of lightning sent rushes bouncing back and forth from my head to my feet. The wind instantly blew harder.

Four big lightning strikes surrounded us—two to our west, one to our north, one behind us. We altered our course, hung a left, and ducked under Seven Mile Bridge, heading toward the ocean side of the Keys.

I knew we had no time to linger. A radical downpour would soon be upon us. I was edgy and high-strung, concentrating on getting the boat under the bridge, fighting the wind that kept blowing us toward the pilings. I worried about the antennae. Did I put them down? If not, they were sure to be shattered under the bridge. I worried about the way the current wanted to push us to one side, the wind the other. Just before we hit the pilings, I increased the power of the outboard engines. We blasted through, safe—at least from the bridge.

Scott said we had only about fifteen minutes before conditions deteriorated dangerously. Now even he seemed to want to hurry. I maneuvered to the next key and down a human-dredged canal.

Before us were travel trailers parked in straight rows, with their little canopied portals and flowerpots, bicycles, and outdoor barbecues. It would have looked normal at the outskirts of a small town, somewhere other than here. But this was a trailer park by the edge of the raging sea with an announcement blasting through loudspeakers against the roaring wind: "Tonight, ladies and gentlemen, there will be a special barbecue, plus we will be featuring some live entertainment."

Something was definitely wrong with this picture. But if the campers wanted to have a barbecue and music during a tornado, I could handle that. Scott and I headed toward the sound of the loudspeakers.

As we walked along the seawall sniffing for the scent of barbecue, gale-force winds and torrential rain hit. Folding aluminum lawn chairs hurled through the air, crashing into trailers and trees. Rain, sounding like thrown gravel, hit the trailers hard. Palm fronds crinkled, ripped from their trees, and flew around hitting everything. We made a fast dash into a building.

A waitress descended upon us. Her more-than-ample breasts jutted out of a low-cut blouse, and she wore tight jeans that accented her wide hips and narrow waist. "Hope all you campers are all happy tonight," she said brightly as metal garbage cans smashed against the building.

From our table I could see the rain blowing horizontal across the water and hitting land. A plastic garbage can blew over my boat. A trio of brown pelicans were treading water in the slight shelter offered by the *Cooper*. I could barely see the boat.

Our bland barbecue chicken, with the chintziest amount of watered-down barbecue sauce was delivered on a starkly white styrofoam plate. Neither barbecue nor styrofoam should be allowed in the Keys.

The worst lounge singer ever booked at the smallest Holiday Inn could not have prepared us for the entertainer who switched on his amp. He sang some country tune badly, he tortured some Tom Jones ballads, he slayed Frank Sinatra, he tormented us with Allman Brothers that sounded more like Lawrence Welk. But when he moved on to mangle reggae-master Bob Marley, Scott's face turned as dark and roiling as the clouds outside. Scott places reggae music on high and sacred ground.

The light was murky inside the restaurant, even though by now the black cloud front had passed and there was only the gray of an ocean downpour. I noticed two bikers, a man and a woman, sitting at a table in a dingy corner.

The biker woman was the only one who laughed at the singer's terrible jokes. Her face was unlined and smooth and appeared to have seen very few blasts from sun and wind. From the neck up she belonged in a choir loft singing gospel on Sunday. Her big, round glasses circled dark, sensitive eyes. From the neck down, though, this woman was pure biker. On the left side of her well-exposed bosom was a bright tattoo. Her almost two-hundred-pound girth was squeezed into a black leather vest.

The biker chick's boyfriend had a gray beard and long, wispy hair. His pumpkin-shaped body was encased in faded jeans and a sleeveless jeans jacket that revealed two oddly thin toothpicks for arms. He had that "in the world but not of it" look that comes with too many LSD trips at too many Grateful Dead concerts. I wondered where they met.

The comedian-singer sang another reggae song. If there was ever a time to yank a performer offstage with a hook, it was now. Scott was deeply offended, almost sick to his stomach.

Scott and I paid our checks and headed out into the rain before the terrible yet blissfully contented comedian-singer could begin his announced tribute to Barry Manilow.

CHAPTER 6

The
Thrill of
Mating

The rain had stopped and the wind had dwindled to an occasional push. Then it was still. I slept in the V-berth, my sleeping area in the bow. Scott had the bunk directly under the elevated captain's chair and the engine controls.

As we lay there deeply relaxed, Scott told me a story about a diver he knew, a man reputed to be the best free diver on Antigua. This diver, who had muscles on top of muscles, was nicknamed "the Devil" because he would stripe his face with red, black, and white paints before he dove. He could dive to seventy-five feet without air tanks, without a weight belt, and could spear-gun three grouper before coming up. Some local Antiguans thought the man had supernatural powers. Scott promised to teach me to free dive when we got to the Dry Tortugas.

By early morning the wind was howling again, this time out of the north. The sun put a yellow tint on the still riled-up sediment in the water. The yellow-jade color of the waves was stunning against the slate gray sky.

We decided to head to Key West on the ocean side, so the south-curving Keys would shield us somewhat from the northerly wind. We would stay as close as we could to shore.

The agitated water surface made the boat ride rough at any speed, so we kept the motors at only 2,900 rpms—going about twenty miles per hour. We navigated past the flats near Big Pine Key, then worked through wave trough after wave trough, past Ramrod Key, then Sugarloaf Key, and finally into Key West.

I'd been to Key West once many years before, but now it looked completely unfamiliar. I was quickly learning that all places look very different when you see them from the water, their ocean profile. There's seldom a way to know you're in a place you've visited before unless there is some overpowering object on the horizon, like a bay-spanning bridge or tall building. Key West had no such outstanding landmarks.

We found an entry into a sheltered bay. This would be our last fuel stop. The way I had it figured, if we left with both tanks completely full—197 gallons of gas—we should have enough to power us the 150 miles to the Dry Tortugas and back. But I hadn't ever needed to stretch the boat to squeeze every last sea mile out of her fuel. I really didn't know whether there would be enough.

At the marina I struck up a conversation with a man who obviously lived in the Key's sun. Though his fishing hat shielded the back of his neck, it was leathery and deeply lined. He thought we were a bit too daring to head out in such weather. The winds were shrieking, and I had my own questions about why we were pressing on. But I said nothing. By now I had complete faith in Scott's judgment and survival skills.

Scott knew the man with the leathery neck. He was a famous guide who sometimes took people to fish around the Tortugas. Scott asked him which would be the most protected route.

"You sure you want to go today?" the man asked with a worried look. "Why don't you go party some in Key West? Maybe this wind will die tonight."

"That'd be nice," Scott replied, "but I guess we'll give it a try anyway." Scott spoke with the never-get-excited tone of a combat pilot. I'd soon find out why.

The guide told Scott that there were three routes to the Tortugas. We could go north of the uninhabited keys directly off Key West. We could go around the same keys to the south. Or we could try to weave our way through them. "Through them" was what the locals called the Lakes Passage. There were no lakes here, but the calm shallow waters shielded by the circling keys looked like small lakes.

We decided to take the third option. The average depth was four or five feet (though our depth gauge sometimes registered three). There were a few red and green buoys to watch for, some indication of sunken boats, submerged stakes, and coral heads. But in this weather the relative calm of the Lakes Passage would be worth the risk.

We popped away from Key West, got the *Cooper* up to thirty-five miles per hour heading west. From there it would be about a thousand miles straight across the Gulf to the nearest continental shore in Mexico.

Immediately through the tight passage, the punishing wind returned and almost blew us onto a sandbar. Scott studied our indispensable charts and said, "We've got to cross the Boca Grand Channel to the Marquesas—that's about six nautical miles. We'll have plenty of deep water, but I'm afraid it's going to be rough and slow. You still want to try to make it to the Tortugas?"

I looked west in the direction of the Marquesas Keys. I saw only whitecaps on agitated lime green water and not another boat in sight.

"Let's go," I finally said.

We headed west across the rough channel, hoping to find the cut into our next protection, the Marquesas Keys, a true tight circle of keys. During the six-mile run, Scott kept glancing down at the bouncing compass: "Let's hold our course right on 280 degrees." At one point I thought I saw a dark brown shape the size of a small boat just under the surface. A tiger shark? Scott said that it could have been a migrating hammerhead shark. Sometimes they grow to fourteen feet or longer.

"Peter, this is interesting," Scott said, peering at a chart as we bounced along. "Did you know that this whole part of the Gulf beginning at the eastern edge of the Marquesas is a naval bombing target area?"

"A what?" I blurted out.

"It's where navy jets drop bombs, practicing—oh, and it's a strafing area."

"A what area?"

"A strafing area is where pilots practice flying low and using their wing-mounted machine guns. This stretch of ocean is called the Quicksands because of the thick sand on the bottom. I can only presume they use this area because the undetonated bombs and stuff sink out of reach. But this would be a bad place for a shrimp boat to drag a net."

I was thinking it wouldn't be a real fun place to anchor either. But we were going to have to anchor somewhere around here because the sun was getting low. We were definitely not going to make it to the Tortugas tonight.

Once we were past the breakers, the water's surface calmed somewhat, and we could see an opening into the circle of islands. Then we were weaving our way into a hidden, magic water place that remained beautifully warm and peaceful while the winds raged outside.

"Tide's going out," Scott yelled from the bow as we searched for a spot to anchor in the mile-wide natural harbor. Then he waved his hands wildly. My reaction was a touch slow. Scott yelled, "Stop!" I punched the controls into reverse, but the wind caught my bow. Instead of going straight back, I went back at an angle.

Scott yelled again, "Put it in neutral." He ran back to the cabin, moving as nimbly as a fiddler crab on a narrow dock.

"I just saw a big coral head, just six inches below the surface. I don't know how we missed it!"

The receding tide turned large sections of this natural harbor into exposed mudflats. Sea birds were everywhere, their screeches competing with the sound of the winds smashing the outside of the protecting circle of islands. They surrounded every muddy pothole, which squiggled with stranded dinner. This circle of mangrove-covered islands was apparently a nursery for all kinds of sea life that would someday return to the deep. But low tide left the potholes filled with thousands of juvenile snappers, silver-sided minnows of all kinds, young crabs, baby eels, and who knows what.

Scott and I watched as long, tall, white egrets by the hundreds waded in, stabbed at dinner with their canary yellow beaks, and gobbled. Noisy terns darted and dived and were happy. Pelicans leapt into the air above a pothole and, boom, slammed themselves into a dive and hit the water. It always looked to me as if they'd broken their necks. Sometimes the young ones did. If they survived the dive, though, every time they came up with something wriggling or flapping.

Scott and I cooked our dinner, cleaned up, then sat on the deck, me sipping coffee, Scott enjoying a Guinness Stout. It grew dark. Suddenly Scott said, "Look at the water, quick, look!" It was alive with squiggling lights.

"They're saltwater worms," he explained. "Little segmented worms about two centimeters long that usually live down in the sediment. It's really a little early, but they're coming up to spawn. They like nights like this. All right, that particular bunch is kind of fading from us right now, but I see some more coming near us.

"What you have to look for," he told me, "is this kind of long fluorescent blur in the water. Those are the females; they emit this glowing mucuslike secretion that attracts the males. If you see a female release this mucus, then you'll see anywhere from one to seven blinking lights heading toward her. That'll be the males, racing to spawn with her.

"Look! There goes a female. Now let's see if there's any blinking. I see some blinking lights! There's two of them, and the first one beat the second one. You see that? Now, watch again. OK, there's another female coming up here close."

I couldn't believe what I was hearing. This reggae-loving captain who reveled in danger now seemed to have entered a heightened spiritual and emotional state over sea worms mating.

"This mating normally occurs in the summer," Scott was saying. "Now, look. See how there's a heck of a lot of females putting out their glow! And then the males will come in and blink and hit the female and they'll both release. Here comes a male right here by the boat. Here's a female, there goes a male. See him blinking? Look, there's about eight males. They all hit her at the same time." Even I was beginning to feel the mass arousal of this nighttime mating dance.

"They're really going at it now. Look, the whole surface of the sea is sparkling. It's glowing in the dark!"

Just below the surface of the black and silky water the fluorescent lights danced as the male worms raced to the long glows secreted by the females. It was incredibly beautiful. But without Scott, I would have had no idea what the glows, secretions, and blinks meant. I felt as though I was on another planet and Scott was my wise interpreter, cracking open a new world just for me.

After the intense excitement of the mating worms we settled down below in our bunks. When it's just-right cool and the salt air smells pure and moist with just a hint of warmth in it, there may be no better sleeping. Especially when the boat rolls and moves like a cradle.

Maybe the wind would finally be gone in the morning.

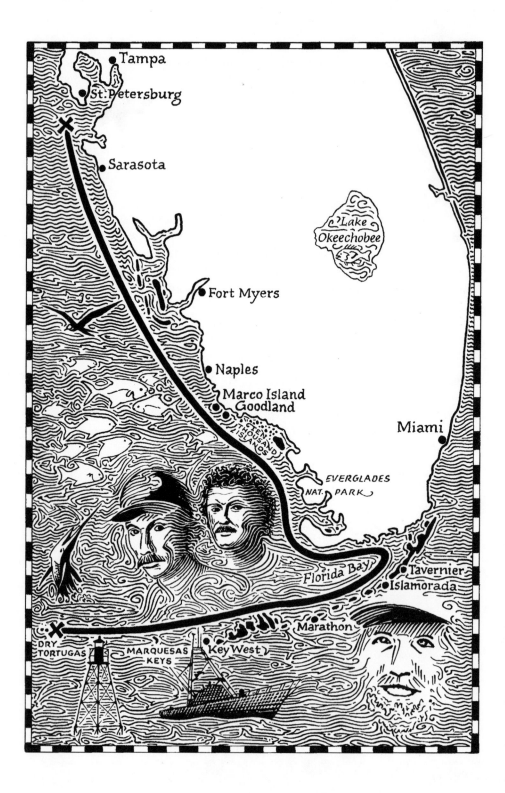

Tampa

St. Petersburg

Sarasota

Lake
Okeechobee

Fort Myers

Naples

Marco Island
Goodland

TEN
THOUSAND
ISLANDS

Miami

EVERGLADES
NAT. PARK

Florida Bay

Tavernier
Islamorada

Marathon

DRY
TORTUGAS

MARQUESAS
KEYS

Key West

CHAPTER 7

Breath–Wasting Attackers

Thirty-five miles of open ocean lay between us and the Dry Tortugas. Scott noted that the wind was slacking up. If it was, I could not tell, though on land I could usually detect wind shifts and faint changes in weather patterns. I was uneasy about venturing that far out into the sea. If we missed the Tortugas, took a wrong course, where would we end up? Adrift where? For how long?

Scott seemed totally at ease, invigorated by the yellow sunlight and the Viking blue sky. I wanted to feel that way, but I did not. I still kept thinking about running out of fuel, about hitting the jagged steel tower of an uncharted sunken shrimp boat, sunk purposely to avoid the Coast Guard, and about capsizing in the pounding, uneven waves. I wondered if we had enough oil, enough drinking water.

Scott's sun-bleached hair and beard and the deep lines at the side of his blue eyes spoke of supreme confidence. I was irritated with myself. I hated to feel fear.

The excitement of being overwhelmed by a place was something I hadn't experienced for several years—not since I'd been to China. For a while, as I'd waited for my life to improve without any direction from me, I'd wondered if I'd ever have it again. Now it was back, with even more excitement than I wanted.

Scott must have sensed my trepidation, but he also knew how badly I wanted to make the Tortugas. As we drifted, the motors idling, the waves rolling us along, he said, "Why don't we head that way? If it's too rough, we'll just turn around. Then at least we will have tried."

On our way to the Dry Tortugas, not far past Satan Shoal, Scott and I anchored for the night in the center of the Marquesas Keys for protection from a blasting wind. The next morning we headed south to Cosgrove Shoal, past the site of many shipwrecks, and saw this very old warning light set atop a boat-killing coral reef.

"All right." I answered meekly.

I powered the *Cooper* onto a plane that kept us slicing through the waves. Scott told me to hold a bearing of 280 degrees, just slightly southwest. Scott distracted me with a few of his stories. Gradually I became more relaxed.

In front of us, just a few inches below the blue-green water, was something huge and brown and almost round. I immediately stopped the boat, thinking it was an uncharted coral head. But Scott pointed: "Look, that's as big a sea turtle as you'll ever see. It's a monster loggerhead, maybe 450 pounds."

The turtle sank out of sight, its dive reminding me of Scott's promise.

"Scott, you think we'll be able to free dive once we get to the Tortugas?"

"Maybe. But this water's going to have to settle. All this stirred-up sand and particles of shell will have to fall back to the bottom first.

"One time in the Caribbean, I was snorkeling along the edge of a drop-off and I saw a very large Nassau grouper, about twenty-five pounds. It was swimming along about sixty-five feet down, below the lip of the drop-off. I was floating on the surface, and I could see him cruising along down there. It was very clear water.

"The way to get down to the fish, you bend at the waist, and make a perfect ninety-degree angle. Then you lift your legs up above you so that you become perfectly straight, and the weight of your legs pushes you down and begins your free dive. You gently work your way down, and once you get down forty or forty-five feet you're pretty negatively buoyant. So then you sink, and you sort of steer with your fins as you descend. All these are energy-saving techniques that give you more bottom time.

"Anyway, I got down to where the grouper was, but it eased into a cave in the side of the ledge. Some fish see you and try to get away. Some are smarter than others, and their behavior differs with depth, too. They're usually not that sharp unless they're in an area where there's a lot of spearing. But a fish that's managed to get to be the size of that grouper can't be all that dumb, either.

"I could see when I got beside the cave that it was a pretty large cavern. I stuck my head in very slowly because I didn't want to spook the fish. Gradually my eyes adjusted until I could see about twelve to fifteen feet. There he was—all the way back in the cave.

"My knees were sort of touching the rocks, and I took aim just like with a bow and arrow. For a long shot like that at a grouper head, which is very bony, you've got to shoot hard.

"So I got a good power shot. I took one of those long distance shots and smacked him real good, but I could tell it hadn't killed him. With a kill shot they just go limp. Then you go and pick the shaft up and that's it. It's good when it works that way because dead fish don't attract sharks as easily."

Attract sharks?

"Well, like I said, he wasn't dead. The spear was all the way through him, and he was just kicking around on it.

"So then I'm looking out. I look out behind me to make sure that a shark hasn't heard us and isn't going to come in the cavern with us. I'd already had a shark stuff himself inside a cave with me the day before."

"You had a shark wedge itself in a cave *with* you?" Just the thought made my blood run cold.

"Yep. That was not fun. The fish I'd shot that day was bleeding badly, and it was in a real sharky area. So I quickly went down to shoot the thing again and pull him out of the hole and get all that fish blood out of the water. I was just backing out when a big gray snout slammed in right in on me and just crunched me up against the coral. He was a good-sized shark, too—about a seven-footer. So I backed out, and he kind of backed out with me, and as I came up he was whipping around my legs and stuff because this cloud of blood was still all around. He could have easily bit me, but he was definitely tuned on the bleeding fish and he didn't. But he was rubbing his head between my legs, and he was bumping my legs and everything else, and I was smacking him with my spear and trying to scare him off. Finally he left. I about ran out of air on that free dive."

Scott paused. "Now where was I?"

"Back in the hole with the wounded grouper," I quickly answered.

"Well, I got the fish and just hugged him close to me . . . just worked myself out the mouth of the cave and got up out of there into the water.

"I held the fish low, looked around and didn't see anything. There were no sharks coming, so I squeezed out with the fish and headed for the surface. I had about twenty-five feet more to go when I saw the shark coming. He was one of those reef sharks—seven to seven-and-a-half-footer, kind of potbellied, a known man-eating species. And he was swimming on autopilot; he had a line on me and that bleeding grouper."

The gray fins of four or five dolphins broke atop the fluorescent water. I barely noticed.

"So the shark's kind of picking up speed, but he's not that excited yet. I said to myself, I'm going to give him the grouper. Then the shark kind of gave one push with his tail and—it was just like magic—he traveled like fifty or sixty feet in no time at all. He grabbed my grouper—now *his* grouper—just three feet from my right arm—just distended his jaws and he whacked him.

"Now, you gotta remember, this was a twenty-five-pound fish. You could hear this big pop when the shark's teeth hit the backbone. He didn't quite sever it that first bite. He hunched up his body, and he's right in front of my face, and I'm just going ahhh—

"He hunched up his body again and whomp, he swallowed the whole thing just like that. Little scales and particles and stuff were flying out his gills. Then he just hunched up again, shivered all over, turned tail, and left. After that, I'm saying to myself, that's it for me. I'm going to take a break for a while. You get a few things like that happening, and after a while you can't dive without every little shadow catching your attention."

I was breathing hard and taking a whole new look at this free diving thing. A seven-foot shark swallowing a twenty-five-pound fish in two bites. How much does my arm weigh, my leg? Did I really want to learn how to do this?

Scott spoke, and now he was back in marine biologist mode. "Actually, it's good when there's a lot of sharks around a reef—it's an indication that the reef is healthy. There has to be a lot of food fish to hold a lot of sharks." Then he added, "There are loads of sharks in the Tortugas."

I didn't say much for a while, just kept trying to keep the *Cooper* running smooth and looking for some sight of land.

CHAPTER 8

Like
Warm
Black Velvet

T he endless, agitated wind changed course again. It was out of the north now, creating new waves that fought with the waves coming from the southwest. The resulting surface confusion made it difficult for us to find a smooth ride. Many times the *Cooper* smashed down into the trough between the waves, and saltwater spray washed over the entire bow, blurring our view till the lone wind-shield wiper did its work.

The fuel gauge, which was reading the amount of gas in my biggest tank (125 gallons), started blinking, indicating we were down to the last eighth of a tank. This was not a good sign. *If* the gauge was accurate, we had burned at least 110 gallons of fuel, more than half of our two-hundred-gallon total. And we had not gone halfway yet; the Dry Tortugas were not even in sight. Now I remembered someone's saying when I picked up the boat back in Pensacola that some of the fuel in these tanks was inaccessible. Another thing to worry about. Even Scott seemed concerned about the fuel.

Scott pointed. A surfing loggerhead turtle was directly in front of us, the crystalline, Coke-bottle-colored water washing over its massive shell. It did not seem to notice us; I had to steer around it. Scott said that some-times loggerheads eat massive quantities of Portuguese man-of-war jellyfish and are blinded by their poisoned tentacles.

Not long after we saw the turtle we saw land. It made me wonder how seafarers of old felt upon seeing land after months at sea.

The turbulence of the waves was calming rapidly, as was the wind. Finally. We had to decide where we would anchor for the night. If the wicked wind picked up again, Scott said, we'd have to anchor behind one of the keys that make up the Dry Tortugas. But he thought it was going to slack off and be calm, and if so we could anchor anywhere.

Whatever we did, we needed to do it soon. It was almost dark.

Our chart revealed there was very little hard land to set foot on in the Dry Tortugas. The few keys that make up the group are far apart; there is no secure circle of islands like the Marquesas. East Key came first, only two hundred yards long by a hundred yards wide. East Key was by itself in the lower end of Pulaski Shoal. We anchored for the night on the other end of the shoal, right at the point where the water drops off from twenty to seventy-five feet.

What happened next was one of several deeply enchanting moments in a night impossible to forget. I felt a familiar tightening in my chest, a quickened heartbeat as my traveler's instinct told me to focus all my attention on the next moments and hours, to feel the place, to stare at it, to be overwhelmed. As many hundreds and thousands of nights that Scott had spent on the sea, he too commented on how beautiful the evening was. Then we both grew quiet, staring toward where the sun had been inhaled by the purple-black Gulf.

Warm breezes puffed from the Caribbean current. The *Cooper* swayed gently on anchor, rocking us into relaxation as we gazed skyward.

The sky was the blackest I'd ever seen. It was blacker than the ebony skies of mountainous Idaho, where I had camped out while walking across America. This night sky was not cold and endless. It was soft, embracing, like warm black velvet. Somehow it seemed rounded on the edges. Against this backdrop the stars and shooting stars, the planets and flying satellites shone with a diamond-pure glitter, every one of them thrilling. The sea was black calm, gleaming like hand-rubbed black marble with the slightest tracing of gold. The black sky and the black Gulf seemed to blend together. Then a moon made of ivory and gold rose majestically out of the darkness.

The days and nights on the big waters take much, hurt much, but they also give much, too. We'd been beaten around and blown around getting here, but what a reward the night was. If heaven has night, it will be like this one.

"Too bad we don't have a light to hang over the side," Scott said after awhile. "A light would attract a lot of marine life to it."

"I've got a spotlight I can clip onto the boat's batteries and shine off into the water."

"Might work," he said. I went to fetch the light.

The spotlight turned the water a ghostly aqua blue. I was staring into the circle of light when a log about as thick as a twenty-year-old pine tree drifted by. That couldn't be a log. Scott came over. We waited for it to come back.

Meanwhile, flying fish darted through the light; one glided across my view and one hit the boat. A little snake (a snake!) slithered across the top of the water, and I scooped it up with my small bait net. But it wasn't a snake after all. Scott said it was an uncommon chain moray eel, only about eight inches long, with a dotted white line down its back. Scott said that kind of eel sold for quite a bit of money to saltwater aquarium keepers. I let it go.

The ghost-colored log was back. Scott took a look and said it was a bruiser barracuda. He hadn't seen one that long and that thick in a long time. Usually barracuda get caught before they can grow this big. He said these reefs must be loaded with fish.

"It's so interesting to be able to anchor in a pristine area on an outer reef," Scott said, "because you can observe so much more than when you're in an enclosed, fairly barren anchorage.

"This is just one of those special times," he added before he went down to his bunk. But there was no way I could go down below and sleep. It had been years since my head, my body, and my spirit had been soaring so high. I felt practically weightless. So I stayed outside with the purple-black sky and the crystal stars, letting my mind wander free.

Ever since I reached the Keys I had wondered just where the U.S. part of the Gulf begins and ends. The waters mingle, one dominating the other depending on the tides and winds. Sometimes the Gulf's water is smothered by the Atlantic. Sometimes the Atlantic water is pushed back, overwhelmed by the green waters of Florida Bay. Often when the winds blow strong out of the southwest, green-white water from Florida Bay is sucked through the passes between the Keys and spews out into the ocean, sending streams of iridescent aqua blue into the Atlantic's deep purple depths.

Here at the southern end of the Florida Keys the Gulf Stream is born. Currents carry warm water up from Mexico along the Texas shore, past the Cajun coast of Louisiana, past Mississippi, past the brief stretch of Alabama beachfront, steadily looping until it's running due south past Tampa and along the rest of the Florida coast, finally swinging around the Dry Tortugas. And from there a stream of warm, life-filled water flows north along the eastern U.S. coast before it heads out to sea. As it crosses the Atlantic it splits into many currents, bathing Greenland, Iceland, Scandinavia, the United Kingdom, Spain, and Africa with warmth and life.

This voyage would be different from any land voyage I had ever made. This wasn't going to be like climbing Everest, where you start at the bottom, get to the top, and you're there. Water's not like land—you can't grab it, stomp on it, hold it, or conquer it. When I thought how different this water world was, sometimes I was frightened to the point of feeling paralyzed. Other times, like now, I was so pumped up I was flying without a plane.

In many ways, though, I felt the same beginning this journey as I'd felt when I began my walk across America as a twenty-two-year-old boy-man. If life goes in circles, this could be the beginning of another loop.

When I'd begun my walk, my quest, I had not the faintest hint of what I'd find in America. I expected the worst, the image I'd gotten from the media and my music in those turbulent years of the 1960s. But I was surprised thousands of times on that five-year walk, and most of the surprises were welcome and renewing. But now, twenty years later, I was deeply concerned about what was now becoming of my country. Would I be surprised again?

Almost forty now, I could for the first time understand my Grandfather Robies's annoyance when, at eighty-seven, he could not take his long walks anymore, much as his heart and spirit still wanted to. My own yearning to explore new places and their people shouted at me to go. And I thought I was up to it. So what if my knees crunched inside when I walked? So what if my back hurt so much that sometimes I had to lie down? And maybe those white-looking hairs in my beard were not really bleached blond but gray white. So?

My body would hold up, I was sure. It would be better for taking the risk, feeling all the adrenaline required to fight the fright.

The *Cooper* would hold up, too. With her sturdy fiberglass hull, her cozy cabin, and her potent engines she could serve as both protector and companion, just like the first Cooper had. This *Cooper* would carry me to new places and to new people and, I hoped, to a fresh sense of who I was.

The *Cooper* was a little bit more than twenty-five feet long, and her beam amidships was nine-foot-six. (I had no idea what "beam amidships" meant at first, but it means the width in the middle of the boat.) The hull draft was nineteen inches. That meant it could float in nineteen inches of water, and that would allow me to get close to islands and beaches. She weighed about five thousand pounds. (How could a "she" weigh five thousand pounds?)

Down below, every inch of the small cabin was used for something. At the foot of the four little fiberglass stairs there was just enough "floor" for one person to stand. Standing in this main "foyer" and facing the bow of the boat, you'd see on the left a fiberglass sink and water faucet. Next to the sink was my "refrigerator." Its strong cover doubled as a cutting board and, when filled with ice, it served as an old-fashioned icebox.

Underneath the sink was a cabinet stuffed with all manner of cheap metal cooking pots, blue plastic dishes, and Comet cleanser. All of it usually fell out when I opened the little black Plexiglas door, just like things had fallen out of the under-sink cabinet in my first college apartment.

Right behind you as you stood in that one spot was the one-burner cook stove, which folded back into the wall. It was fired by an alcohol-soaked piece of material much like the wick of a candle. Scott promised to make some incredible fish stew out of fresh snapper and rice on that stove. Also on that wall was an electrical panel. (Everything on the boat was powered by two car batteries.)

Tucked into the pointy bow of the boat was a cushioned area called a V-berth—my bed. The light blue cushions (my mattress) were covered in scratchy, non-dirt-revealing fabric. Underneath the cushions were compartments with removable tops, best for storing canned goods. On top of the cushions I had a couple of pillows and some blue sheets. (Some days I folded the sheets, some days I didn't.)

On either wall of my V-shaped bed were racks for fishing rods. I had eight different Shimano rods and reels. There were a couple of rigs for mega-sized grouper and sharks, a few medium-sized ones for snapper and redfish, and some light spinning tackle for speckled trout, maybe freshwater bass. There was no wall space for framed pictures, no plugs for a television or a VCR.

The walls of my "sleeping cave" were fiberglass, two narrow sliding windows trimmed with still-unvarnished mahogany. There were a few small lights, but I rarely used them because they tended to drain the batteries. I counted on the battery to power up my Sci-Tex water-resistant cassette player. Fine music played at a low volume has a special purity when heard on the water.

If you got down on your knees in the cabin back toward the stern, you'd see a white-cushioned sleeping compartment—Scott's place to crash. It was extremely cozy in there—definitely not a berth for claustrophobics.

On your right, as you still looked toward the bow, was a door to the bathroom. It had a toilet and a flexible shower hose connected to the sink. I could stand there, take a shower, and brush my teeth at the same time. The shower got its water from a thirty-gallon freshwater tank that I filled with a hose when I was docked. There was no water heater. Since the Gulf Coast rarely was cold and more often was sticky-warm, there would be no big need for hot water. After a searing day in the Gulf-Coast sun, in fact, a cold shower was wonderfully refreshing.

Not that I needed the shower now. My mind was finally beginning to slow, to mellow. After another gaze round at the velvet darkness, I went below and crawled into my bunk.

When I woke up, all I could think about was fishing. Scott said that there was a good current flow, so I got out the gear. Within minutes there was no time to talk, except for a few excited words here and there.

"Get the gaff, big fish coming up."

"Wow, look at this slammer."

"This thing, I can't budge him off the bottom."

"This one's wrapped around the anchor. What do I do?"

We were catching three fish at a time, and there were just two of us. A few of the fish we caught tried to pull me overboard. Saltwater fish are so incredibly strong. When you catch one, you and the fish are attached to each other—power to power, finesse to finesse, finesse to brute power.

I seldom knew what was on my line until it came to the top. You eventually learn their movements, their tugs. Many fish do not want to leave the bottom. Some are so powerful you feel like you have caught the bottom itself. Sometimes while we were in the Tortugas we both had a pole in each hand, fighting potent fish, shifting, tugging, keeping the tension on the line.

When I first hooked into the large shark, I could not budge it, even when I pulled with all my strength. At first we assumed it was a big, big grouper. Then it decided to make a run for the depths and it zoomed toward the front of the boat, taking me with it. I had to run along a narrow walkway to get to the bow, and normally that required holding on with one hand, but I could not hold this thing with one hand. I just knew that fish would pull me over the stainless-steel railing. It would have, too, if Scott had not grabbed the waistband of my sweatpants.

I fought that shark for what seemed like an hour, until the muscles in my arms and back felt ready to snap. But finally the fish broke the line with one last, great lunging run.

"This place is a very healthy, very active reef," Scott observed while I rubbed my aching biceps. "These black tip sharks are following the yellow-tail snappers we're catching. They were buzzing in. One shark grabbed a yellowtail that I had on a line, but he let go of it, and I got it back."

It was time to clean ourselves and the fish. The fish did not need to be filleted, just have their entrails removed so they wouldn't spoil. Before we did it, though, we decided to work our way closer to East Key. The sediment, agitated from the four or five days of relentless winds, still clouded the water where we had anchored, making the diving unsafe. Sharks are most dangerous when they are confused about what they are smelling, seeing, or not seeing.

In near the key, however, the water was shallower and clear as clean air. Coral reef was everywhere, dotting the clean, white, sandy bottom—you could see it clearly from the deck. The contrast between bright white sand and the rainbow colors of coral and fish thrilled my senses.

We showered and washed our hair with buckets of saltwater. (Scott said Lemon Joy was the soap to use when bathing in saltwater.) Then Scott put on a wool cap, like the ones the Rastafarians wear over their dreadlocks, and volunteered to gut the fish while I did some snorkeling around the island.

We anchored in six feet of water, just fifty yards from a virgin beach—not a footprint on it for days, weeks, maybe even months. The only human touch was some lobster buoys that had washed ashore in a high-water time. But before I jumped overboard we cleaned the boat—only a hard-core fisherman can understand how nasty and dirty a boat can get after a day's fishing. It looked like Hells Angels had had a party, including a few knifings. Scott savored the remaining Guinness, and then he pulled out his prized collection of reggae music.

We listened to a compendium of the best stuff the reggae group Third World has produced over the years. Songs like "Legos Jump," "Sense of Purpose," "Moving Up," and "A Spiritual Revolution" sounded forth. This music was perfectly suited for this place, this moment. Before long we were jammin', mon. Dancin', cleanin', guttin' fish. We were cookin' fish stew, moppin' the deck—the winter sun soakin' into our necks.

I mopped and scrubbed while Scott threw the fish entrails overboard. I glanced in the water and saw at least twenty monster barracuda circling the boat. The biggest of the big ones were directly behind us, scarfing up the fish guts. I seriously reconsidered the idea of snorkeling.

"It'll be all right," Scott told me. "Barracudas have long teeth, but they're really no problem. Just make sure you don't have any bright shiny metal rings or watches on. If you don't shine, they won't bother you."

Oh, OK.

Jumping into that water was not a relaxing moment; I'd never swum with fifty to a hundred guts-inhaling barracudas before. As I looked around they did not seem to be coming at me. Could one be coming at me from behind? Their teeth!

Tensely I swam to the beach, where bleached staghorn coral, chunks of brain coral, and all kinds of coral were rolling in the easy waves, slowly being ground to sand.

I walked across the island of no human tracks to the other side, the side of no silver barracudas. There I waded in to glide peacefully atop the shallow water, snorkeling from one coral garden to the other. They grew their own islands of life, and their colors were so unbelievably vivid and varied they made a double rainbow jealous. For a moment it seemed too beautiful, too perfect, too solitary, too wonderful. I guess it was because it had been so long since I'd felt so joyous.

Never did I feel more at peace than while floating or swimming or lying alone on a deserted beach, as I was doing now. The blazing clear water touched the virgin beach easy. My whole being was renewed, intensely alert and deeply relaxed. My eyes were closed as if they would never open again. My spirit left my body lying there and soared away. It headed for places I'd already found on other trips. I flew over New England, the Appalachians, the Smokies, Tennessee, Alabama, the lands of the Cajuns and the Texans, the Rockies, China.

A dense-sounding splash brought my spirit back to my body there on the tiny island. Scott had just thrown in an entire five-gallon bucket of yellowtail snapper guts to the long-toothed barracudas. They attacked the guts and each other in the confusion of it all while Scott's reggae pounded its island rhythms.

We had an easy journey back from the Tortugas to Windley Key, with the weather fine and my navigational skills improving. I even managed to maneuver smoothly into the tiny little dock where I'd been tying up the *Cooper*. There was a hot glow in my face and dried saltwater on my body.

CHAPTER 9

Man
o' War

S cott and I had made that kind of rare connection, a friendship that would last. While I lived on my boat in the Keys I went out on many charters with him. Ordinarily I'm not much of an observer, yet just *being* with Scott on his boat was stimulating. Some days the clients were so hung over or so seasick that I got to fish in their place.

On such a morning I was in Scott's boat headed to a fishing place called the Hump, an undersea mountain. The sky was a soft silver, and the sun filtered through just enough to paint the crests and curves of the medium rough sea a deep gold. The rest of the undulating water was dark silver. Out of the water behind us came flying fish after flying fish. And above them, more than a hundred feet over the water, flew two skydiving man-o'-war birds.

Scott explained, "Most predatory birds have a very high density of cones throughout the back of their retinas. We have cones just in the center part of the retinas, which is why things that you look directly at are in perfect focus but the things you see out of the corner of your eye are fuzzy. Now, the man-o'-war birds can see 180 degrees of detail or more. That's why they can cover such a large area when they're flying.

"And that's why I'm always looking for them. There is nothing in the natural world that can give me so much information as these birds. When they dive down and start hovering over fish, that's a pretty sure indication that the predator fish we seek are there, too. Those birds locate marlin, sailfish, dolphin, mako sharks, great whites—any fast-moving predator fish that chases prey to the top of the ocean.

"My boat's named for those birds," he added. "Larry Dukehart named it. He thought, The man-o'-war has to catch fish to survive—we have to catch fish to survive. So Larry named the boat after the birds. I kept the name when I bought her.

"Fact is," Scott mentioned, "you can even tell what kind and size of fish the man-o'-war is over by the way it flies. For instance, we use the birds a lot to find schooling dolphin—that's the fish, not the mammal. The little schooling fish move erratically, and a bird that is following them will swoop and move from side to side. The bigger fish will tend to move in a straight, deliberate course. So when you see the birds just swooping and not doubling back or varying too much from a straight-line course, then you can almost be assured they're either on the bigger, solitary dolphin or on a billfish like a sailfish or a marlin.

"If it's following a billfish, the man-o'-war will get right over the fish and just hover. The billfish generally move slowly and deliberately, and the bird will look like he's standing still; he'll just be flapping his wings and hanging there. I've seen them where they were not more than a foot or two off the top of a marlin's head. They are just following that marlin right along, waiting for him to run the small fish up near the surface so they can go fishing, too. They are incredible birds."

On our way out to the Hump, Scott told me story after story. But we were interrupted by an excited voice crackling over Scott's VHF radio. It was another charter captain, Skippy Nielsen from the *How About It*. The transmission was scratchy and intermittent; I had trouble following it.

"Skippy's saying that right there where he is, near shore in ten feet of water, there's an eight-hundred-pound tiger shark," Scott interpreted. "They say he's just swimming around. No one on the boat wants to catch him, so they are just having fun watching him. It is a little unusual to find one that size in that close."

"Where exactly are they watching him?"

Scott told me, and my mouth suddenly went dry. I'd been snorkeling in the very same area yesterday.

"A tiger shark that large has a big potbelly," Scott told me. "It'll also have a blunt head, a very large mouth, and triangular teeth. Tigers clamp on a piece of food and shake their heads and just sever whatever they've bitten.

"They're very aggressive, too. That would be a bad shark to encounter in the water.

"Other than the great white, which I've seen at the Hump, there is no shark I would be more afraid of," Scott continued, steering deftly around a floating log. "A tiger shark like they're talking about is a bona fide maneater. It could just snap you up like a snack—no problem.

Ten miles out from Windley Key a man-o'-war bird, also known as a frigate bird, soars over the storm-lashed ocean. Experienced fishermen can tell what kind of fish the man-o'-war has sighted by how it flies, whether it flutters, dips, darts, or dives. I agree with Audubon, who said that he thought this bird was one of the most expert fliers in the world. I saw this one catch flying fish in midair.

"You ever see a tiger that size," Scott said, looking directly at me, "you'd be out of the water real quick. You be doing everything you can to ease over to the boat and get out."

I didn't answer him. What if yesterday were today? Could I have slowly eased over to my boat? Would I have become a two-bite snack for the potbellied, bona fide man-eater?

"I've caught several sharks like that," Scott finally said. "And I'm always sad afterward. I'm never really happy to see them die."

CHAPTER 10

Night
Sweats

T he wild green parrots came often to Allison and Bill's dock, where I kept the *Cooper*. The parrots, the descendants of pets who had escaped and thrived in the mild climate, rested in palms Allison had planted and added their shrill cries to the slapping of the fronds in the wind. Scott's boat was just a block down, past the bait store that had a stuffed tiger shark hanging outside.

From this key of coral where people and parrots perched, every morning for weeks I would go off with Scott to search for fish—living creatures that are unbelievably fast, exquisitely colored, and incredibly strong and rare. Every evening we returned with the sea-exploring birds to rest till tomorrow.

"What we need to do tonight is go over to my house, slam in some reggae, and get you to eating some raw tuna," Scott decreed one day after we got the *Man o' War* clean. We had caught some blackfin tuna, and Scott said the fish would be perfect for sushi, then some tuna steak. "We'll knock back a salad with some fresh bread first."

Scott owned a small home in Tavernier that he sort of lived in but did not sleep in. The upstairs was rented out to a long-haired, sad-eyed carpenter from Minnesota. In the downstairs Scott had an office, a bathroom, and a kitchen with stacks of fishing and sailing magazines where a dining table might have been.

Scott slept on his sailboat, the *Elan,* which was tied up at a canal at the end of his back yard. I could understand that. I loved sleeping on my boat. I'd pass up many an invitation for a guest room to remain in my small cabin on the *Cooper.*

Kenny Hildebrant's lobster traps are stacked on Upper Matecumbe Key at the fish house where he also docks his boat, Reel Freedom. At one time in the Keys, drying piles of traps like these were considered a funky-beautiful part of the Keys "look." Many newcomers now find them unsightly, and zoning restrictions have been created to keep them out of sight. This is just another hardship on those who have to pull their living from the sea.

Scott's library was full of scholarly books on fish behavior. He also had copies of his master's thesis and doctoral dissertation. I thumbed through a volume entitled "An Investigation of the Effect of the Protogynous Hermaphroditic Life History Strategy on the Population Dynamic of Groupers."

"Yeah, that's my dissertation. Basically, I studied the sex life of groupers. I found out that as long as sperm is not limited in the population, then males are expendable; the female groupers are what counts when it comes to the population's health; females are capable of bearing young; and in most biological populations there is usually an excess of sperm. I also found that groupers are sexless until determining which sex is most needed in their population. I got a couple of articles out of that study before I decided to hang it up."

By now I had seen Scott kick into his marine biologist mode many times, but I was always amazed by the extent of his knowledge. Scott laughed and then explained why he had left it all behind.

"If you do a research project, you milk it for as many publications as you can. There's a whole little game associated with all that. It becomes a real rat race. A lot of the fun went out of it for me when I realized what it took to succeed and saw that it doesn't have much to do with the work involved. You miss a lot of time at sea while you're climbing the academic ladder. You're behind the computer or the word processor too much of the time. That didn't appeal to me. So I got out."

We polished off the blackfin tuna and talked about the next phase of my journey, which was just about a week away. Even with all my recent experience on the sea, I still felt unprepared for the voyage I was about to undertake.

Scott reminded me that one of my biggest challenges would be to learn to read the water. In the Keys I would need to see its colors and know what they meant, because navigation in the Keys often depends on the color of the water.

The waters of Florida Bay, for example, are normally a brilliant emerald green. An area of brown water means steer clear immediately; the water could be a foot deep or less. Often you can see a path of startling green water cutting between areas of brown water. If you stay on that green path, you will usually be all right. To venture into the brown is to potentially destroy your boat—or at least run it aground.

To me, one of the most enchanting places in the Keys is the spot on Plantation Key where Tavernier Creek empties into the Atlantic. There it is easy to see the dramatic changes of color that indicate different underwater conditions.

The channel in this place is relatively deep and narrow. On either side of it are flats of shallow water where bone fishermen come to pole their boats. The channel water is neon-bright green near the key, but at the end it turns a Caribbean blue green, clear as light from the sun. Another couple of miles out, the water doubles in depth and gets a touch bluer. Then, at five miles out, the reefs end and the bottom drops off radically. Down it zooms from about fifteen feet to two hundred, four hundred, seven hundred, a thousand. At this depth the light cannot penetrate very far, so the water turns deep cobalt and then violet blue as it becomes the endless Atlantic.

The weathered dock I lay on trying to relax was only big enough to tie up a small boat; the *Cooper* was far too big for it. My boat was tied up just across from me on the roadside of this cramped inlet. The graying dock was connected to a wall of coral rock, and the water around it was as vibrantly bright and clear as the best diamonds I could never afford. My eyes could not get enough of the beautiful blue-green Keys water.

But for all the beauty around here my mind could not relax, even while being seduced by the palms that slow danced with the breeze. The parrots sat in the tropical trees above in the perfect-feeling, South Florida winter sun, now on its way toward the horizon. I was not having end-of-the-day peace, but end-of-the-day bad dreams—daylit nightmares.

People came and went, crossing my peripheral vision without a direct look from me. Then I saw someone pass on the dock where the *Cooper* was tied, no more than fifty feet from me. I'm not sure if it was the bright turquoise shirt and the nicely fitting gold jeans that caught my eye or the good-looking woman who wore them.

The woman was tall and blonde; she moved with a calm assurance. She was not the only beautiful woman walking around this place, but I had not been able to notice any of the rest of them. I was too preoccupied with other concerns. In three days, if I could keep my courage high enough, I would be leaving the Keys—alone.

The woman with short blonde hair got another look from me. She carried a baby in her long, winter-pale arms. It couldn't have been much more than six months old . . .

What?!

How had I not recognized them instantly, even though they were not due for another couple of hours? My wife, Rita, and our little baby, Julianne, had come to spend a few days with me. The sight of them thrilled my anxious heart, charged my weakening will with an instant shot of confidence.

"Honey," I shouted. "I'm over here."

I ran to them, and we held each other, the three of us. Julianne looked and looked at the big, sunburned man now three inches from her bewildered face. She hadn't seen me in six weeks, so I was practically a stranger to her. Her expression seemed to say, Who is this strange man, and why are there tears coming out of his eyes?

Rita and Julianne had flown from Nashville to Miami and rented a car. Rita said that she'd heard there could be terrible traffic getting out of Miami and then long slowdowns on Route 1, the mostly two-lane highway that connects the inhabited keys. But traffic had been very light. That was why she was early.

In an instant my feelings of being alone vanished; I was made whole. How could I feel so much better so quickly? But that was the effect Rita had on me. When she looked at me I felt I could do anything, overcome anything, patiently achieve what was necessary.

There wasn't really a lot of news to catch up on. Since we talked almost every day on the phone—even when I was on the boat, we used the marine operator when I was in range—I knew everything that was going on at home. But it was obvious that Rita had something important to say—and she wanted to say it now.

Rita is not a compulsive talker. She rarely, almost never feels compelled to blurt out anything that can wait. Maybe it's her Danish heritage (her maiden name is Jorgensen) or her Midwest farm background. A farmer's daughter is raised to take things as they come—both the inevitable downs and then the good times of making one's living from the land.

At any rate, it was unusual for Rita to be in such a hurry to tell me something. But it was clear that she wanted me to stop talking right away.

"Peter," she began, her voice as calm as usual. She keeps her cool always. It is a matter of pride to her family.

I really didn't want to hear whatever she had to say. It had to be something serious. My mind raced to anticipate the absolute tragic news that was compelling Rita to make a big announcement so soon.

"I decided on the way down here that Julianne and I are not going to drive back to Miami when we go home." Her green eyes seemed even bigger behind her glasses.

"Oh," was all I could come back with.

"We are going to come with you on the boat and travel with you past the Everglades to wherever you're going. We can fly home from Fort Myers."

"Oh." I was not believing this. Not only would I have to get myself past the Everglades and the Ten Thousand Islands, some of the most treacherous coastline in America, but now I would have the responsibility of the woman I loved and our seven-month-old baby.

I was already worried about having to make the trip solo, without a guide. But if something happened, at least I could swim, even tread water, or hang on to the floating, flipped-over hull of the *Cooper.* The underside of the hull would be slippery, difficult to balance atop. How could I ever hold on to it and baby Julianne at the same time?

I was searching fast for a positive side to this turn of events. I knew from Rita's stare that she had made up her mind and there would be no talking her out of coming with me.

If anything, I told myself, having Rita and Julianne come along would make me even more observant, extraordinarily cautious. I would plan out my every move, plot my course, check out every buoy and landmark ahead of time. I would study the depth charts, the danger zones (coral reefs, sunken vessels, whatever). I would make a list of what to watch for.

This last part of my plan shows just how nervous I was. I never make lists. Usually I am confident of my abilities to respond to whatever comes up. But not this time. Not with my family aboard.

Julianne was still nursing, so she had her dinner on the boat before we set out for a restaurant I had chosen. Rita had not seen the boat before, she looked it over and asked me about it while JuJu nursed. Now Rita is not easily impressed by machinery. She grew up with John Deere tractors and combines, considered by most to be the best farm machinery made. She could see how well made the *Cooper* was and could appreciate the crafts-manship. As I watched her appraising gaze sweep over the boat, I was dou-bly amazed that she had decided to go with me before she even laid eyes on it.

Somewhere beneath my layers of worry, it occurred to me to be thankful for that kind of love.

We got in the rental car and went to eat some Florida lobster. Normally we would have wanted the ocean view, but tonight we sat back by the kitchen door. Rita knew my mind was not on the dinner, not on her.

"You ready to go?" I might have heard the series of sounds she made.

"Peter, are you ready to go?" She spoke louder now. But her voice was almost always soothing; it desired to be compassionate.

"What? Yeah, yeah, let's go on back to the boat." In the Keys there are few side roads, basically just Route 1. I knew we needed to take a right to get back to the *Cooper*. With my current state of mind, it was good there weren't too many turns.

Julianne was asleep before we pulled up to the boat. Just making the long step onto the boat with her made me nervous. What if I slipped—we slipped—and fell into the water? I held her like a football with one hand, using my free left hand to grab hold of the side railing. She never stirred, just slept sweetly with her face pressed into her blankie, a small quilt with pink hearts given her by her Uncle Skip and Aunt Winnie.

Her life was in my hands now. And soon it would really be, once the ropes were untied and we shoved off into what was for me the great unknown. We laid Julianne down in the smallish extra bunk, the one Scott had slept in on our voyage to the Tortugas.

"Peter, what's wrong? You act like you're not glad I'm here. I feel like you hardly notice me." Rita touched the inside of my right arm with her long fingers. Her touch yanked me from where I'd been. I hadn't seen her for more than a month. She should never have had to say anything to me.

Later I heard feral Keys cats howling, clawing each other. Then later came the soothing sounds of the sea lapping against the bow, the sound of dry palm fronds crinkling in the dry, sweet wind. I was lying on my back. Rita was asleep—she falls asleep faster than anyone I've ever known. She rubbed her head on my chest and settled even closer beside me. I was sure I would drift through the night in the most satisfied of sleeps.

I dreamed I heard some people laughing hysterically . . . but it was no dream. My eyes were open. I glanced at my little battery-powered clock: 3:45 A.M. I stood up, peered through the window. Three people, a guy with a black ponytail and two woman, were sitting under the safety light at the dock, having a loud and wonderful time.

The Keys can be a terrific place to party, but I was not in a party mood. I lay there brooding until they finally left. By then I was fully awake, alone with my worries.

I remembered lying awake like this for months before I married Rita, scared that failure awaited me again. Sometimes I was sure our relationship wouldn't work, other times I was sure it could. Often I felt we should wait a few more years to get married. Some days I worried about what other people would think. Most days I knew all that really mattered was doing the right thing for me and my children. But what was the right thing? Too much of the time, finding the right thing and then knowing when it was there seemed to be an unsolvable mystery.

I might have gotten an hour of restful sleep that night.

The events of the next day didn't do much to improve my state of mind. I decided to take Rita and Julianne for their first ride on the *Cooper*. But getting in and out of the tightly narrow channel that led into this tiny inlet should have been outlawed to anyone who didn't have years of boating experience in the Keys.

The first thing we had to do was navigate between two car-sized coral boulders. Then there was a hard left to make, and three or four more boulders that looked like mini-mountains to me. A bamboo stick protruded from the water to mark the next set of coral rocks, but I couldn't remember for sure if I was to go to the left or right or it. To the left—no, the right. Yes, the right.

After that portion of the obstacle course I had to take another hard right to find the ten-foot-wide channel that paralleled the coastline through an area of sand flats. The other charter fishing boats that docked here kept the shallow channel clear of the sediment that wanted to fill it in.

As I was untying the *Cooper* that morning one of the captains, the tall, hawk-nosed one who drank whiskey for breakfast, took me aside.

"Listen, Peter. You've made it in and out of here a few times now. Remember what I told you before. Do not be afraid of this boat. You are the one who controls it. Relax. Think."

He put his deeply tanned right hand on my shoulder. "You have any trouble, call me on the radio."

As hermit crabs search for a shell to live in, in the Keys many people search out wrecked boats to live on. This one in Little Basin is past its prime.

"Thanks." I said, grateful for the advice and the moral support. Maybe I could manage it after all.

I made it past the coral boulders that loomed menacingly in the clear water. Now I was in part of the channel that went through the flats. There were no markers; I was supposed to head for the middle buoy in Whale Harbor Channel a few hundred yards away.

Quickly I recognized that today I had at least two major problems. First, the wind was blowing briskly, continually trying to push us off course. Second, the sun was at just the wrong angle. It cast a bright glare on top of the water, camouflaging the color variations that should have helped me navigate.

I squinted and peered, but the surface was like a blinding mirror. I could not make out the darker water of the channel.

I slowed the boat, then stopped. I still couldn't see. I lifted the motors as high out of the water as I could while keeping the propellers under water. But that just allowed the wind to blow me right out of the channel and onto the flats.

Now I was stuck. Rita and Julianne were stuck with me. What a dope. What a great impression I'd made on Rita. Maybe she would decide now that if I could not go one hundred yards over familiar water without getting stuck, maybe going more than a hundred miles with me would be too risky.

I got on the marine radio and called my friend the captain. He didn't sound surprised—said he had come close to being stuck himself a couple of times. In a short time I saw his charter boat emerging from the inlet.

Now the rescue began. The captain's deck hand tried to throw me a rope, but they could not get it close enough. I had to jump overboard, sinking up to my knees in soft sand. But I finally got myself and the rope back to the boat and tied us to our rescuer. He pulled us off the sandbar and then out into Whale Harbor Channel. I thanked him with an upraised hand, then we went on our ride. It went well, and I did make it back in without getting stuck.

The captain was waiting for our return and gave me the good news— "Good job coming back"—and the bad news—"Pulling you off the sandbar bent my new propeller. I'm afraid you're going to have to pay to get it repaired."

Even after getting stuck, Rita still wanted to come with me on the voyage to north of the Everglades. Either she had more faith in me than I had in myself, she was even braver than I thought, or there was some part of her character I was not aware of that craved extreme risk. Maybe all three.

She slept her usual oblivious-to-worry sleep that night. I lay coated in a mist of sweat, surrounded by a cloud of doubt.

Could I really learn to read the water? Would I be able to navigate the pounding waves and the tricky channels? Could I survive if the savage sea overtook me?

I had so far to go, probably more than two thousand miles before I finally reached the Rio Grande on the U.S.-Mexican border. But I was so blown away by the beginning of the trip that I couldn't even imagine the end.

I finally gave up trying to sleep. While my wife and baby slumbered peacefully in the gently rocking *Cooper,* I turned on a dim light and worked on my uncharacteristic list of places to watch out for in the upcoming trip.

Rita was talking in her sleep. The only word I could decipher was "stop."

CHAPTER 11

Danger
Circle

On the bleak, anxious night before we left Windley Key headed to Goodland, Florida, the wind blew hard out of the southwest. I found myself hoping it would continue blowing in the morning so I could delay my departure for another day. Maybe it would even blow for three or four days.

I had a set of eighty-nine full-color reproductions of U.S. government nautical charts that listed landmarks, navigational aids, and hazards. I studied them intensely.

This trip to Goodland would take me and the *Cooper* west across shallow Florida Bay, then north past the Everglades and up to the northern edge of the Ten Thousand Islands, an exotic water wilderness where experienced boat people sometimes get lost for a long time. More than half of the keys in this area are unnamed, seldom seen. Almost all were uninhabited except for a few hermits. At Indian Key Pass, I'd been told, people sometimes heard screams bouncing through the tangled mangroves and over the water passageways. Panthers still scream there, too.

I would have to negotiate nearly eighty miles along this slash of little-seen Florida. The chart advised mariners to use caution along this route. I read this warning one more time: "The shoals and passes were obtained from reports and have not been verified by field surveys. Stakes and piles, marking passes, are not shown due to their frequent change in position."

Why did my eyes go to every phrase that sounded bad: "warning," "stranded wreck," "dangerous wreck," "danger circle," "obstruction," even "missile debris, unexploded ordnance exists in this area"? The last note I read was especially encouraging: "Warning! The prudent mariner will not rely solely on any single aid to navigation, particularly on floating aids." "Floating aids" meant numbered buoys, on which I would be relying heavily in the morning when I left. Now the chart was telling me the buoys might not be reliable.

OK, terrific. What was I supposed to do if I couldn't trust the buoys or even the markings on the charts that designated shoals and passes?

After awhile my eyes seemed to spin in circles inside my eye sockets. I couldn't focus on the charts. Inside my little cabin, light on, winds quieting, I battled against my dread. There was no way I would ask Scott to come with me. But there was a guy who wore a red bandanna and lived on a deserted boat with a dog that looked like a coyote. I probably could buy that guy a case of beer and hire him to navigate. Nobody would know.

Finally, sighing, I stowed the charts and crept into the bunk beside my sleeping wife.

We woke to a bright, windless morning—no excuses for putting off the trip. While Rita nursed the baby, I made one more last-minute check of equipment and supplies. Then I said good-bye to Allison and Bill, fired up the engines, and pulled out my list. I felt foolish and fearful. Underneath the dread, I felt a quiet excitement. I was under way at last.

All right, what was the first item on that list? It felt strange to be this organized. Lists are definitely not me.

1. *Leave Allison's. Get into Whale Harbor Channel, go about 2 miles from bridge to red buoy #80. Go too far, and water comes up to 1-foot depth. Hit that, and I won't be leaving the Keys. (Appealing, in a way.)* So far so good. I made it through the channel.

2. *Go through Steamboat Channel. Well marked with buoys.* I managed that, too, though slowly. It helped that I'd already been through here with Scott.

3. *Head 244 degrees, almost due west, for almost 4 miles to red buoy #93. Buoy needs to be on my left. Here begins Bowlegs Cut. Narrow but well marked.* Bowlegs Cut is the way through Peterson Key Bank. Scott and I had gone through here on our way to the Tortugas. I remembered it and squeezed through with no problems.

4. *Once through Bowlegs Cut, keep the Coops heading at 244 degrees about 6 miles to red buoy #1 (Old Dan Bank). Stay to right of the buoy—6-inch-deep water and rocks to the left.* I did that. At buoy #1, I watched a bigger cruiser come through a half mile before I did. That gave me confidence I was on course.

5. From buoy #1, turn to the north, 296 degrees, for about 3.1 miles to sight buoy #2. This is the Yacht Channel. I made it through the Yacht Channel to buoy #2. This passage was like threading a needle. The shallow water came close together and at an angle, which meant I had to reorient my direction to get through. I made it through. So far so good.

6. Head north 6 miles to Oxfoot Bank—keep it on the right. To my left the water was ten feet deep; to my right, it ranged from four feet to two inches. My boat could run full speed, over forty miles per hour, in three feet of water. On board I had a gauge that continuously reported the water depth.

By now I was feeling fairly comfortable. The wind and the extreme power of my two Yamaha motors, and the smoothness in which the *Cooper* sliced through the water made for a feeling of liberation. On my own in the boat, I'd not felt that way before. I tried out my version of Warren's war cry. I high-fived the sky. I woke up the baby. Rita was her usual mellow self.

7. After Oxford Bank, continue north to buoy #3. It was seven miles of open Gulf to the buoy right before the mainland, just two miles south of the east cape of the Everglades. The *Cooper* and I made that with no trouble at all.

8. 10 miles to next buoy, #4, red. Good water about a mile and a half off shore—7 to 10 feet. I found the good water and kept on course. "I be cruisin!" I shouted over the wind. This time Julianne laughed.

For the first time on this segment of my journey I thought of my lobster tails, iced down and waiting. Scott's friend Kenny Hildebrant, a Keys lobster fisherman, had given them to me in return for helping him pull his traps.

9. From Northwest Cape, longest open-water run—37.7 miles to buoy #5 (Gullivan Bay). Here I had to leave the security of being close to land and cruise fifteen miles offshore. Everything I passed on my right was still the Everglades National Park, the least inhabited shore along the entire Gulf Coast. I kept my bearing to 321—mostly north but leaning slightly to the west. I figured that at my average, twenty-five miles an hour, this run would take me an hour and a half.

One by one I passed the landmarks on my chart: Shark River, Lostman's River, Porpoise Point, Clam Point, and Chokoloskee Pass. Beyond the entrance to Everglades City, I passed Tiger Key, West Pass, and Panther Key. Soon I would be in Gullivan Bay, from which I could find the north passageway into the Ten Thousand Islands.

It was a mind-expanding concept to think that I was going 37.7 miles through the open, signless Gulf, heading for a buoy that was only two or three feet wide and four feet tall. In fact, one of the most difficult things for me about navigating at sea was the lack of landmarks. On a road you keep your vehicle between the center line and the side of the road. Here I was moving on an unmarked course with massive expanses of water on all sides. There was often nothing to aim at, just a compass heading to follow.

Finally, I saw buoy #5 about a mile ahead. It was a gratifying moment. I had completed my list.

But there was little time to be glad. I was still eighteen miles across the bay from Coon Key Pass, a slender passage into the north end of the Ten Thousand Islands. Now other, off-the-list problems could develop.

First, without any buoy, I'd have to navigate across Cape Romano Shoals. Some of the water in this area was nineteen feet, but the depth could drop in an instant to five feet or less. There could be eleven feet and, *boom,* one foot. On the chart, little pictures of sunken ships indicated where these shoals were. I decided to stay a bit to the right of Coon Key to avoid the sunken-ship traps. Right under the words *Cape Romano,* the chart warned, "Area is subject to continual change."

Ahead I could see waterways, most slim as a flamingo's neck, curling through the endless horizon of Ten Thousand Islands. If there were ten thousand islands, then there were fifty thousand water passageways. If there were ten thousand islands, there were at least twenty thousand inlets, baby bays, big bays, and indentations that very possibly could be dead ends. No wonder everyone got lost here sometime. At night, I had heard, the mosquitoes and gnats were bad enough to drive a person insane.

I was looking for a place called Marker 7 Fish House in the little town of Goodland, on Marco Island. There, I'd been told, were people who could find their way in and out of the Ten Thousand Islands on moonless nights, so imprinted in their genes was this maze of waterways.

I passed Coon Key on the right and threaded my way into the narrow pass. The top of the water shone orange and purple from the setting sun, and the narrow-branched mangroves, whose roots arched up out of the water, lined the pass with deep green. It would be dark within an hour.

Right at Tripod Key I heard a sound over my easygoing engines, a tremendous series of splashes. I immediately put my boat in neutral. Another more rowdy series of splashes, and then something emerged from the water onto the exposed mud bank. There were two dolphins, light gray in color. They wiggled backward off the mud bank and disappeared. Then I saw two well-defined wakes in the water. The porpoises were swimming very fast, just underwater, back toward the bank, until they were almost

Marker 1 is the first man-made sign that you've made it to the channel that will bring you in from the sea. It was a finer sight this day, near the northern portion of the mazelike Ten Thousand Islands, because of this osprey with the fish in its talons.

beached. Then one of the porpoises flipped a silver-sided, foot-long fish into the air, and the other one caught it.

They did it again and again while Rita and I watched and tried to show the baby. They were herding mullet into the shallows, where I guess they were easier to catch.

Right before I left, one porpoise became stuck. Not until the other porpoise made a run toward the bank, using its mass and speed to push water in front of it, was the marooned mammal able to wriggle its way back into the channel. By now the water had turned a deep pink and dark purple.

I was searching for Marker 7. I passed 2, 4, 6. On 6 an osprey landed with a trout, flipped water from its tail, and tore into its catch.

Marker 7 was green. I had made it. Behind it, on shore, were several small, weathered buildings—houses, I supposed. There was no sign for a Marker 7 Fish House.

I anchored at the head of Goodland Bay, and we quickly began boiling water and melting butter for the lobster tails. As the late light turned to black, Rita and I ate our lobster tails with some tough French bread and sampled the very different scents of this place. Warm and sweet and salty smells, highlighted with a fishy aroma, blew back and forth across our faces. We fell asleep to a cassette of Don Henley singing a song about forgiveness.

Tattoos
of
Flowers

Hey. Is anyone aboard this boat?"
Voices tried to creep into my
sleep.

"Hey, buddy, you in that boat or not? We're about to come aboard." I
heard the groggy sound of an outboard motor.

"What do you want?" I called from deep inside the cabin of the
Cooper.

"We're drug enforcement agents; we want to search your boat," the
voice from outside penetrated clearly. The man had an odd accent. Only
then did I remember that we were no longer at Allison's dock, but floating
in the water outside a place I'd never been before. These people must be in
a boat themselves.

Rita was awake, too. Not exactly alarmed, but very alert. She reached
for her glasses.

"OK, OK, I'm coming," I called.

I hurried into a pair of black sweatpants and up the little flight of stairs
to the deck. From there I saw a wooden boat with two rugged men looking at me.

The one doing the talking had black shoulder-length hair and a black
untrimmed beard so long it almost hit the chest of his dirty white T-shirt.
He looked more like a member of ZZ Top than a DEA man and wore
white rubber boots.

"We will need to come on board and look through all your equipment. You're suspected of smuggling drugs."

"I'm what?"

"You heard me, mister. Now move aside; we're coming aboard." This guy's body was very strong. He was densely tan and wore a bright orange baseball cap.

As I stepped back, he said, "You are Peter Jenkins, ain't you?"

"Yes, I am."

"Do you really go around claiming that you write them books?" He seemed angry.

"I don't claim to. I do. What's going on?"

There's nothing more vulnerable than being on a boat out of sight of help. Anyone can board your craft, even kill you, and chances are no one will ever find out. There is so much in the waters around the Ten Thousand Islands that likes to eat dead meat.

"We have received information from a reliable source that you ain't no writer, this writing thing is just a cover. We're here to find cocaine on board. Ain't that right, Thomas Lee?"

Thomas Lee wasn't saying a word. He must be the enforcer of the two.

"I have no idea what you're talking about—wait a minute! Don't you need a search warrant?"

"Not in the middle of these here islands, Bubba. We don't need nothin' but our smiling faces. Ain't that right?" He looked at Thomas Lee, who looked like he'd been in the South Florida sun too long without a hat. Thomas Lee nodded.

The black-bearded one came toward me. I tensed. Then he stopped less than a foot from my face, looked me over, and said, "Now, you gonna tell me where you done got them drugs hid, or we gonna tear this new boat a'yours apart?"

"I have nothing illegal on board this boat."

"I don't believe a word you say, boy." He stepped a few inches closer. Was he going to hit me?

Then he almost whispered, "We ain't no drug agents, man. We're fishermen. We done heard from that friend of your sister's up in North Florida that you was comin' this way. We been lookin' for your boat a couple days now. Winky is your sister, ain't she?"

I must have looked confused. Then I laughed.

They had to be serious about my sister—no one could make up the name Winky. My redheaded sister, the one who looked like the duchess of York, knew a man, now a computer software executive, who had once done time for smuggling boatloads of marijuana. I couldn't guess what he had to do with these fishermen masquerading as DEA agents so many, many miles south of my sister's home. I was relieved to be greeted with a

Marker 7 Fish House. My boat's the one on the left with the twin Yamaha outboard motors. The other boats are a type of fishing craft called bird-dog boats and are used throughout the Ten Thousand Islands. These boats can travel over shallow water sometimes only inches deep. Many have outboard motors mounted in the front.

practical joke instead of a loaded shotgun, relieved to find someone who knew me in this unusual water world.

Smuggling has long been a prime source of income along the Gulf. Boats have smuggled in stolen gold, stolen women, slaves, whiskey, immigrants, embargoed cargo, and billions and billions and billions of dollars worth of drugs. The influx of illegally attained drug money contributed tremendously in fueling Florida's remarkable growth in the 1970s and 1980s. And there have always been—still are—many undercover narcotics agents planted among the locals, sniffing out the dope runners.

During the high, wild '70s and money-hungry '80s, countless millions of pounds of pot were smuggled into small fishing towns like Everglades City and Goodland and hundreds of others in Alabama, Mississippi, Louisiana, and Texas. These mostly subsistence fishing towns had one advantage; strangers rarely came there and locals rarely left. The outside world considered them unattractive and brutally rough. They were perfect for smuggling, bad for a stranger like me.

Although this wake-up call from the black-bearded man was a joke (I do think there was always a lingering doubt in many of my ports of call about what I really did), it would not be the last time on this journey I would be suspected of being involved with drugs in one way or another—although usually I was accused of being on the other side. Everywhere I went, people would tell me that at first they thought I was a narc, and that was not good news. Getting caught by certain people who thought you were a narc was a guarantee that you'd use your health insurance to its limits. Quite possibly, you'd just disappear.

I realized that everything I did added up to narc for the people in these little fishing towns. I asked too many questions, took too many pictures, moved around too much, said I lived in Tennessee yet talked like a Yankee. These things, plus the fact that I was obviously not an expert at running my boat, didn't add up in the isolated ports or the river communities I visited. Eventually I took to carrying copies of a couple of my books and showing them as soon as I could to the people in each community who had the loudest mouths and the most influence.

"My name's Larry Thompson," the black-bearded man in the baseball cap was saying. "Come follow us. Marker 7 is right across this water, but it's tricky getting into the place your first time." We shook hands. His hand was about as hard as an anchor.

I followed him, squeezed my boat between two others, and tied up with four lines. During different cycles of the moon, Larry said, the tide rose and fell many feet here.

Marker 7 Fish House was a white, rugged two-story building constructed of concrete blocks and wood. In the two months I spent in Goodland, it became my entrée into the lives of lower West Coast Florida natives. The descendants of the original Florida settlers I met here are increasingly rare and hard to find.

Marker 7 stood at the end of Pear Street in the small piece of high ground on Marco Island that comprises the town of Goodland, Florida. Several of the residents here rode bikes because their drivers licenses had been revoked, either forever or for a while, for one too many "driving under the influence" convictions. I saw more than a few cases of wobbly bikes from time to time. A lot of the people went barefoot.

Goodland was the kind of place where people stretched their fishing nets between trees in the front yard to repair them. It was one of the last places in South Florida where independent fishermen could live on their small and sporadic income. It was also the kind of place that might scare many travelers.

Downstairs at Marker 7 the day's catch was sorted, weighed, and stored in a walk-in cooler. There was a washer to do laundry and a screened-in

Barb and Bob, managers of Marker 7 Fish House. It is at the end of Pear Street if you're coming by car or Harley, or across from Marker 7 if you're coming by boat. Bob's life's story is told by the tattoos on his body, both those that are visible and those that have been removed. Billy and Red Parker, Larry Thompson, Gary Weeks, and a few others brought all the fish they caught to Marker 7.

place for tired fishermen to hang out. Upstairs the managers of Marker 7, Bob and Barb, lived with their two pit bulls and a bunch of parrots.

Most of Bob and Barb's parrots related to Barb best, except for Peeper. Peeper, a pretty red lory, had the hots for Bob. When I arrived, it was parrot breeding season, and her parrot hormones were surging. According to Bob, she'd turned into a "biting bag of feathers."

Bob had a white beard and long white hair, usually worn in a pony-tail. He looked like a thin Santa Claus except for the fact that most of his right buttock had been shot off in a barroom brawl out in California dur-ing the '60s. Bob rarely wore a shirt, and tattoos covered much of the top half of his body. When he looked at his upper body, his life's story was told

While fishing south of Marco Island, Gary Weeks throws a shovel-nosed shark as he sorts through his catch.

in tattoos—in the aged, fading ones; the new, vivid ones done mostly by a guy named Tennessee; the old ones touched up by Barb; and the new ones also done by Barb.

Bob got his first "skin art" in the 1950s, when he ran away from Georgia to San Francisco at age sixteen. He had been placed in a foster home a few years before because his aunt had killed his mother in a drunken brawl, stabbing her some thirty times. The killing had been a feature story in the magazine *True Detective*.

Bob's first tattoo was an eagle with his name in the center that he had acquired in the '50s. Just the week before I arrived, Barb had re-inked that first tattoo, tribal-style like the Samoans do, using only black ink. His second tattoo was originally the name of an early girlfriend, but that had been covered over with tattoos of flowers. A heart pierced by an arrow and embroidered with a different girl's name had also been covered by another tattoo. He could have saved himself some pain if one of those early girl-friends who rated tattoos had been named Barb.

When Bob ran away to San Francisco, he settled in with some bikers who call themselves "one-percenters." Bob told me: "A one-percenter is someone who belongs to a motorcycle gang like the Hells Angels. They are the 1 percent of the people on earth that don't care about nothin', ain't afraid of nothin'." He used to be one of the baddest, and he went by the name of Spider Bob. To commemorate that period of his life, he had a sizable spider tattoo and, right on the top of his chest, a large etching of a Pan Head, a famous Harley-Davidson motorcycle engine built from 1948 until 1965.

Bob and Barb met when Barb was living around Daytona Beach and Bob was working there. He proudly mentioned that he used to be a top-rate big-crane operator and that he helped build a lot of the bridges cross-ing the Florida interstates. At the time, Barb had her jaw wired shut—she and her prior boyfriend had had some arguments before he left her stranded. Bob and Barb started having coffee together and soon married.

Both Bob and Barb were recovering substance abusers, proud of their sobriety. They told me the main reason they had chosen this quiet lifestyle was to get away from the temptations of the fast and rowdy living in the city, any city. But "quiet" is in the eye of the beholder. The owner of Marker 7, a native and descendant of a local pioneer, had hired Bob and Barb and moved away because he couldn't stand the growth and develop-ment that was drawing near to this former wilderness. When condos began appearing on the north side of Marco Island, the owner had moved himself and his family to rural South Georgia.

Bob and Barb's two pit bulls didn't take to strangers like Rita and me, and neither did some of the guys who fished out of here. Mostly these fish-ermen caught mullet, pompano, shark, trout, sheephead, Spanish mackerel, any fish that someone would buy. Much of the fish was shipped to New York City. But their biggest money comes when the mullet swim to the ocean to spawn, away from the protection of the Ten Thousand Islands. The females are filled with eggs then, and their roe are prized by the Japanese, who pay a lot of money for them.

Dave Osceola, a pure-blood Seminole, fished out of Marker 7. Everyone told me he was explosive, had a bad temper. "Just stay out of his way," I was warned. I did.

But I couldn't stay out of everyone's way, especially two intense-looking brothers, Billy and Red Parker. They either were arrogant, had a chip on their shoulders, were angry with the whole world, hated Rita and me at first sight, or never smiled. Probably all of the above.

Rita and Julianne went home two days after we arrived in Goodland. Bob gave them a ride to the Fort Myers airport. After that, I waited for my chance to get to know Billy and Red better. I had guessed that they wouldn't talk to me, take me in, until Rita left. I was right. Even after she left, it took a few weeks before they'd do more than nod when I said hello.

CHAPTER 13

The
Parker
Brothers

Almost everyone at Marker 7 could think like a fish, feel the wind, and know where to go. They could watch the top of the water and know if they should drop their nets. They inherited this knowledge from their fathers, who got it from their grandfathers. It was a fact that the best of the fishermen were part Native American.

Here at Marker 7 Fish House, right off Coon Key Pass, I would be docking my boat and making my home for the next several months with people who knew the Ten Thousand Islands better than anyone.

My first thought upon hearing about the Ten Thousand Islands had been that they would be something like the Keys—islands of hard, rocky ground with beaches, land to walk on, places to camp or even build a house. But there is almost no place for a human even to stand on these islands. So it is true that no humans live on them but a few hermits—and huge numbers of egrets, pelicans, ibis, wood storks, and an incredible number of other exotic and rare birds. Decades ago this was one of the main hunting grounds for the feather hunters.

From the air these Ten Thousand Islands look like green lace laid on top of the water. It is one of the most important marine ecosystems in the world. But these islands and this place are absolutely nothing like the Keys. There is no coral, the water is not clear, and the islands themselves are not really land but masses of mangrove roots, which spread out and grow in the saltwater. The original natives called the mangrove the "walking tree" because its roots "walked" farther and farther out into the water and made "land."

The early Indians built land, too, by piling up huge mounds of oyster shells. Some think they did so by accident, but I think they created oyster mounds on purpose. Back then, when the coast was pure, oysters were one of their best and most convenient foods. But oysters shells are heavy, so why would the Indians just happen to carry their harvested shells to the same place for years on end? I think they threw the shells in one place because they needed high, strong, hard ground.

Many oyster mounds rose fifty or seventy feet or more. They lifted the natives high enough above the mangroves to catch the sea breezes, which blew away the clouds of mosquitoes, sand flies, and other biting bugs. More important, they must have offered the only place of refuge when hurricanes attacked the area. (There was no Weather Channel then.) High water does the killing when hurricanes hurl black winds and rain. And ordinarily these coastal people would have no place to escape the inundating waves. But if they could climb to the tops of their oyster mounds, hunker on the down-wind side of them, and hold on to the small children, then they had a chance.

The Parker brothers, who fished out of Marker 7, were half-Seminole, half-Irish. On the Irish side, they were descended from one of Florida's first settlers. Prior to the Civil War, when the area was still brutally inhospitable, the Parkers homesteaded and built plantations in what is now the Everglades National Park.

Billy and Red Parker didn't look much alike, but they were the most connected brothers I've ever met. They were both married, and Red had children and stepchildren, but they still spent most of every day together—either fishing or hanging out in the Marker 7 Fish House.

Billy, the eldest, looked more like their dark-haired Seminole mother. Red, four years younger, was broad shouldered and barrel chested, red-headed and freckled like his Irish father. There was a touchable edge of danger up close to these men. After awhile they took me in, but they watched me for a few weeks before they'd talk with me.

The Parker brothers grew up like many pioneer Floridians did before the elderly and wealthy from the North discovered their state. Untamed Florida is not an easy place to live in, especially "if you ain't got a buncha money," as Red said more than once with an angry edge to his voice. Red is the brother who is quick to boil. Billy, you better hope he *never* boils.

I grew up not much more than a mile from the Atlantic. Red and Billy grew up on the Gulf waters. In 1991 we met just as Billy and I were about to turn forty. We couldn't have lived more different lives. In fact, the difference was stunning to me. As children, they lived with mud-caked

Near Blue Hill Bay, not far from Goodland, mangrove tree roots spread like thousands of snakes. These roots create a protective home for an amazing number of newborn and immature fish and other marine life. The Indians called the mangrove the "walking tree." The mass of roots and its ability to grow in saltwater make the mangrove one of the most crucial and productive marine environments in the world.

heads to protect them from the sand flies. They dove for alligators their dad had killed with a hatchet and salted their mullet down in wood barrels. They sailed in an old wood-plank fishing skiff from island to island during the same 1950s when I was growing up among cars that weaved in and out of the endless suburban streets. Heat, humidity, and hurricanes ignited human passion and incited wildness in a way that life in suburbia could never do.

"Mama come off the reservation," Billy said, "and Dad was just a poor fisherman. We moved from island to island depending on how good the fishing was. Later on, when I was still young, my father acquired a house-boat. Back then they were called lighters."

We were sitting around Marker 7 waiting for one of the Parkers' out-boards to be rebuilt by an ex-drug-addict mechanic from Vermont when they first began telling me their story. Billy and Red's stories kept me awake—both while they were telling them and long after they stopped.

When their dad was in his twenties, Billy went on, he fished a lot on the slow dark-brown waters inside the Seminole reservation. One morning he was poling his skiff down a channel surrounded by salt grass marsh, and he came upon a little Seminole settlement. An amazingly beautiful Seminole woman was standing on the bank, and in less than a few seconds, the family story goes, he had decided to marry her. He did.

Billy and Red's mother was a descendant of a small band of about one hundred Seminoles who escaped to these watery places prior to the Civil War. These were the only Seminoles our relentless government, in three wars with them, could not kill or march off to Oklahoma. They became the nucleus of today's tribe, which is headed by women.

The Seminole people had not wanted to retreat to these South Florida swamps. In the 1770s the Seminoles were settled around what is now Gainesville on good, high, fertile land. They were descended from the Upper and Lower Creek Indians, who early on had roamed into northern Florida to hunt during the winter. A group of them stayed and became independent from the Creeks. They were given the name *Seminole,* which means "wild, runaway."

"My family all lived on the islands, mostly in the Ten Thousand Islands, but up in the Fort Myers area, too—around the little town of Fort Myers Beach. We followed the fish, lived on our boat." Billy spoke of these times with a muscular pride. "Dad used to take his skiff and put his poling oar up in the center of the boat and put up a sail, and we'd sail the skiff from one place to the next because we didn't have outboard motors at that time."

Now Red, the younger brother, took up the story. "That whole area changed real fast from total wilderness into what they have now—total condos, high-rises, big, expensive houses. When I was a kid, there was a ferry that went from mainland Fort Myers to Fort Myers Beach. There was no bridge then. Land was almost nothin' an acre at Fort Myers Beach, and it's worth millions now.

"It's hard to believe the way this place was all wilderness, even up around Fort Myers. When I was about nine years old there were about fifty tourists a year that came to Fort Myers Beach. There was nothing there. There weren't no condos. It was all sandy beach, coconut palms from one end to the beach, rattlesnakes six to eight feet long, loggerhead turtles crawling on the beach, key deer running around, turkeys. There's none of that anymore. Only down south of here, on all those wilderness islands, is where it's like it was when we were children. That's why we are living here. Goodland's sorta right on the edge of the wilderness now. Up north of here, it's all gone."

"Mother was dark-skinned, real dark olive skin . . . long black hair," Billy remembered with a faint, sad smile. "She was tall, thin, and had big almond-shaped eyes, black eyes. She had high cheekbones, and I guess I have the high cheekbones and I have the slimness of my mother,"

"Of course, Irish and Indian makes for one mean temper," Red offered.

"Our daddy was a strong, fair man," Billy went on. "Rough in his own kind of ways. He was five-eleven, about 180 pounds, broad-shouldered, red hair, fair-complected. Red favors him a lot.

"Daddy grew up fishin', huntin' gators, eatin' curlew, sellin' feathers for hats. We fished with him as soon as we could go in the boat. We did a lot of our travelin' in a sixteen- to seventeen-foot skiff. We would mainly go three or four or five days at a time to catch our fish. Then we'd just salt our fish down and we'd cover them with the mangrove limbs to keep them from spoiling—keep the sun off of them. When we needed extra income, Daddy hunted gators and coons.

"Those boats then were practically like the ones we're using now except they weren't made of plywood. They were plank skiffs, made of cross planks and caulked with cotton. We didn't paint our boats; we limed them white. We didn't have monofilament netting; we had cotton nets, and we limed our cotton nets to keep them from rotting. We built the nets completely from scratch. We had a push pole, an eighteen-foot mangrove limb or buttonwood limb that we used to push the boat with. If there was no wind to sail, you poled."

I noticed that Billy had very large bicep muscles—the better to pole a skiff with. I also saw that he had a large scar on one of his shoulders that did not tan the same as the rest of his body. Later, when they trusted me more, I would learn how he got that terrible scar.

"To get some cash money, Daddy and us boys hunted alligator. He couldn't afford to have a stainless-steel gun, and a normal one would rust all to pieces. So most of the time we'd hunt the gators with a hatchet. We'd do it right at dark, when they were becoming active. Dad would get in the water just about up to his neck. Dad could make all the sounds a gator could make—bellow, grunt, mating sounds. He knew when the gator was coming cause he could see the wake from the gator coming at him. He hit 'em right between the eyes with his hatchet—he knew right when to drop the hatchet into the gator's head.

"After Daddy hit the gator it was supposed to be dead. But I was the one that had to swim out for the alligators and, of course, a lot times they weren't dead. So I've had to wrestle a few alligators in my time as a young boy. I began doing that when I was seven."

I could just imagine my father telling me to swim out and retrieve a wounded gator. When I was seven, I felt like Lewis or Clark when the back yard flooded and we sloshed in the puddles. A lot of my friends' mothers wouldn't even let them get wet. We felt wilder than *those* kids. I didn't have a clue that there were boys like Billy and Red or childhoods like theirs.

Half-Seminole Indian, half-Irish Billy and Red Parker, brothers

"We went to school," Billy said. "I went to elementary school at Fort Myers Beach when we weren't fishing. My dad would take us in his boat, pull us up to a little canal behind a little brick school down at Fort Myers Beach. He'd let us out of the boat, and I had one good shirt that I wore, a real fine silk shirt—I wore that with cutoff shorts. We went to school barefoot. But sometimes we couldn't get to school—and that's probably why the state came and took us."

Then Billy fell into silent brooding. Red explained that the state had taken all four Parker children—Billy, Red, and their two sisters—away from their parents and divided them up among their daddy's sisters.

"I don't know who thought up that scheme," Red added with vengeance in his voice. "Some city-raised social worker that'd never been sunburned before. I don't know how the state even knew how to interfere with our life. I guess through the school system—that's probably how they found out how we were living. But anyway, they broke the family up. Our mother and father definitely didn't want us to be sent away, but it happened anyway."

Their mother didn't live long after this happened. She died of cancer, although Red and Billy were both unclear about when or where. Billy couldn't even remember how old he was or whether he went to the funeral. And talk about his mother's death seemed to plunge him deeper into a dark well of sadness.

Red spoke, seeking to rescue Billy from his thoughts. "You remember, Billy, the time that ol' bull gator attacked Dad's favorite dog?"

"Oh, yeah," Billy said. "Remember we was living in a place called Duka Ridge. Duka Ridge is the locals' name for a place called Punta Rassa, near Sanibel Island. The reason they call it Duka Ridge is because of duking—you know, fighting. Those people used to fight a lot.

"Anyway, in the other side of Duka Ridge was a freshwater creek, and there used to be a big, big gator in that creek. It was probably about twelve feet long. We had a dog named Lady, and Lady went down there one day and got caught by the gator. She got free, but the gator bit off one of her ears. Well, that made my dad mad. So Dad grabbed his ax and called me, and we went down there to where that gator was.

"The gator went up in his cave inside of the ridge, and Dad got down there and started grunting for him. That gator came to Dad, and he hit it right in the tip of the nose. But he didn't kill it right off. He could see its wake and some blood coming from underneath the water. Then Dad got down in the water and finished off that gator.

"Dad said he went after that gator because me and Red played down there on that creek. But I think it was because of Lady, too. Dad didn't like anything that tried to hurt his family, and Lady was family."

Red's strategy seemed to be working. Billy pulled a knife out and began sharpening it slowly on a whetstone while he reminisced. "The next morning I woke up and Dad and me were in the skiff, and I was in a box with the gator hide, and Dad was poling his boat to the man who bought the gator hides. Considering the times, a gator skin got good money. I think Dad was getting like six to eight dollars a foot. Mullet was a few cents a pound, so even after they outlawed gator hunting, we still gator hunted to supplement our income. Any way we could make a dollar, we would, other than steal or rob from people. We didn't do that. We just kept on doing the things that we were raised doing. Be damned with the new laws."

The sun was now blood red, and clouds of mosquitoes were coming out to feed. I asked if we could talk some more tomorrow. Already the mechanic had found more wrong with their motor than he'd originally thought. It would cost them more money; money they didn't have at the moment.

So Comfortable
in the
Blackness

After dark I was going out to the islands with Larry, the black-bearded man who had claimed to be a drug enforcement officer. We were going, that is, if Larry's banana tree told him to.

Larry used his banana tree to gauge fishing conditions. When the banana leaves brushed up against the kitchen window, that meant the wind was up and it would be too rough to fish. If the banana tree was still, that was a sign to Larry that the conditions were good to find fish.

The banana tree had been scraping against the window early in the afternoon, so we sat in the kitchen and drank coffee while we waited to see what would happen. Doug, Larry's fishing partner from Everglades City, waited with us. If the winds laid down (as they said), then we would leave the hill, which is what these people call the land, and go searching in the night for fish. We'd head into the maze of gray-black sky, the still darker islands, and black, shiny water. There would be no moonlight. Larry said he would navigate by discerning different shades and shapes of black in the night.

Evening approached, and the winds seemed to be calming. Larry and Doug were getting excited. These fisherman, everyone of them, became visibly stimulated whenever the waters and winds and temperature gave them the chance to try again to catch the always anticipated, almost never realized net full of fish. Larry and Doug loaded up the boat with ice and cold water and windbreakers. Larry cleaned out his little coffeepot. He knew we'd be needing it.

Saltwater fishermen love these moonless nights because they can see the fish as they "fire." Like neon lights, fish glow an eerie pale green underwater. The darker the night, the more visible the "fire" beneath the water. Because of the glowing shapes the fish made underwater, and because Larry knew how to read the shapes and movements, we could see the fish far better at night than anytime during the day.

Depending on the way a fluorescent green shape moves and the size of the shape, Larry can tell what kind of fish it is. If it's a ladyfish it darts wild and crazy, fast and confused. If it's a mullet it's more stationary; it goes up near the surface and then sinks down. If it's a smaller shark and it's spooked, it flares off to the side of the boat—or if it's a really, really large shark and not startled it will just ease away, moving in slow motion, a seven-foot-long lightning bug. Pompano show as little squatty shapes that sink in deep water or dart and skip in shallow water. (Pompano are very fast and smart.) And a school of big black drum can look like the Fourth of July underwater.

All of this I would learn before the night was over. But it was all completely new to me—fishing on the blackest of black seas, with the green glow of different-sized fish here and there, alone and together, darting off, or staying in one place.

We started out about eleven-thirty, heading south toward a fishing grounds called Camp Lou Lou. It lay around Gomez Point, right at the border of the Everglades National Park. I was stunned at Larry's ability to navigate by feel, by the time traveled, by the sound his propeller made, and by the many shades of blackness.

Past Panther Key, we went in behind Round Key. It was a long run, almost ten miles. Then we slowed down to about half speed. Larry turned on a little light bulb on the back of the boat, which he called a skip light, and we began to look for pompano.

The surrounding black night air rushed by me as my eyes began to adjust to the darkness and recognize shapes in the black on black before us. Everything was in textures of black—dull black, shiny black, reflecting black. The islands covered with mangrove trees looked like black camouflage cloth. The sky was a clear, darker black. The water was a shiny black, and there was a barely perceptible difference in blackness between channel water, shallows, open bays. Larry acted so comfortable in the blackness.

Larry eased the boat here and there, and suddenly in the glossy water there was an incredible light show, phosphorescent shapes flickering and darting. The fish were making a lot of fire. Finally, we saw a couple of pompano skip. One jumped out of the water at our side, two flew out of the water toward the back of the boat, and one fired off from the front of the

Pompano are the best money fish that can be caught by the fishermen at Marker 7. These were caught by Gary Weeks and his brother-in-law on his boat, Family Tradition.

boat. Larry went a little ways and curved hard to the left, all the time trying to figure in which direction these pompano were moving. Pompano are fast swimmers and easily spooked.

These guys needed pompano badly. Pompano is the big money fish; it brings three dollars a pound as opposed to thirty cents a pound for mullet. These fisherman were used to living on the edge of poverty, their financial well-being dependent on the luck of the catch. Many I met would never consider taking welfare or asking anyone for help.

Larry and Doug released the net with an air of excitement and anticipation and wonder. I'm convinced that the thrill of anticipation is one of the main reasons these men keep fishing. They never know when they might hit the mother lode, that two thousand pounds of pompano, the six-thousand-dollar haul.

It was beautiful to watch and hear the net flinging off the stern—the upper line of cork and the lower lead line and net in between—as we zoomed around and cut toward a small beach.

Round Key was between us and the open Gulf. I could hear the waves crashing on the other side of the mangroves. Every noise out here told Larry and Billy and Red and all the rest of the fishermen something.

Even I was cataloging away a whole new file of sea sounds, fish sounds, and Gulf night sounds.

After we got the net in the water, Larry anchored the boat and we waited. The tide was falling, and he hoped the pompano would ride the current right into the net. He turned off the motors to hear the pompano skipping, and pretty soon we also heard some heavy splashing and thrashing. Larry figured some big sharks were hitting the net. If they didn't spin up in the net they'd rip right through.

We waited there twenty or thirty minutes, letting the tide continue to fall and hopefully letting the money-fish swim into the net. We heard some excited churning in the water. If it was sharks, we were in for a destroyed net and a nightmare getting them untangled. Larry didn't have a gun with him.

Finally it was time to pull in the nets. What began as excitement turned into the endless sorrow every fisherman knows. The net was filled with black drum. And most had to be thrown back because they weighed ten to twelve pounds apiece—breeding size. Larry and Doug knew that releasing the fish was right and the legal thing to do. But they had spent all this time, all this money, all this gear, and had caught almost nothing they could sell.

Larry shrugged. There would be other chances. There always had been. At least all that thrashing hadn't been sharks. The nets were still in one piece.

We left the bay where the pompano had escaped and where they'd released many black drum to spawn again. Then we ran a long distance back to the north, near the Romano Shoals. Not far away, on the intensely developed end of Marco Island, we could see lights as people slept secure in the high-rise condos. That image did not fit this black-on-black, water-on-sky night.

The sun was already rising when we tied up again at the Marker 7 Fish House. We'd fished from eleven-thirty at night until seven in the morning and caught no pompano whatsoever. An entire night, eight hours, had yielded four drum and a couple of sharks—a few dollars. The fuel for the boat had cost far more than they made that night.

Pretty depressing. I was exhausted. But Larry and Doug forgot about it a lot sooner than I did. The next day Larry's banana tree wasn't stirring. And Larry and Doug were at it again.

CHAPTER 15

Little Fingers
in a
Shark's Mouth

I was working-on-the-water tired after fishing all night on Larry's boat. I slept till the sun warmed my cabin on the *Cooper,* then walked to the local cafe for biscuits and gravy and some coffee. Billy and Red were there, too. Neither liked to talk much around other people, but no one else was around. Billy started right in with more of his story. I'd been wanting to hear more.

"A lot of times our whole family would sail down the coast toward the Keys. We'd tow the skiff. When we'd get to an area where we were going to fish, then Mama would make camp right inside the boat. She'd build her campfire in a little stove, and she'd cook our groceries for us. We ate grits and pan-fried bread and fish. Sometimes Dad would shoot a few curlew, maybe some white ibis. It was legal then.

"Say we'd leave here at Goodland and we'd sail to Panther Key, maybe a day's journey if we were sailing. We'd stop there, and Dad would check out the territory for a day or two, and if the fishing was good, then we'd stay. Most of the time, our destination would be around Lostman's River, right in the heart of the Ten Thousand Islands.

"Lostman's River was excellent fishing, but it's all national park now; we're not allowed to fish in there at all. I thought it was a great life. I didn't see any harm in it. We were a happy family, a real close-knit family. We ate good and we had a lot of freedom.

"Mama and Daddy, they took real good care of us. Mama would make beds for us in the bottom of the boat, and Daddy had a tarp he'd throw over the whole boat during the day to keep the sun off of us. At night Mama would make a smudge pot of burning cotton to keep the mosquitoes and the sand flies away. She'd rock Red to sleep and fan us three older kids to help keep the bugs off. There was a lot of bugs. Lots of bugs.

"We were usually barefoot. My first pair of shoes was made out of coonskin. My mama made them." A tone of gentle longing overcame Billy's voice every time he spoke of his mother.

"Dad would pole us up to the headwaters of a creek and drop us off. Then he'd go back to the mouth of the creek, which he would block off with his net. We were supposed to move around in the water and run the fish toward the mouth of the creek.

"A lot of times this happened at night, and of course kids have their fears. There's always a bogeyman, which for us was black panthers. There were plenty of black panther running around then. But the mosquitoes and the sand flies were the real problem. We'd rub oil on us, to keep 'em off. When the sand flies would get too bad, Dad would take the mud from the bottoms of the creek and pack our heads with the creek mud to keep the bugs from driving us crazy.

"Sometimes we were up to our necks in the water. Most of the time we'd be right under the edge of the mangroves close to the shoreline because that's where the fish try to hide, not in the middle of the creek. Just us moving through that water was enough to run the fish up toward the mouth of the creek."

I almost missed what Billy was saying at this point. I had gone off into my own world thinking about what he had said about being a close-knit family, a happy family. Growing up, I had always wished that our family had a farm we could all work on together instead of us all running down our own separate paths.

Billy was still talking about fishing. "The fish we drove down would mill about in the deep hole at the mouth of the creek. Dad, he'd take his cast net, and he'd net the fish right into the boat. Then us kids would take the fish up and we'd lay our fish out, the mullet in one place and the trout in another. A lot of the mullet we'd pack in rock salt. You slice them down the belly and lay them open, leave the scales on, and then you pack the salt in 'em and dry 'em in the sun. We kept some like that, then we pickled the rest in barrels with saltwater.

"Some of the real small sharks became our pets. All of us kids have been bit by baby sharks because we played with them. If you're a kid, you've just got to stick your finger in a shark's mouth."

When you grow up sticking your little tan fingers into a shark's mouth and diving into the dark water for a partly dead gator, what's the big deal about going off to Vietnam? It was just another adventure, Billy thought. Most importantly, his country was calling him. So he answered.

"I wasn't drafted, man," he told me later that afternoon. We had moved our conversation back down to the fish house. The motor still wasn't ready, and both brothers seemed to be growing edgier. Maybe that's what moved them toward the edgy subject of Vietnam.

"Down here in Florida when I was a kid," Billy said, "we sang the national anthem. We said the Pledge of Allegiance to the flag and the Lord's Prayer in school. I was real patriotic-minded. I believed in my country. I believed I was supposed to go to war for my country, any time, anywhere."

Billy paused, clearly undecided about whether to keep talking. I just sipped coffee and waited. Then he seemed to make up his mind and continued. "When Vietnam came about, I was afraid that the war would be over before I had a chance to help my country. When I turned seventeen, I volunteered for Vietnam."

"That second ambush is what near killed him," Red added in a quiet voice. Red could be loud and even obnoxious, but he spoke now as if he were in the presence of God. "When Billy went over he weighed 185 pounds. He was some specimen of a man, even though he was really only a boy. He came back weighing 94 pounds. And he wasn't the same person at all. When he first came back, everybody thought he was crazy, wanted to put him away. Even my father thought he was crazy."

Red shook his head. "Billy had always been my hero growing up. He was still my hero when he came back from Vietnam. I didn't care how crazy he acted. He was my brother." Billy watched Red closely while he told this part of the story. "Later, I found out maybe he was crazy for a while. But I still wouldn't go for putting Billy in a mental institution. I have never agreed with any of them about Billy—that's why Billy and I really separated from the family.

"I told myself that I'd take care of him even though I was awful young when he got out of the VA hospital." Red's eyes narrowed and opened, narrowed and opened. "And I did. Really, we took care of each other. Probably neither one of us would be alive today if we hadn't stuck together."

Red looked off through a torn screen toward the mangrove islands they fished and lived among. Billy was staring at him as though he'd never heard Red say some of these things before.

"He was so different," Red said again. "I don't know how to explain it, really. He was detached from this world as we know it. You see how we are here, but Billy wasn't like this then."

Billy stopped staring at his brother and said, "Sometimes I still sleep with my eyes open. I learned to do that over in Nam. I read a story about this Italian woman in Sicily who taught herself to do that to keep the Mafia from sneaking up on her and killing her son.

"I thought, If that woman can do it, so can I. So I just taught myself how to sleep with my eyes open and not to snore. I slept quiet, made no noises. I fought quiet, too."

Billy told me that a lot of things still made him remember Vietnam. Certain kinds of rain. Certain trees. The jungle at the edge of the Everglades where he and his wife lived in a camper-trailer. A certain kind of a quiet, dark, humid night. Smells.

"One particular battle I remember a lot. We were at the DMZ—just rolling hills. I was pulling guard duty. All our base camps were built in a circle, just like the old-time wagon trains. In Vietnam, your enemy was all around you, and you didn't have any front line. We formed circles so that our fire zone could cover 360 degrees."

"The battles where you got overrun usually happened at night, under the cover of darkness. That's the way it happened this time. It was the second year I was there, when I was eighteen."

I had another one of those moments when I suddenly saw the Parker brothers' life up against mine. Billy was eighteen in 1969. If he had not dropped out of school, both Billy and I would have been graduating from high school that year. Billy was about to describe a night of horror that had happened about the time of the "freaked-out" days I had spent at Woodstock, partying in the mud.

Now Billy was getting engrossed in the story. "I was on guard duty in my foxhole. Protecting our outer diameter was concertina wire, which is like razor blades. You have several layers of that. Outside of the wire we had about three hundred yards of open ground. You clear everything away so it's all open ground and there's nothing for your enemy to hide behind. Inside that concertina wire you've got claymore mines. That's a little concave mine with several thousand ball bearings in it, so when you push a little magneto in your hand, that claymore blasts all those ball bearings into your enemy. Then you also have a mine that's filled with napalm. You ignite it the same way as the claymore.

"Now what happens when there's an attack is the zappers—that's what we called the first gooks—they would try to come through the wire, and they would trip some trip flares in the wire. That night when the trip flare went off a call went out, 'Gooks in the wire . . . Gooks in the wire.' We shot off some more flares to light up the area. I was manning the sixty-caliber machine gun." Billy's dark Seminole eyes quit blinking. They became as wide as they could. His breathing was relaxed.

"The zappers came first, crawling through the wire, trying to get inside our compound. The zappers are some of their baddest dudes. They want to get inside with us and get us confused, get our eyes off the perimeter, fighting a few of them so we would not be able to take out what came next, the second wave. I guess you could call them a suicide wave. They just come in a mass, running at you. They're shooting, you're shooting back—those guys are falling down over that wire. The third wave just uses the dead and terribly wounded bodies like a bridge to run over.

"What they did with that suicide wave, they psyched up a bunch of the young ones, got 'em loaded up on opium, then sent them in. They sacrificed themselves in that wire—it cut 'em to pieces. The whole thing was booby-trapped; they were setting off mines, grenades. Thing is, they were so numbed on opium they couldn't feel anything.

"I don't think they *all* got stoned on opium, just the ones with the red bandannas. They had had 'em tied like tourniquets around their wrists, their arms, and their legs.

"When the trip flares started going off, they would light up everything like daylight. Then it might get dark for a moment. There was a lot of screamin' and shootin', explosions.

"I was real aware of what was happening around me. It was kind of like a movie in slow motion. It just sort of slows down, and you can kind of take it all in. That was the way it was for me. It was kind of like I was in a protective shell. I could look around and watch whenever the flares had things lit up.

"For instance, I seen this rocket explode, and I seen this guy running—one of our guys running—and I could see that hot piece of metal coming up behind him. And he kept running and that piece of metal was low to the ground. And he was running and that piece of metal looked like it was chasing him. Just as he dove into the foxhole, that piece of metal caught him right on the heel of his boot and cut off his heel right behind his ankles—boot, heel, and all.

"I could see the enemy comin' at me like that, too. Screamin' with knives and shootin', sometimes with their arms blown off, the red bandanna tourniquets keeping them from bleeding to death, the opium keeping them from feeling. They acted like they didn't even know their arm was missin'."

At that point the fish house cat jumped onto my lap, and I almost dove under the table. No wonder Billy and Red had come back here to where their happiest, however brief, childhood memories were.

"Then when your planes start coming over, they're dropping flares, too. So the sky just lights up. It's just daylight out there. It's kind of eerie because it's flashing like a strobe, but it's going dim and light, dim and light, as the flares burn out and then a new one lights up. Of course, those flares are like a thousand, two thousand feet up. They're coming out of the airplanes and they're floating down on their own little parachutes. The funny thing about those little parachutes was that they were all coated with talcum powder. We'd keep the silk parachutes because they smelled of talcum powder and it was like a scent of home."

A flying bug hit the light overhead. I jumped again.

"The Vietcong sacrificed a lot of their people just to get through our concertina wire. They lost eight hundred of their people that night."

It seemed like a long minute before he continued talking, and then his voice was so low I could hardly hear him. "In combat like that you're not thinking about 'I'm doing this for the United States, I'm doing it for South Vietnam.' All you're trying to do is stay alive. You're not doing it for anything except to save your own skin, just to stay alive. Forget about the United States. Forget about Vietnam. You're just trying to make that year so you can get home."

All that madness, all that killing, all that terror. Billy did stay alive, but he came home to a place where no one wanted him. No one but Red.

"I've got to go," he said. "Got to get me some sleep." He appeared exhausted. So was I. But I didn't think I would get to sleep that night. I kept seeing those opium-dazed North Vietnamese warriors charging, tourniquets tied around their wrists, elbows, and knees. Some missing arms or legs; many falling, getting up, coming, screaming. How could Billy sleep—ever?

I sprayed myself with insect repellent and stayed a long time in the fishermen's lounge, watching *The Tonight Show,* David Letterman, and the ever-repeating CNN.

I didn't see Billy and Red for a couple of days.

CHAPTER 16

Thousands
of
Outstretched Arms

Billy and Red fished most of the next two days. Their motor was finally fixed, so they caught a lot of sheephead and some mullet and earned enough to survive a couple more days. A week later we talked again. Billy said he hadn't even told the Veterans Administration shrink some of the things he was telling me. As in our earlier conversations, Red and Billy took turns talking.

Red hated that he and Billy had been separated when they were small. "We didn't get to finish growing up together, but I did get to go visit him every now and then—about once every three months. I usually spent a couple of days. When I saw Billy he lived on a farm, and he was a lot of fun. We'd ride horses, and he had an old car. He couldn't drive it nowhere—old battle-ax aunt wouldn't let him take it off the property. But we'd drive around and around on that ten acres of hers. We'd go milk the cows and go swimming and play and have a good time. It was all fun. We just had a good time and he wasn't mean . . ."

Now Red hesitated as if he did not want to say what he was about to say. He glanced at Billy. Billy seemed to want to hear it, too.

"When he came back from Vietnam he *was* mean. He was a real efficient killer when he come back, man.

"Well, he didn't get out of the hospital for a long time, till his wounds healed up a little. He'd been shot seven times. When I first saw him he came to my father's house—that's where I was staying at the time. I was kind of shocked at his appearance. He was all skinny, and his left arm was all crippled. But he wasn't dead. That was something. And I was glad to see him."

Billy broke in. "In '68 or '69—I don't remember the exact dates when I got wounded—I got hit two times. That last time I really got it, five rounds at once. A piece of metal went through my neck and down to my right chest. My forehead was broke. My nose was broke. Three cracked vertebrae in my back. My left hand was almost blown completely off, hanging on by a few fragments of skin. A bullet wound in my left leg, my right leg, one in my shin."

"That day, when I got hit the second time, we'd run down Highway 1 for a ways to observe and check for possible enemy movement. That time the enemy detonated a five-hundred-pound American bomb under us—one that had been dropped but hadn't exploded. I never knew what hit us, but that's what they said it was. It went off underneath the jeep, and then they opened up on us with machine-gun fire.

"I was standing in back of the jeep with an M-60 machine gun. There was a driver and a shotgun rider in the passenger side, and it just blowed them away and blowed me out of the jeep and I was—I don't know how far I got blowed away from the jeep. I saw a flash of red, and I thought everything was blowing by me, but I realized I was going with it . . . with the blast. Then I hit the ground and the jeep hit me. That's how I broke my forehead.

"For a long time I was lying there thinking I needed to get hold of my rifle because they were going to come over there and finish me off. Then two Vietnamese did walk over—I thought that was the Vietcong, but it just happened to be two South Vietnamese medics. They did what they could for me and then they called in a medevac chopper to take me out.

"I remember it all, every bit of it. I was in shock, but I was aware of what was going on. I wasn't really aware of the condition of my body, though. I felt no pain. I felt like I was all in one piece. The first time I understood what had happened to my body was about four days later, after I came out of surgery. I was in the hospital eighteen months that time."

"When I first saw him after that," Red said, "I guess I was awed. I was still pretty young, and it wasn't so much shock as it was awe that my brother had gone off to fight and gotten hurt. I had tried to enlist but they wouldn't take me because I was too young and also because I already had a brother in a combat zone.

"He was my hero," Red repeated. "But I had a lot to learn, because when he got back he was so different. Even with only one arm, all he wanted to do was fight. He just didn't care about anything.

"I realized pretty soon after Billy got home that we had to get us a boat and go shrimping. Staying on land, he was going to kill a bunch a people, maybe get killed. I figured I'd get us both out to sea, stay out and shrimp. I don't know how he shrimped with me as good as he did with his bad hand. Sometimes he'd get so upset with it not working—all shriveled up and numb—he'd beg me to chop it off."

"When I first got out of the hospital," Billy said, "I tried to go back to Vietnam because I didn't feel I belonged here in the United States. I had adapted to livin' over there. I felt like that was the way it was supposed to be for me. This life wasn't real no more.

"When I couldn't go back, that's when we went shrimping. I had to get away somewhere. Man, I'd just left combat, and they shoved me right back into society with no readjustment period. There was nobody to talk to, nobody to tell you how to readjust, nobody to help you readjust back to society."

"You never knew what would make him think of something that happened over there," Red said. "Even something beautiful we might see out on the Gulf might make him start thinking of something bad.

"I remember the time we were coming across the Gulf, coming back from Texas. We were in sixty fathoms of water. It was real pretty—beautiful rolling seas. We stopped the boat and looked over the rail and put this spotlight over the side. On top of the water just as far as you could see there were just millions and millions of tiny shrimp. Just millions of them. It was unbelievable. That was a beautiful thing.

"But when Billy saw that, he began talking about Willie, his black friend. I guess you could say we grew up pretty prejudiced. But this guy was his best friend over there. And then Billy started thinking about when Willie got killed, and then he got crazy again."

Nothing Billy told me seemed to torture him more than Willie Austin's death.

"My friends, Paul and Willie, they was both working with this self-propelled weapon, like a tank except it was a big canon. Paul was the controller of it, the one that drove it and fired it. A 122 rocket hit it and blew out the hydraulic controls that raised the barrel of the weapon up and down, left and right. The weapon caught on fire. Paul was dead instantly. Then another rocket hit the ammo bunker, the powder bunker where Willie was. It blew both of his legs off at the knees. From his hips to his knees there was no muscle, just bare bone. From the knees down there was no legs at all, and his intestines was wrapped around those bones and stuff."

Billy fell silent, deeply moved, but there were no tears. There were never any tears, only white-hot rage.

"I picked Willie up in my arms and carried him to the medevac area," Billy continued in a monotone, his dark eyes staring. "He was unconscious. I never got to say anything to him. Of course he died.

"I used to write poetry, sometimes," Billy told me. "One thing I remember I wrote went,

> Thousands of outstretched arms
> all lined up down a long road
> all reaching out
> none of them touching me.

Billy and Red stood up and went to a rusted sixties-style refrigerator in the fisherman's lounge. They were looking for some no-brand sodas, but Red's kids had drunk them all.

Billy and Red's wives walked in; they'd been grocery shopping. We stopped talking. Billy and Robin and their three small dogs went to bed in their van outside. Red and Janet and their kids got in their boat and headed to their houseboat, which was anchored near Brush Island. And I got up and stretched and headed back for the *Cooper*, my heart terribly saddened, crying for Billy and Red and crying because I'd been wasting too much time the last several years focusing too much on me.

CHAPTER 17

It's Freaky,
Man

e hit the Gulf, man, we were shrimping and fighting. Man, did we fight. Usually I started it, man, and Billy, he done finished it."

We were back in the fish house, in the early evening, as Red spoke. We had gotten to the point where we all looked forward to being together and talking more.

Today the wind had been too disruptive to allow the brothers to fish, so they and their families had come in to take care of some domestic chores. While we talked, Red's wife, Janet, sat nursing their baby and watching television. She had just taken a shower; there was one in the laundry room. Only occasionally did she seem to pay attention to our conversation.

"I would be going wild, fighting anybody, no matter how big, and Billy would just be standing there cool, calm, smacking people with a pool stick as they charged me. He'd go back to shootin' pool until another one charged to jump on me. He would knock 'em out; we'd tear that meat house down.

"I became bad from hanging around him. I mean I was tough enough before, but I wasn't bad until Billy came back from Vietnam. You've got to be like your heroes. So I became bad, too."

Red reminded me of my younger brother, Freddie. Freddie looked up to me the same way Red looked up to Billie. I went to college. He wanted to go. I'd been to Woodstock. He wished he'd been old enough to go. I listened to Jimi Hendrix, the Allman Brothers, Stevie Wonder, Sly and the Family Stone. He did, too. If I had come back from Vietnam in the same shape as Billy had, Freddie was the type who would have stuck by me no matter what, just exactly the way Red did. Red and Freddie, they loved their brother no matter what.

Red said, "We was raised not to abuse women. One of the fastest ways for someone to get hurt was for Billy or me to see someone beating on or cussin' a woman."

"One time in Fort Myers Beach," Billy countered, "Red even went so far as to stand at the front door of a bad bikers' bar and tell 'em all to come out on the street so he could tear 'em all apart. He hates the way bikers treat their women."

I asked the brothers what else they did in those bad, fighting days. "Me and Billy, we done a lot of things from construction to painting to roofing, all kinds of land jobs you can think of. We've worked iron and on oil boats, but shrimping's about as tough as it comes. It takes a special breed to be a shrimper.

"There was this storm one time, and it wasn't blowing but 116 miles per hour. We was about eighty-five miles offshore of Morgan City, Louisiana, and the seas were really bad—fifteen, eighteen-footers crashing across the bow. I was trying to move back inshore so the boat wouldn't get sunk. We were already taking on water. And every time a wave hit us, the boat sounded like it was breaking in half.

"We'd lashed everything down and those waves still tore us all to pieces. Tore off the running lights and broke windows, busted doors off where seas crashed into the side of the boat. All the canned goods busted open, the doors flew off the cabinets, everything just shattered where the canned goods had bounced around in the cabin.

"We had this ex-marine on the boat as a crew member. He had his life jacket on and was crawling around the deck. 'Are we going to make it? Are we going to make it to Cameron?' 'I guess so, man; I don't really know. We're going to try with everything we've got.'

"Like I said, man, Billy and me, we were tough. We could take anything came our way—the notorious Parker brothers. We were young, we were ambitious, we were mean, and we were going to be the best." Red's face turned the color of his name when he talked like this.

What eventually stopped them from shrimping was an invasion of sorts. The Vietnamese, fleeing the aftermath of Billy's war, moved by the thousands to the Gulf Coast, and many of them became shrimpers. The Vietnamese now dominate shrimping in the Gulf, the most lucrative fishery in U.S. waters.

"Can you imagine that?" said Red. "Here Billy goes over there to fight for these Vietnamese people's freedom from communism. Then our stupid government don't let us win the war. So Billy sacrifices his sanity, his body, his whole outlook, his friends—goes over there and fights for almost two years. Then he comes home and goes back to what he done growed up with, shrimping. And what does the government do? They let these Vietnamese flood in here and give 'em all kinds of help—housing, food stamps, real cheap loans. They give 'em ten years where they don't have to pay any taxes. Did they do that for Billy? No way! It's freaky, man, the way it happened."

Billy sat upright with the great dignity of a Seminole warrior through Red's flood of righteous indignation. He sat that way a lot, never said a word. Red wanted to get his hands on the bureaucrats who had inflicted all this idiocy on him and his brother. But then he added, "It's weird, man, but I can't say as I really ever had any trouble with them Vietnamese myself. Actually, I've always gotten along with them pretty good. At first I really hated them because of my brother. But I try not to be a narrow-minded person. I tried to give them a chance. And when I did, I found out that they were basically a good people. They work hard; they're real family oriented. I have to give them a lot of credit."

At this point Billy's wife, Robin, appeared. She'd been doing their wash in the fish house's laundry room, next to the ice room. Billy's eyes locked on her even as he continued our conversation.

"I'm not mad at the Vietnamese," Billy said, his face blank. "They just took what was offered 'em. I'm pissed off at this idiotic government. When are they gonna get anything right?"

Robin was the one thing that pulled Billy away from the nomadic and wild life he was living on the shrimp boat. The people who know Billy well say the best thing that ever happened to him was the day he stepped out of the chicken coop behind Odie Love's house in Freeport, Texas, and saw Robin walking in the front yard.

"Odie had this chicken coop out in a little barn where he could keep a couple of bales of hay and his chicken feed and stuff like that. I was living there. I just put me a bed in there and a fan and built a partition to separate me from the chickens. Robin, she lived right across the street in one of the Loves' rental trailers. Whenever she'd come over and pay her rent, while she was talking to Miz Love and Miz Love's back was turned to me, I'd be making eyes at her—you know, flirting.

"She had a boyfriend at the time, and I guess he wasn't too good to her. I ended up taking her away. We couldn't go far, though, cause I didn't have much money, so I got a job and made enough money to come back to Florida. I asked her if she had her stuff packed. She said, 'Matter of fact, I do.' She had her stuff packed right there in a suitcase beside the door.

Gary Weeks and his brother-in-law, Earl Moore, haul in the net on his largest boat, Family Tradition. *"My people were some of the first settlers of Marco Island, before tourists ever even knew of this place,"* he told me. On this March day, they cast and hauled in their net six times; only one had captured any pompano, the money fish. One net load was filled with stingrays, and they spent more than an hour untangling and releasing them.

"So we jumped into my Monte Carlo, used about two cases of oil to go three hundred miles. I kept asking her to marry me and she said, 'No, you don't know what you're doing.' But we ended up getting married anyway. She has kept me out of trouble these last seven or eight years."

Robin had sat down next to Red's wife and was gently rubbing her hand across the head of their new little pit bull puppy. She was about thirty-five years old, with blonde hair, a round, gentle face, and a sweet strength about her.

Red had been talking a lot, and he had one last thing he wanted to say. He seemed to want to say it before Robin left to put her wash in the dryer.

"I wasn't a real good influence on Billy. Robin, she's the only person that's ever been able to tame him down, and how she does it I don't know. I guess it has something to do with Billy. It's not *her* keeping Billy from fighting; it's him trying to keep her from seeing that rage that's inside him. I think it's him keeping his inner self from her so that she don't have to see the way that he can be. Whatever it is, he's calmed down considerably."

Robin leaned over to whisper something to Janet as Red continued. "Thank God, man, I found the right woman, too, 'cause we both calmed down. You know what they say, what I heard all my life. A bad woman can destroy a man, a good woman can make him. We both got good women. No doubt, man."

Billy acted a little embarrassed, as if he wanted to change the subject. Red said that we had talked a whole lot longer than he'd ever expected. He was surprised at how much he and Billy had told me. He said it was time for them to get in their boat and get home.

"Right now, we're back to the way we started as kids, livin' in a houseboat. I have it in a little bay. It's probably four or five miles from here. We kind of have to stay away from society because I'm not a real society-type person." Their salvaged houseboat was anchored at the south side of little Brush Island in a little cove near a small white beach. Red said that the mosquitoes got a little bad sometimes, but his wife and kids really loved it there.

Billy and Red and their wives and children and dogs haven't lived in Goodland all that long. They can't live in Fort Myers Beach anymore; it's been taken over. The fact is there's almost no place for people like the Parker brothers to live on the water in South Florida anymore, except Goodland and Everglades City. Billy and Red, like the Seminoles before them and a lot of other native Floridians now, are being driven farther and farther into the inaccessible places, the places few want to live.

I heard Red's outboard engine crank up. Instead of pulling away, it seemed to be idling too long, tied up to the dock next to us. Red came back inside. He said he'd thought of something and wanted to say it now.

"Me and Billy, we don't talk about it much, but we sure think about it. What kind of future do people like us have here in Florida anyway? I've thought about it long and hard many nights because when you're out there fishing you have a lot of time to think. I've done a lot of other things in life and I've been a lot of other places, and I guess you have the tendency to come back to where your roots are no matter what. I've tried to get away from the Gulf, but I can't.

"I hope to be a fisherman all the rest of my life," Red said as Billy turned the television off. "I want my children to be fishermen. I hope they can be. But in all honesty, I don't think we're going to make it. I don't look for us to be fishermen for very much longer. I think that probably the government is going to put us out of business. I don't really understand how they can do that to us, but that's what I believe." There is a strong movement in Florida to ban all fishing with nets.

"I mean, I may have to end up having to become a fishing guide to make a living. It just seems really contorted. All's I really want to be is left alone, to be able to fish like my people always have."

Red and Billy are not the type to say an official good-bye. So Billy surprised me a few days before the *Cooper* and I shoved off to my next destination. He walked over to my boat, which I was hosing down, and said, "Listen, man. You have any kind of trouble on this trip, you give us a call. We know this Gulf, man. We know how to get out of situations."

I felt very honored by this offer from Billy and Red. But most of all, I felt indebted to them for trusting me with their private worlds. With their honesty they changed me forever.

A Real
Sensitive Man

The morning I left Goodland, I went upstairs and knocked on Bob and Barb's door. Chainsaw, their male pit bull, still barked at me like he wanted me for a snack. But Pinky, the white female, wagged her whole body. I could see her through the glass sliding door, and I could hear Piglet going through her morning screaming ritual. Piglet, the parrot Barb had gotten when it was twenty-four days old, always talked a lot when Barb got up and had her first cup of coffee. Every morning I could hear Piglet screaming out, "I LOVE YOU . . . Good morning . . . What's the matter, huh? . . . What's the problem?" Then Piglet would start screeching for the dogs, calling them by name, and for all the other parrots. She just had to wake everybody up.

I said good-bye to Barb. When I asked where Bob was, she told me he was still asleep. He'd been up real late, all upset because they'd taken the red parrot, Peeper, to the vet and found out that she had a cancerous tumor. "Bob may not seem like it, with his tattoos and motorcycle and all," she said, "but he's a real sensitive man."

So I did not get to say good-bye to Bob face to face. But Larry the fisherman gave me a great sendoff with a mullet breakfast. The whole time I was in Goodland, Larry had been telling me how delicious fresh mullet was. Now he filleted some for me and cooked it up in the fishermen's lounge. It was my last meal at the Marker 7 Fish House. There were no fancy plates or napkins, nothing but the mullet, hand-caught and hand-filleted, as good as any fish I've ever eaten.

And then I said good-bye. I had been here two months, and it was time to head north, up the coast toward Fort Myers and beyond.

My father would be flying down from Connecticut tomorrow to join me on the boat—the first time in our lives we would be alone together for any length of time. I had so much to do to get ready, but I wasn't ready to think about that yet. First I had a challenging trip ahead to Pine Island, not far from Fort Myers.

I had my choice of routes to get to Pine Island. I could either head for the open Gulf or choose a more protected river route behind a growth of mangroves.

"The Gulf is gonna eat you up today," Larry had said before I cast off from Marker 7. The northwest winds were creating something called a quartering sea, where waves would hit the boat from the side and toss it about. I opted for the protection and calm behind the tangled trees.

Behind the mangroves, out of the wind, it was a perfect Southwest Florida day in late May. I wound along the snaking, handsome Big Marco River, past haunting Turtle Island, under the tall and expensive Marco Island Bridge. When I got to Capri Pass I put my potent, metallic blue Yamaha engines in neutral between Coconut Island and Sea Oat Island and reconsidered my course. I could see plenty of whitecaps, the waves smashing over and over, frothing at the top of their crests. I decided I would stay inside the protected waters longer. If I kept Keewaydin Island on my left and Rookery Bay on my right and headed north, I would be in a natural backwater route that would keep us—the *Cooper* and me—from the pounding of the Gulf.

When I got to Dollar Bay, I was almost to Naples. And by now all I could think about was my father.

For the year I spent planning this trip and for the last five months I had been at sea, my father and I had been talking about his joining me on the boat for a week or so. I knew from past experience that he'd probably try to get out of coming. But I was determined not to let him.

Throughout my childhood I had wished that my father and I could do more stuff together. But Dad was always working, struggling to feed, clothe, and house six energized, rowdy Jenkins children. When he managed the hardware department at Caldors, he usually didn't get home till after the store closed, and he worked six days a week.

A couple of years back Dad had taken advantage of an early-retirement buyout deal from Pitney Bowes, where he'd gone to work after Caldors. Now, at age sixty-five, he was free to do whatever he wanted. Mother wanted him to come with me. Dad did, too. But every time we talked on the phone, Dad seemed to come up with problems from every negative angle imaginable. He was worried he wouldn't be able to get around, that he'd get in my way.

It is true that he had fallen at work on some icy stairs and torn his knee up. After reconstructive surgery on that one, he had gone back to work before being fully rehabbed and had fallen again, screwing up his other knee. (Bad knees seem to run in the Jenkins family.) Now Dad walked with a cane, an uneasy sight to me. But I told him not to worry, we'd stay out of dance halls where they did slam dancing. He knew what slam dancing was. He amazed me with what he knew.

Watching Dad age was probably as unnerving to me as it was for him to see his oldest child about to become forty. His still thick, curly hair was now almost white, and seeing him hobbled with his knees, not springing back and recovering like he used to, made me acutely aware that life was moving fast. Growing up, I don't ever remember my father or mother being sick. Now I realize what it must have been like to raise and provide for all six of us. There was no time for them to be sick; our demands were too great.

Thinking about Dad made me remember the time right after my divorce when my older children—Rebekah, Jed, and Luke—came to spend spring break with me. We looked forward to ten whole days together, just them and me. And after an adjustment period—after I learned the trick of keeping them fed and clothed and bathed, pacified and played with and put to bed with prayers said and concerns talked out— then we really enjoyed being together. I became a relaxed Mr. Mom . . . until a cold front blew in. The yellow daffodils got hammered by a killing frost and my tractor got mired in the mud. The pasture grass iced over, and I had to feed my cows by hand. And then I got sick with a bad, shivering fever—the worst sort of winter sickness. It was the kind of flu that flattened me to the bed, made me see two of each kid. I felt like I was already dead, seeing everything in one of those after-death experiences. But the kids still needed me.

"Daddy, I'm hungry," Jed would say.

"Daddy, Rebekah won't let me play Astro Warrior," Luke would complain.

"Dad, tell these boys to stop picking up the phone; I'm talking," Rebekah would shout down the hall.

"When are we going to eat?"

"Dad, please come get me a glass of water."

It was all I could do to stand up. I took care of them the best I could. That was when I really began to realize what Mom and Dad must have gone through with six of us. I understood all that they'd sacrificed, putting their own desires aside to fulfill our needs.

I liked the idea that Dad and I were going to be spending time together as two men, two fathers. Never again would he be the overpowering physical and psychological force, in control and all-knowing, standing on top of the mountain, with me, the slighter, inexperienced one near the bottom looking up at him. Now it seemed that we were both about halfway up the hill, standing together. We both now voted for the same party, leaned the same way on just about every political issue. He didn't despise rock 'n' roll anymore, and at times I liked Tony Bennett, Glenn Miller, and Nat King Cole almost as much as James Taylor, Steely Dan, and James Brown. Maybe we could move beyond father and son and become friends.

I'd not been around Dad on a day-to-day basis since I left home to go to college in 1969. Now he and I had lived apart for more than twenty years. Since I'd settled on my easy-rolling, pasture-covered Tennessee farm some nine hundred miles from their little blue home in Connecticut, we didn't see enough of each other.

Where had all the summers and falls and winters and springs gone? Lately a year seemed to last a month. We'd both been in our own worlds, routines taking over, everyday challenges taking priority, eating up precious time. I have always felt attached to my family, no matter how many miles away I was from any of them. I have always felt we'd be a part of each other far beyond our deaths. But that good, long-distance feeling of togetherness wasn't enough anymore. I was hungry for Dad and me to spend some of our priceless time doing something together.

I thought about our upcoming time together so much that I was nervous. I told myself that was stupid. Dad was always so accepting of all of us kids, what we did and didn't do. It didn't matter what I told myself; my stomach still fluttered. A few times I even felt like copping out on the experience, creating a reason not to get together. That had to be how Dad was feeling, too. That's why he kept thinking of reasons not to come.

Dad worried that his knees would give out on him, and he wouldn't be able to help me on the boat. I told him I could do almost everything—and that if he had trouble getting off the boat I'd hire a crane. He wondered if he would get in the way of my meeting people. I told him I didn't care about meeting anyone while he and I were together. He asked how well the boat was running, and he wanted to know all its specifications. (I knew he would be checking with his half-brother, Morgan, who lived next to the Greenwich Yacht Club, to make sure the *Cooper* was up to snuff.)

Dad wondered about the weather. What clothes should he bring? Where would we eat? How far out of sight of land would we be? He wondered how I was going to come pick him up at the airport. I wondered the same thing, but told him I had it arranged.

My worries were different from Dad's, but they were just as strong. What would it be like for him and me to be together, sitting inches apart in the *Cooper?* We'd have hours and hours and hours with nothing to do but run the boat and be near each other. We could talk, maybe. But we had never been all that comfortable talking before.

There were so many things I wanted to know—questions about people and events of my childhood that I had never understood. I had questions about my Grandfather Jenkins, who'd died of cancer when I was five, and about my grandmother, who'd died of cancer when Dad was eighteen. (Now I realized why Billy Parker sometimes reminded me of my father. Billy got that same pained, confused, tortured look on his face that Dad did whenever he spoke about his mother.)

I thought I wanted to ask Dad about why he had chosen to work where he did, why he had chosen not to take a couple of jobs that would have brought in more money. I wondered why we had lived so many years in Wilbur Peck Court, a federal housing project, when we were supposed to be descended from a long line of New England blue bloods. I had a lot of other questions about the way we had grown up.

I hoped most of all that during our time together Dad and I would be able to make the move from our outsides to our insides. I've always been one family member who tried to lay off Dad, tried not to criticize him. I always felt it was my role to protect Dad. Maybe by playing that role, I had missed out on some of the confrontation it takes to begin the journey toward openness. I felt that for us to grow closer we *needed* to talk about some uncomfortable issues, and I worried whether I would be able to ask my father anything that I felt might make him uncomfortable.

What would we talk about? What *could* we talk about? This was like getting ready for a first date, a first job interview.

I had to stop thinking about Dad's visit every once in a while and navigate. The buoys were close together, easy to follow. There was no coral to worry about, and the dolphins knew to stay out of my way. But I did need to keep focused for signs of the slow-ambler, the vegetarian manatee. And I needed to keep an eye out for Marker 73, where I had planned to stop and study my charts.

I zoomed past 71, surprised that all my thinking about joining up with Dad had consumed so much of this run, that I was still feeling so anxious. I made note of Marker 72, then pulled up close to Marker 73.

I saw that now I had no choice but to brave the Gulf and its side-smashing waves for the next leg of the journey. The *Cooper* had to move powerfully through Gordon Pass to the sea, where the incoming tide was funneling through. On my right were mansions of millionaires in a part of Naples that rivaled Beverly Hills, Greenwich, Palm Beach, or East Hampton. Black-haired gardeners amid automatic sprinklers scurried to get their jobs done. One tinted-glass palace was getting a new ceramic tile roof.

The open seas stole what little tranquility I had left after my worries about Dad. It was all I could do to hold the boat on course, almost straight north. I had more than twenty miles to travel with pounding waves and ocean spray washing over the bow.

These were the waters of the outside, where today's rough, tough, pounding sea challenged me to fight back, to find a way. I loved the outside for what it was. But the inside had been a lot more comfortable, much more secure, easier on my tired spine.

When I finally reached the protection of Sanibel Island, I brought the four hundred horsepower of my two roaring 200s to a halt, shut the motors off, and just drifted a few minutes, relieved to be out of the struggle. Once past Woodrings Point the waters gentled even more. My boat now felt like a magic carpet fluttering over the top of Pine Island Sound. The feeling was the opposite of the open waters. Being alone in the boat on mirrorlike salt-water, in perfect air just the right warmth, the engines in a high whine mixing their sounds with the passing winds was a soothing thrill. I felt as if the sea had been created just for me.

I was running the *Cooper* with confidence, navigating through narrow buoys at thirty miles per hour. I would never have imagined doing this when I was goofing up in the Keys.

This feeling was unlike anything I'd ever had before, a new one for the feelings catalog. I felt like a pelican gliding a few inches over flat water, riding the warmth, powered by the low wind, every so often dipping its wingtips into the water. Airborne, seaborne—I was free.

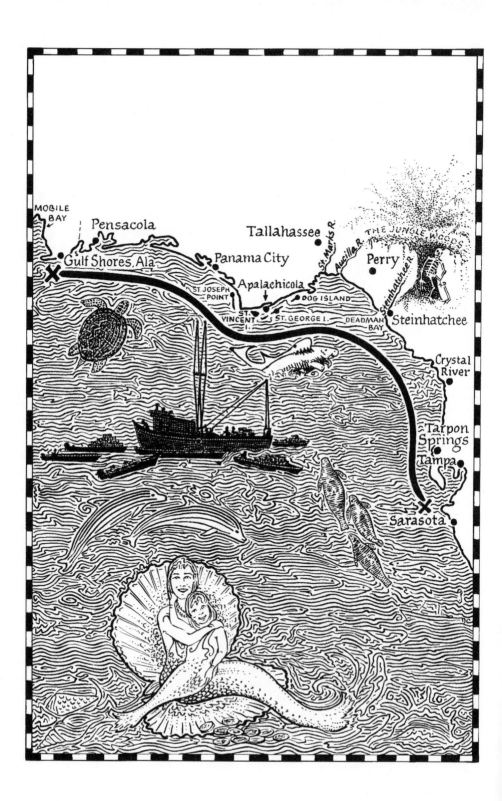

MOBILE BAY

Pensacola

Tallahassee

Gulf Shores, Ala.

Panama City

St. Marks R.

Aucilla R.

THE JUNGLE WOODS

Perry

Apalachicola

ST. JOSEPH POINT

DOG ISLAND

Steinhatchee

ST. VINCENT I.

ST. GEORGE I.

DEADMAN BAY

Steinhatchee

Crystal River

Tarpon Springs

Tampa

Sarasota

CHAPTER 19

Man
Beside
Man

Driving a borrowed truck to the Fort Myers airport felt unexpectedly strange. After five months at sea, all that solid ground felt too stable.

Dad finally came off the plane just when I thought he must have missed his flight. He leaned on his crutch and moved more slowly because of it, yet that mischievous sparkle in his eyes still flashed through his shyness. We gave each other a hug, kind of a stiff one. He told me he'd brought me a copy of the *New York Times,* and he said he was glad to be away from Mother. It was a family joke. What he really meant was that he missed her already. I knew the way Dad had acted when Mother came to Tennessee for a month every time one of the babies was born.

We stopped at a grocery store before getting back to the boat. Dad has always loved food shopping. He gets into it so much that often he will go to another store to save thirty-two cents on a package of paper towels. Now he wanted to pay for everything. I was determined to do the same. Although he fought me, he let me win.

First thing Dad said as we rolled into the store was that I needed sunscreen. He certainly didn't. He's always been dark, with the kind of skin that tans easily, and he had always loved the sun and the water—even been a lifeguard. As a freckle-faced, redheaded kid, I would turn the color of a red Corvette but fight and resist when Mother tried to make me get in the shade. I wanted to be in the sun all day like Dad.

Dad had taught me to swim underwater by letting me lie on his back. Together we'd slip under the water, I felt like a baby whale. I have taught my children the exact same way. They want me to carry them on my back all day, just as I once wanted. They seem to think I never tire, never wear down—just like I thought about my father.

Once we were finally in the boat, Dad seemed overly concerned. When I got out into the open water and accelerated, the quiet idling gentleness of the *Cooper* changed to throwback power, and the speed pushed us both backward. Then he asked, "How do you know where we're going?"

"I'm headed for that red buoy over by that island," I answered. "We stay in a channel, using the red and green buoys as guides." That seemed to satisfy him.

Our first night together we both seemed tense. I certainly was. We watched ospreys fishing for their dinner in Pine Island Sound. We talked about the family, about brothers and sisters—but only the aspects of their lives that were not potentially painful or controversial. Dad seemed to want to talk about the trip. That was fine for now.

"Well," he said, "you have any close calls yet? Have you gotten yourself into any trouble on this thing?" At first, as if reverting back to junior high school, I said no. But then I told him about the first time I took the *Cooper* out solo.

"I decided to go snorkeling at a reef. I had to go through a creek and under a bridge to get to the reefs. Vertical clearance was only fifteen feet, which meant I could not get under it with my antennas raised. I needed about eleven feet of clearance to get under the bridge with my two antennas down.

"Almost to the bridge, I heard these big bad engines powering a boat behind me. It was the kind of speedboat that wanted to be seen and heard, and it was crowding me. I was fighting a strong current; I could feel it trying to grab hold of my boat. I wanted to stop and collect my thoughts, but that obnoxious boat was pressing me."

"Why didn't you wave the idiot off?" Dad growled. "Give him one of those New York City driver hand signals." Dad can be a rowdy and outspoken driver.

"I was too uptight. It was all I could do to keep from crashing into the bridge. I told myself to breathe deep. Just give it a bit more power, lower my motors, steer toward the middle of the bridge, don't slow down.

"I did all that, and as soon as I got under the bridge I heard a snapping crash. At first I thought the bridge was falling, then I realized what had happened. I had forgotten to lower my antennae, and that sound was the fiberglass shattering as they smashed their way under the bridge. What an idiot—and with two boats behind me. I got out from under the bridge, let the boats by, surveyed the damage. One antenna was splintered but not broken; the other seemed OK. One was for my VHF radio, which is my only way to communicate. The other was for my loran, the navigational system that uses radio waves. I wasn't sure which one had splintered."

"Did you fix them?" Dad blurted out.

"I think so. So far they seem to be OK." Actually, I was enjoying messing with my father. I couldn't remember when in my life I'd heard this tone of concern in his voice. No matter what I seemed to do, he had never seemed surprised.

Why did I feel like this was the first time I'd ever been with my father? Was it because Dad and I had never developed a relationship just between him and me alone? Growing up in my family it was always the group—all six of us kids, plus mother and father. There was me, the eldest, supposedly doing everything first. Then there was Winky, the brain, the good student, Mommie's faithful helper. Scott was the blond, artistic one, a bit intense. Freddie, the cute dark-haired one who lost the sight in one of his eyes in a rock fight at five, was the athlete, the musician, Mr. Popularity. And then came Betsy and Abbi, the cute little blonde and brunette sisters too young to apply their emerging personalities much while I was still home.

Just because we were father and son didn't mean that we were automatically close. We'd lived together for about seventeen years, but so what? There was me, kid, and him, man. Now we were man and man and stumbling and stammering around each other.

OK, Peter, relax. Take it easy; don't push. Whatever's going to come—just let it come. I realized I had a tendency to be too intense, too pushy. I needed to lighten up.

We anchored at Useppa Island and sat around late into the night as a snooping, damp wind blew weakly into our cabin. I plotted our route and explained it to Dad on the nautical charts. We were going to blow by a big slash of Florida's most populated coast. Once we made it to Boca Grande Pass there would be an endless blur of buildings and boats—Gasparilla Island, Venice, Siesta Key, Sarasota, Long Boat Key, Bradenton, Tampa, St. Petersburg, and Clearwater.

Tomorrow we planned to make it to Tarpon Springs, not far above Tampa/St. Pete. Tarpon Springs is still basically a Greek fishing town transplanted into Florida. It is populated with a lot of Greek-American sponge divers, fishermen, sponge dealers, other descendants of Greek settlers. I had been told that some of the best seafood in Florida can be found here.

I'm not quite sure why, but I decided to take a calculated risk with our route. Tomorrow was supposed to be a calm day. If it turned out as nice as

predicted, we would go through Boca Grande Pass into the open Gulf and
then make about a sixty-mile run to the mouth of the mighty Tampa Bay.
I'd been telling Dad about my loran, and he seemed really intrigued, his
interest more than a father's attentive ear. I guess he realized that his life too
now relied on the loran. This long offshore stretch, well out of sight of land,
would show him how this navigational machine worked—*if* I used it right.

One entrance to Tampa Bay, a place called Southwest Channel, had a
big old buoy, a horse of a buoy, with a bell that rang every two and a half
seconds for nighttime orientation, especially helpful in fog. It also had a set
of numbers that marked its exact spot at latitude 27 32.5 and longitude 82
47.9. No other spot has these numbers anywhere on this earth. With my
Raytheon loran, I could head us directly for that buoy over miles and miles
of unmarked Gulf. All I had to do was punch the latitude or longitude for
this buoy into my loran. It didn't matter that the buoy was only a few feet
wide and sixty miles away from us, bobbing in the midst of Gulf waters.
Give the loran a few moments to make the calculations, and it could tell
me exactly what heading to take—in this case, 336 degrees. It also told me
how many miles I had to go. Once I got going, the loran would calculate
my speed and constantly update me on how long it was going to take to
get to the buoy.

We left Useppa Island and eventually entered the Gulf through Boca
Grande Pass. But first we lingered in the pass to watch one of the most
awesome animal gatherings in the world. The water in Boca Grande Pass is
naturally deep, in some places forty-five feet. And this time of year, every
year, the big-scaled tarpon gather here by the thousands to pass through
Boca Grande. They have wintered to the south—no one seems to be quite
sure where. Dad and I saw them leaping in unison—sometimes twenty,
even one hundred at a time. Following them, and eating them, are giant
sharks. It takes a pretty big shark to eat a hundred-pound tarpon.

After watching the tarpon awhile we headed north across the open
Gulf. Looking out over the vast expanse of water, Dad wondered out loud
how we possibly could go sixty miles and hit our target. He seemed
relieved when I mentioned that the loran was manufactured by the same
company that built missiles used in the Persian Gulf War. He watched the
numbers change on the screen as we sliced through the smooth Gulf
waters. We had been given a rare day of peaceful weather, and the wind was
far away, in someone else's face.

We reached the entrance to Tampa Bay in two and a half hours.
During that time, Dad looked around a lot. He asked me at least three
times where the life preservers were. (I told him I had eight—four for him,
and four for me.) I assured him that the *Cooper's* hull was filled with foam

and would not sink; we would always have something to cling to. I asked if
he would enjoy getting rescued, and he gave me one of his ha-ha looks.

"How do you know we're not going to run out of gas on this run?"

"Well, it won't be the first time. But we'll be OK."

I told him I'd run out of gas on my first solo trip—the same time out
that I'd smashed the antenna. The Coast Guard had called me a tow boat;
that had cost me a hundred bucks. And it turned out I wasn't really out of
gas after all. I just didn't realize that to switch over to my second fuel tank I
had to turn a switch *and* a lever.

"Actually," I admitted, remembering my experience on the way to the
Dry Tortugas, "I really don't think the gauges are accurate. But we should
still have just enough gas to get us where we're going."

"OK," he said with hesitation in his voice.

We had another thirty-five miles to go before we reached the channel
that would bring us to the port of Tarpon Springs. I mentioned to Dad that
we needed to make sure to stay well off of Three Rooker Bar. (We both
noted the "we.")

Soon after that we saw the end of the Anclote Keys and began a cautious entry into Tarpon Springs. We eased in behind a slow-going Greek
sponging boat. She was laboring low in the water, her wooden decks
loaded with fresh sponges. We followed her until we spotted a marina
where we could tie up for the night.

We feasted on excellent Greek cooking that night. I had my first
smoked mullet. After the first taste, I wanted to eat nothing else for a year. I
brought my charts to the restaurant, and we plotted our next leap north.
The next day, if the weather held, we would travel eighty-five miles over
the open Gulf—all the way to Florida's Big Bend, where the coastline
curves and begins to head west. Our destination was the Ideal Fish Camp at
the mouth of the Steinhatchee River. My sister Winky lived only a half-
hour from there by car.

Of course, as I explained to Dad, all these plans depended on the Gulf.
Everything I did on the *Cooper* depended on the Gulf's mood that day, that
hour, that season. On a good day it could be so tranquil, so sweet. But
when it was badly agitated, the *Cooper* and I had no business anywhere but
in port. In the past few months I had become keenly aware both of the sea's
power and of my own limitations.

Dad really enjoyed figuring our route that night. So did I, even
though this leg of the journey would take us farther off the coast than I'd
ever been when I was in charge of the boat. Maybe it was the influence of
the smoked fish, but I felt quite confident. It felt good to feel in charge, to
be the captain.

The next morning presented us with another gift of a day—bright, sunny, and still calm. We weighed anchor and paraded down the Anclote River in line with other departing boats. I was at the wheel. Dad was using my binoculars to scan the horizon for our destination buoys, and he also kept track of the buoy numbers. We quickly became a smooth-as-silk team. We were a natural. Never had we been together this long without some tension.

On our second day out, even though we were fifteen miles offshore, Dad didn't ask where the life preservers were. There wasn't a boat or green coastline in sight. I spotted a couple of huge orange-brown sea birds with wings that looked eight feet long. Dad excitedly pointed out two dolphins that leaped at the exact same second.

I could not remember when I'd seen my father so relaxed, so at ease. I was amazed at how quickly he'd adapted to life in a boat, and I felt honored that he felt secure with me. We hit buoy number two perfectly on course, after 29.6 miles of subtle waves. Dad was impressed with us. So was I.

Now we were ten miles west of the Crystal Reefs. We'd just passed the Homosassa River, spring fed and clear as window glass. Because it is fed by giant springs, the Homosassa maintains a constant temperature, and my friends at Marker 7 had told me that many manatee wintered there. It wouldn't be long before some of those gentle sea mammals would begin the migration farther up the coast to rivers loaded with aquatic plants. Some would calve there, some would have their babies before they left on their migration. Some would give birth along the way.

And then, from out of nowhere, Dad began to talk. He said he was very proud of me, that he had missed me since I'd settled in Tennessee. We talked some about my divorce, about my new life with Rita, and about my kids and my brothers and sisters. And then he really surprised me by asking, "What do you want to know about me?" It seemed that he'd been waiting a long time for the right moment to ask that question.

Now, suddenly, I had the chance to ask my dad anything I wanted to. And suddenly I wasn't sure what I wanted to ask. Some of the questions I'd mulled over before picking Dad up now seemed none of my business. Other questions seemed to have lost their importance in the days we'd spent together.

I asked about my Grandmother Jenkins, who had died when Dad was so young. He didn't say more than a sentence about her. And that felt like enough. His pain over losing her when he was so young still seemed unbearable to him.

I thought I wanted to know why he didn't take the job offer with IBM when he was young . . . no I didn't. What difference did that make now? What good would it do now to bring up decisions that Dad made when we were kids?

It was amazing to me how different I felt about a lot of issues after a time of being alone with my father. This past week there had been no interruptions, no grabs for attention. There had been no wives, no kids, no brothers or sisters, no one to enter our world. Before, when I'd been around Dad, I'd almost always felt agitated—something seemed wrong, out of tune. Now I was looking at our relationship in a whole new light.

In our family Dad had often been blamed for doing this or not doing that. For instance, we could have bought a house one time, but he was too stubborn, too proud, too something to borrow the money from his step-mother. So we had kept on living in the projects—and resenting his inaction.

Now, as a result of our time together, I was seeing that circumstance in a different light. I realized that growing up in Wilbur Peck Court had created within me a drive to succeed, a determination to someday have my own home. Yet growing up there had also taught me I could be happy anywhere, no matter how crammed in or humble. And spending most of the first seventeen years of my life in a federal housing project had taught me to relate to all kinds of people in a town where, at that time, basically only one kind was esteemed. Our WASP family had gotten along fine with neighbors who were Italian, Polish, Southern Black, Jamaican, Russian, or just plain Catholic. And now I was also remembering how Dad always got along with everyone, talked to everyone. Sometimes we wished he wouldn't talk to everyone so much—it seemed we were always waiting for him as he talked to one of our neighbors.

And now I was remembering other things about Dad. He may have given me bad knees, but his knees had been weakened by decades of standing on them, working long hours in a factory or a store. He had stood on them to work, hours on end, days and weeks and years without end, standing on them so that he could spend practically every cent he made on us. He never seemed to buy anything for himself.

I looked over at Dad, trying to disguise a sense of perplexed wonder. I looked at him the same way I looked at my children, amazed at the connection of blood and experience. Did I really come from that man? And I saw so clearly that not only had Dad helped to create me when he united with my mother; he had also shaped me by the way he acted, the decisions he made, the emotions he felt, the things he said. I could cop out and blame him for who he was, what he did. Or I could choose to accept him and honor him.

I knew I was now having this kind of impact on my children. I hoped that my children would come to the same place I was with my father. I so wanted them to love me for the imperfect man I am, not to blame me for the mistakes I had made. And I hoped that someday they would come to an appreciation of the good things I had given them, just as I was coming to a new appreciation of all my dad had done for me.

I looked over at Dad, the binoculars still hanging around his neck, an expectant look on his already tanned face. And suddenly I wished I could just run up to my father at full speed, with absolutely no hesitation. I wanted to just spring up to him like I did when I was two, like my children did to me when they were two, and jump into his big arms and shout, "I love you."

I used to get so excited when Dad came home from work. Nothing mattered then except that at that moment he was home with me, with us. And that was all that mattered now. Dad had come to be with me. We had overcome our hesitation and made what seemed like a huge effort just to be together. All I could feel was gratitude and the strong desire to make the most of our remaining time together.

When we reached my sister's house, our time alone together would be over. Once we walked into Winky's home, Dad would have to share himself with Winky and me, with her kids (his grandchildren), with Randy, Wink's husband. I'd had more than my share; I would stay in the background, let Winky have the most of him.

I felt something now that I'd not felt before this week. For the rest of my life I would know that Dad and I had come to love each other for exactly who we were, with no blame, no hesitation. We had a bond that could never be taken away.

Smoke was everywhere as Dad and I walked into Randy and Winky's kitchen. My sister's husband was preparing blackened fish. Randy, a computer programmer, still looked like the hippie he once was. He had always reminded me of a frenetic scientist. He was always taking computers, cars, boat motors—even fish—apart.

Winky, now a teacher of children with severe learning disabilities, had always been the straight-A student of the family. She had also been mercilessly harassed by me, her older brother. Now, seeing her for the first time in a long time, in her world, I was struck by how beautiful and self-assured she was. Her red hair was streaked almost blond in places by the Florida sun. She wasn't chubby anymore, and she was dressed in stylish greens and rusts, just right for her coloring. I was surprised by how excited I was to see her.

When I reached out to take Winks into my arms she seemed startled. We hugged. I looked for Dad. He grinned and scooped up Tyler, Winky, and Randy's youngest.

Dad and I stayed for a couple of days, then it was time to take him to the airport in Tampa in Winky and Randy's van. Dad and I didn't say much on the way to the airport and didn't talk a lot while we waited for his plane. A glow of contentedness surrounded us. This time together, the first time we'd ever been alone together for more than a few hours, would grow more important as time passed, as Dad and I went back to our separate lives. Our days together were a giant gift that had already brought a deep sense of peace. That ever-present uptightness created by a swirl of unresolved issues was gone. I felt like things were settled between us, that we'd created a sense of oneness we'd never had. Our time had been like a holy week, time spent with forever consequences.

We promised that we'd spend time together like this again. (I also promised myself that I'd do the same thing with my kids.) Then we gave each other a hug, and Dad walked onto the plane. He did not use his cane, the one he had so relied on the first few days after he'd arrived.

Right as Dad was about to disappear up the jetway, I realized I had not told him out loud that I loved him. But even as I felt the regret I also felt a comforting realization. I may not have told him. But I had definitely shown him.

CHAPTER 20

Blonde
and
Curvaceous

H ow do you find a manatee? They don't leap acrobatically out of the water like dolphins. I've not observed them mating, but even then I doubt they're acrobatic. About the only way to find them is to watch for their stubby snouts sticking a few inches out of the water to breathe. If the water's calm, they can be seen from at least a hundred yards.

Some people call manatees "sea cows," but they don't look much like land cows. To me they look more like walruses. In a beauty contest I would definitely pick a land cow over a sea cow, but then I'm prejudiced. There are several land cows that I love, many I like very much, a couple that make me nervous, and none that I despise.

Sea cows live in the shallows and never leave the water. They are vegetarians and the gentlest of creatures, rarely moving fast. They don't bellow or roar; they slowly munch and chew, munch and chew. They have a helpless quality, with gray skin like an elephant and the features of a basset hound. Whoever once thought a manatee was a blonde, curvaceous mermaid must have been years at sea on an all-male ship. Even then, they must have seen the creature from afar. Very far.

There seem to be more people who love the sea cow than love the land cow. That's probably good, since the manatees are an endangered species and need all the friends they can get. But land cows have their good points, too. On my Tennessee farm, which rises into hills from McCutchon Creek, I have land cows that I consider my friends. I've helped deliver some of them when they were stuck in their mother's birth canal, then watched them grow up to have their own babies. Many of them have names. And all have distinct characters.

Miss White is the leader of our herd and is more stubborn, more perceptive, more aggressive than the rest. Pretty Girl is Miss White's daughter. She is the softest tan color, almost as tall as a horse and with dangerous-looking horns, yet she is as gentle as a teddy bear. Shy Bent Horn was not pretty, but she was a better mother than the rest and gave a lot of milk. Unfortunately, she died last spring. And then there's Zebra-stripe. She's striped black and brown, like a part Brahma cow can be, and she sometimes tries to kill you the first week or so after she's had a calf. If a cow can suffer from paranoia, then this one does. I've seen her jump a five-foot fence to avoid being caught in my pens.

Manatees are not all the same either. I learned that from being with them on the grass flats off the mouth of the Steinhatchee River. One afternoon, not long after saying good-bye to my dad, I snorkeled for hours alongside a few manatees as they grazed.

From the mouth of the Steinhatchee River, I knew to head just right of the setting sun to reach the grass flats about eight miles offshore. There was no way to miss them really, because they covered a couple of square miles out in the open Gulf. The water was very shallow here, sometimes only a few feet deep. (Occasionally at low tide the flats would become a sandbar.) And here the undersea grass grew into lush water pasture, a green haven for animals like the manatee.

For many thousands of annual migrations, gray sea cows had come to these Gulf Coast flats in the summer to graze on the delicious sea grass. The location of this bountiful, unpolluted dining place is stored in their memories and somehow shared with the newest baby manatees, who pass the memory on and on.

They used to come closer to the coast, to even shallower and probably safer waters. But closer to shore, much of the once luxuriant sea grass has been poisoned by the fifty million gallons of waste liquids pumped daily into the Gulf down the now grotesque Fenholloway River. Up this obscene river is a cellulose mill, a foul-smelling, smog-belching plant that harvests the fast-growing local pine trees and turns them into an essential ingredient for disposable diapers, plastics, cellophane, and rayon fabric. The daily discharge from the manufacturing process oozes down the Fenholloway to the Gulf, killing the grass flats and oyster beds where the river becomes part of the sea. The high level of dioxin is also creating mutant fish; scientists have found female fish becoming biologically male. Fortunately, the manatees seem smart enough no longer to graze there.

The last time I'd been out to the grass flats, folks in another boat said that they'd seen two manatees. Today I was back, hoping some might be around. I assumed they were moving north.

I turned off the boat and drifted when I got on the western side of the flats. The water was clear and lit by yellow-gold sunlight. I sat as still as possible and watched the bright surface for signs of a manatee snout.

I saw something. It was the head of a sea turtle. They come to graze here, too.

I looked for almost an hour. Finally I noticed some lumps on top of the water—three adult manatees and a smaller one, probably last year's calf. As fast as I could, I threw out my anchor, made sure it was secure in the sandy bottom, pulled on my flippers, mask, and snorkel, and joined them. I floated easily on the sensually warm water above them.

The manatees were heavy enough that the current did not affect them. They casually flapped their rounded-off tails and ate as if the flats were all theirs. The smallest one had a little green moss growing on its body but no scars—so far it had managed to avoid the near misses with sharks and boat propellers that had marked the bodies of its parents. It swam close and looked me over. I probably could have touched it, but I didn't. It moved back and forth and up and down in the water with the inefficient movements typical of immature mammals.

I would never have thought that anyone could get excited about grass, but these manatees did. They ate it passionately. The beautiful purity of these offshore pasturelands must have produced sweet-tasting, delicious food. The manatee was only one of hundreds of creatures that fed here.

Grasses and other plants cover the rounded hills of my farm, too, providing nourishment and protection for just as wide a variety of land creatures. Land cows eat it, and so do the whitetail deer. Cottontail rabbits that have survived all their predators live off of it and in it. Field mice eat it and build nests in it. Meadowlarks eat its seeds and weave the grass into carefully hidden ground nests. Cautious woodchucks nibble and gorge on it. The gray squirrel and the fox squirrel weave the dried grass into their nests of oak leaves as they feed on the walnuts, acorns, and hickory nuts. And the trees that drop those nuts grow in abundance, thanks to the nutrients put back into the soil by the clovers and the cattle droppings.

Just as on the Gulf grass flats, predators swoop and slash atop the land grass to catch their living from it. The night-flying great horned owl, whose favorite hundred-year-old cedar was blown down by the last great wind to hit the farm, grips the mice and rabbits in its curved claw. The coyotes who often howl on the back ridge by the Williams farm catch and eat everything that lives off the grass or dies upon it. (They also try and sometimes succeed in killing the wobbly calves born on it.) The foxes come, the red-tailed hawks dive down. The killing-machine weasel terrorizes the creatures of the grass.

This same circle of life also exists in the Gulf grass flats. The grass flats serve as giant food factories for marine animals; they produce vast amounts of enriched food for this entire Gulf coastal area. One marine scientist compared the grass on the flats to peanut butter on crackers. The sea grass leaf is like a cracker. And the microorganisms that grow on it are the peanut butter for many of the creatures who graze from blade to blade.

The grass flats also serve as a big safe house, a place for small fish and marine invertebrates to live where they have less chance of being eaten. And yet they also attract their share of predators—from ospreys to sharks—who find good hunting in the area.

It is estimated that there are twelve hundred square miles of dense, fairly contiguous sea grass along this Big Bend area between Tarpon Springs north of Tampa and the mouth of the St. Marks River south of Tallahassee. This little-known coast is a low-energy coastline. It doesn't get a lot of heavy waves or strong currents that transport sediment and sand. So the marshes and sea grass beds in this area are not strongly disturbed by the moving seas.

The manatee trio swam at a pace I could keep up with. Most fish that swim out here leave people far behind. I floated on top of the water, my snorkel directing the air to my lungs, my two flippers easing me along. I stopped when the manatees did and then dove down to get on their level. Mostly I followed the adolescent. The manatees surfaced several times for air during the hour and a half I stayed with them.

The shorter of the adults was very much rounder than the other one. I wondered if it was pregnant, or if they both were. It was early summer—about time for them to calve if they were going to. The spunky yearling wasn't feeding, just picking at the sea grass. Young manatees stay with their mother for up to two years. A small school of bloodthirsty, hyper bluefish flashed their silver sides in front of me, startling me.

The roundest adult manatee had dark green algae all over it except for the area between its eyes. The algae on the long one was a light yellow-green. These adults almost certainly had migrated here from different wintering places. Maybe they met on the way. The longer one with the light green back had three deep slash marks across the top of its back, healed over, but light gray. It probably had been hit by a boat, cut by its propeller. Boats are a significant danger to the slow-moving manatees.

The longer adult glanced over at me quite often. The round one ignored me. Although manatees can live in fresh- and saltwater and every combination of the two, they seem to prefer the serene waters of the Florida rivers pumped full of spring water.

The rotund trio was moving through on their migratory path but they were in no hurry. I don't think they ever are.

I wondered what the manatees did through the night. How did they rest? They had to come to the surface to inhale, and nighttime is when sharks become most active and move in closer to the coast. Did the manatees head for a river or salt marsh or creek as an overnight stop? When you're as big as a manatee, there is no place to hide. When you're as slow as a manatee, there is no place to run. When you have no offensive or defensive weapons, like fangs or razor-sharp teeth, there is nothing to fight with. Their size offers some protection, but there are plenty of sharks in the saltwater and gators in the fresh that could eat the babies and yearlings and bite killing holes in the adults.

At least humans do not hunt the manatees for food as they once did. The early Seminoles and the tribes before them, as well as Billy and Red's European pioneer relatives, used to consider manatees fair game. A couple of the men at Marker 7 who keep the oral history of their people alive say they've heard they were good eating.

I lifted my head and saw that I had several hundred yards to go to get back to the *Cooper,* so I turned around. The air had a pink tone, the water was a bit duller. In another hour the sun would drop into the Gulf.

I was about fifty yards away from the manatees when I felt my body tensing, my fingers tightening up. I was breathing faster. What was going on?

Swimming with the manatees, I'd felt safe, relaxed, secure in the water. I felt that way when I saw a dolphin, too—some sort of attachment, a sense of comfort. It was an odd feeling, a warm guarantee of safety, like being with friends in an inhospitable place.

Now the waters felt insecure to me. Danger seemed to be everywhere out here. Any minute now a twelve-foot tiger shark could weave into my view. I just knew that at this moment the sharks were smelling me and sensing my every motion from afar. What I'd heard about sharks being able to smell one drop of blood in the ocean and track down its location kept coming to mind. I wasn't bleeding, but maybe they could smell my Mennen deodorant. I felt like a chunk of bait bobbing in the massive expanse of ocean.

It was weird how fast this new, anxious feeling had come over me. But as far as I could tell, nothing chilling came near as I covered the distance to my boat. I climbed out of the warm water into air of the same temperature. The hard fiberglass deck of the *Cooper* felt so fine, so safe.

CHAPTER 21

There Should
Have Been
Some Screaming

The *Wakulla News* from Wakulla County, Florida, has a feature called "Manatee Watch." Its purpose is to list sea cow sightings in the area. Every July, Wakulla County even throws a festival to celebrate the return of its herd of manatees.

I picked up a week-old copy of the *Wakulla News* in the office of the Ideal Fish Camp near Steinhatchee, where I was keeping the *Cooper.* The headline to the "Manatee Watch" column announced, "Newborn Is Seen." The article beneath the headline then explained,

> A 2 1/2 foot pink-nosed newborn manatee was seen on the Wakulla River Friday, June 21. Daniel and Mabalene Hayes of Old Town were collecting plants for their business, Nature's Aquatics, which supplies plants for aquariums when they saw the newborn with its mother. It was maybe 2 weeks old, Daniel Hayes said, swimming on its own. Hayes said the newborn and its mother came within 50 feet of his boat and a male came within 100 yards. "We've been watching them," Hayes said. "My son and I saw both adults but no baby a few weeks ago. They're real curious." The three manatees were seen near the big cypress tree, 3 1/4 miles south of Lower Bridge.

The *Wakulla News* also cautioned, "Area boaters are encouraged to read the Watch weekly and take care in areas where manatees are cited." Boat propellers are a major cause of manatee casualties.

One day after reading these articles, I decided to head over there in the *Cooper* to see if I could find some manatees in the Wakulla River. The journey was about forty miles, maybe more, across open sea. But I wasn't worried. My confidence in cruising now was strong. I was beginning to feel I could handle almost any situation the *Cooper* and I got into. Still, there is always reason never to get too loose out on the Gulf. Anything can happen. And there is probably no stretch of coastline in the Lower Forty-eight that is so alone with itself.

My bow was targeted for Apalachee Bay, southeast of Tallahassee, where the Wakulla and the St. Marks mix their waters with the Gulf. My cassette deck blew loud tunes out of its waterproof speakers. The Allman Brothers had never sounded so good. Their low-down, hazy-woods southern rock and blues was the life-sound of this region, along with Hank Williams Jr., Lynyrd Skynyrd, Travis Tritt, and countless church choirs.

The opening to the Wakulla is guarded by oyster bars. There were two sand islands about three miles out I had to thread my way through. While occupied with this navigation, I heard a sweeping splash off to my right. I put the *Cooper* into neutral, expecting to see a couple of dolphins herding fish into the shallows. The surface of the silvery-smooth water looked like molten glass right before it solidifies.

Then I saw a fin. It moved rapidly. The top fin was too thin to belong to a dolphin, and it wasn't the right shade of light gray.

Another splash blew up from the water, this one sounding as if it had been made by a five-hundred-pound watermelon. The fin moved swiftly in the direction of this second splash. A head lifted out of the water, its snout was blunt, rounded off, and wide. It was a large shark, attacking whatever made the watermelon splash. The splasher's tail showed itself amongst an explosion of water. It was the unmistakable rounded fluke of a manatee.

The manatee seemed longer than the shark, which I guessed was a bull shark. The bull shark is an authentic man-eater and is even found in freshwater, farther inland than any other shark. Blunt-headed bull sharks have been sighted more than a hundred miles upriver in Louisiana. And although their favorite meal is other sharks or rays, a slow-moving manatee would serve as a welcome, easy-to-catch taste treat.

A wide wake appeared underwater—that had to be the shark, moving fast. Then partway out of the water came a small manatee. The shark must have charged it and missed, running underneath it. The big manatee, probably the mother, spun around right next to where its baby had emerged, then part of its head came out of the water, too. I couldn't believe how fast that manatee moved. A lot of water was being displaced by the manatees' large bodies.

Denver Fleming retired to the tiny coastal town of Steinhatchee, Florida, to become a fishing guide and common-sense environmental activist.

I clunked the engines into gear to get a closer look. The shark lunged up. I could see its head lashing out on the top of the parent manatee's body. Shark and manatee, one on top of the other, created a storm of splashing. The shark moved in a crazy-furious way. The manatee sunk down a bit more, and the shark went over the top of it. By now the battle had stirred up such a quantity of sand and sediment that I could see nothing but disturbed water. Where was the baby?

There should have been some screaming, but aside from the splashing everything was quiet. I saw no red blotches in the water. The mother manatee must have been terrified. The baby with its newborn, clean, gray skin was probably radically confused. Maybe the mother gave it some kind of message to swim as far off as it could.

There was nothing I could do to help. I could have so easily shot that shark, but I had no rifle. My gaff was not long enough to reach the shark nor anywhere near strong enough to hold a shark, even if I could sink the stainless steel hook into it.

I ran to the bow. I was right over them. The shark wanted the baby manatee. The brave mother manatee would not let the shark get its bearings. The mother butted the shark, hitting it sideways with its body.

I decided I would pull right into the middle of the frantic surging water and see if I could distract the shark, scare it, anything. But something happened before I got over on top of the shark. The water quieted; there was a slight wave as it settled. What had happened? Had the blunt-headed killer seized the baby in its teeth and swum off?

I was about to run aground, so I eased back into the channel and headed back toward the river. There, ten feet to my right, was the surfacing, whiskered nose of a manatee, headed the same way as me, upriver. At the very same moment a small set of nostrils broke the surface, too.

I let out my breath in relief. Maybe the mother and the baby would soon make it safely into the Wakulla, where they would spend the rest of the summer grazing their fill until the air and water cooled once again. By then this baby manatee would be much stronger.

I spent the day snorkeling up and down the Wakulla River. It was like being in the world's largest fish tank. The freshwater plants swayed in the current as if keeping time to a Bach fugue. Some of the emerald green plants were more than twenty feet tall, creating caves with vegetative walls, the underwater spaces changing constantly as the current took charge. Some idiot zoomed by in his outboard and almost hit me.

Late the next afternoon I made it back to the Steinhatchee River and Ideal Fish Camp. Denver Fleming, my friend who was retired and now served as a local fishing guide and seller of cubed ice, was smoking his usual cigar, standing in the long shadow of a slightly bent palm tree.

CHAPTER 22

Cash
All Over
the Road

Throughout time there has been a
place in Florida that practically no
one has wanted and few knew
about. This bizarre and sometimes brutal place is seen on the map as Taylor
and Dixie Counties. I discovered it because my sister Winky lives there. I
stayed with her and Randy and the kids for most of the summer, looking,
listening, and watching, making occasional jaunts on the *Cooper* from her
temporary home at the Ideal Fish Camp.

A lot of this lonely land is a jungle of scrub and pine woods, with an
almost uninhabited coastline about a hundred miles long. I call this forsaken
yet oddly appealing world the jungle-woods.

The woods of Taylor and Dixie Counties and the wild coastline that
forms their western boundaries combine to shape a region unlike any place
I've seen in the Lower Forty-eight. It seems as isolated as Alaska. This
remote place is part wetland jungle, part scrubland, part dry prairie, and part
swamp, with long fingers of high pine forest crisscrossing it from every
direction.

In the 1820s these lands were considered impassable barriers by white
travelers. Explorer W. H. Simmons wrote in 1822,

> Nothing could be more sterile than the soil; and these tracts are,
> in fact, concealed deserts, as they are too poor to allow cultivation, and
> afford nothing that is fit, even for the browsing of cattle. The growth
> upon these places, from its rough and stunted character, forms a com-

plete live fence, which probably would never have been penetrated
through, but by the Indians, who made the present trail for the purpose of hunting bear.

In the 1990s the region is still relatively untraveled. Before I-75 was built,
fifty-five miles east of the jungle-woods' main town of Perry, people
would drive through Perry on Route 19/27, headed south. From Perry it
is 150 miles to Tampa. It's only 45 northwest to Tallahassee. It might as
well be a million.

Plenty of black bear still roam here, mostly unseen. I followed the
tracks of one along a beach that was half-covered with derelict tree stumps;
its pawprint stretched longer than the length of my camera. Other wild
animals roam and mate in the jungle-woods as well; they are much more
plentiful than humans. Wide-headed bull gators eat an occasional otter;
there are many of both. In the humid early evenings, black-and-white
wood storks fill the tops of crooked, moss-mantled cypress trees, and
dinosaur bones lay by the hundreds in rivers fed by springs giant and small.

The women of the jungle-woods area are known far and wide as fight-
ers; I was told they'd scratch my eyes out in a heartbeat. They raise their
babies to be as tough as they are. One of the first things a true jungle-woods
dweller learns in life is that there is *us* and there is *them*. *Us* is anyone born
and bred in the jungle-woods. *Them* is everyone else. Many early settlers
were deserters from the Civil War, Yankees as well as Confederates, so the
people of the jungle-woods have followed their own set of rules and laws for
many generations. These rules often do not mesh with the generally
despised federal government, which they feel is there to screw up their lives.
In the past refugees from the law were not pursued here, because more than
one lawman who has gone into the jungle-woods has never come out.

Because the jungle-woodsers are set apart from the rest of the world,
they are raised from childhood never to rat or squeal on anyone they know.
To talk, to inform, is to sell out your family even if they aren't your blood
kin. To squeal is to violate the laws of your tribe.

Because the land is sandy and swampy, there were never any sprawling
plantations or large farm clearings here. Natives have always preferred to
stay off by themselves, and they rarely want to leave. Sometimes when in
need of cash to buy something in the outside world, they dig up wild palm
trees, carry them out, and sell them to the new Floridians in Tampa,
Tallahassee, or Orlando who plant them in their gardens for an authentic
Florida look.

The jungle-woods people have always been able to find nearly everything they need right at home. They find mullet, shrimp, deer, turkey, wild

If I hadn't known better, I would have thought this view was somewhere up the Amazon, but it's only a few miles up the Steinhatchee River in Dixie County.

hog—all in abundance. There is plenty of good spring water filtered by the sandy ground. And their daddies and granddaddies taught them how to cut out the hearts of palms and eat them to survive during lean times. People of the jungle-woods have almost always been able to catch and harvest plenty of good things to eat. Death comes from old age, falling trees, boat accidents, and shootings, not from starvation.

Off the so-called Road to Nowhere (supposedly built as a landing strip for drug-filled planes), I discovered a simple graveyard. Most of the graves were adorned by things at hand: neatly arranged bits of green and yellow glass, sun-bleached shells, crosses made out of white plastic pipe. There were lots of plastic flowers scattered about, the blood-red ones especially faded by the all-powerful sun.

In this austere graveyard I found a tombstone with a carving of a small truck bearing a harvest of palm trees. Another rare marble headstone was carved with a shrimp boat. It marked the grave of a man who died in his early twenties. It's very possible that the way he died had nothing to do with shrimping; no one I asked would tell me. The year of his death would have been a high point of drug-smuggling here.

A limpkin, a rare snail-eating bird, preens its feathers high up in a cypress tree growing at the edge of the Wakulla River.

There has always been smuggling in the jungle-woods. But beginning in the 1970s the drug business became big business in the area; a few of the jungle-woods natives were some of the biggest marijuana smugglers in the world. These outlaws ferried the drug by boat into a forbidden, dark-water river. God made it forbidden by placing giant limestone rocks in the most treacherous places, and then he made the rocks invisible because the water is dark brown, colored by tree bark, mostly.

But it wasn't just the geography that made the jungle-woods a smuggler's paradise. When the drug smugglers from South Florida came here looking for deep cover and the mouth of a river to buy, they found both. They also found an ideal labor force: hard-working people who had an inborn genius for boats and the local Gulf waters and who could keep secrets for a lifetime.

Perry, Florida (population 8,254), is the only town of any size in the jungle-woods. For a person with a brilliant mind and a gift for organizing people and information, there are very few job opportunities. But Eric is fortunate that he landed a job with askSam, a leading software firm in an old store-front building just a block from the courthouse square in Perry. The software program he works with organizes huge masses of data. It's used by the CIA, the FBI, CBS-TV, lawyers, doctors, writers. It is one of the most popular programs of its kind.

I saw Eric for the first time while visiting my brother-in-law, who works for the same firm. With his wire-rim glasses, fashionably rumpled linen shirt and slacks, calm face, and relaxed body language, Eric fit my picture of a computer exec. I would have guessed he'd grown up in the north Atlanta suburbs—or perhaps California—and transferred here. Eric shook my hand firmly and confidently. His speaking voice was smooth and assured. Nothing about him prepared me for the fact that he had been a leader in one of the largest marijuana smuggling operations in American history, headquartered right here in the jungle-woods. Eric, by the way, is not his real name.

When I met him, Eric was no longer a smuggler; he was a model, rehabilitated ex-con. He'd gotten started with computers in a classroom at the federal penitentiary, where he was sent following a conviction for drug smuggling.

The feds had just one problem with Eric in prison. He freely confessed to what he did, but he would never—no matter how much they tried to isolate him—inform on the people who helped him. He kept telling the feds that no one else helped him. He could have served less than a year if he would have ratted on all his people—or even just a handful of prime operatives. He refused. The few men who went to the pen along with Eric never talked either. They all did their time, and because they upheld the code of silence, they were allowed to return to live in the jungle-woods.

Some people speculate that almost every family in the isolated jungle-woods has some relatives involved in smuggling. No one knows. I certainly didn't ask.

I was stunned when Eric agreed to talk with me about his former life. I told him never to mention any names and if there were things I shouldn't know, just not to say them. I wasn't born in this place. I didn't want to have to carry anyone's secrets.

Eric said, "All right."

Even then it took me a week to decide if I wanted to find out what he'd done. I was curious about how such a big operation might work. But would knowing bring me too close to that murky, deadly world?

Before we got started on Eric's shadowy life of drug smuggling, he told me a story. There was no buildup, no warning, no explanation—he just started talking.

"One time, maybe ten, fifteen years ago, down in Dixie County, somebody informed on the smuggling operation they had going on down there. It was something like ours; they were bringing in shrimp boats full of marijuana.

"They found out quick who had informed the narcs. It was this ol' boy everybody knew. He wasn't born there; he'd just hung out for a few years. Bunch of them ol' boys down there in Dixie County done taken him into their organization—something we'd never've done up here. It turned out this ol' boy'd made a deal with the government to get hisself out of trouble.

"You know, after the government boys congratulated this ol' boy he disappeared. He never cared a thing for them local boys. Anyway . . ." Eric paused a long minute and looked me over with eyes that became momentarily intense and searching. "A few months later, in the fall, some turkey hunter found that ol' boy's bones in the jungle.

"What I heard happened, somebody took that rat out into the jungle—in the middle of August, now. You know how brutal it would be out in the middle of this jungle in August?"

I knew. It would be like being eaten to death in tiny, vicious, blood-sucking bites.

"Well, they stripped that ol' boy down naked. They put a big ol' chain around his wrist, tightened it, then strung that chain around an old, straight-up-and-down pine tree, one that escaped cuttin'. That ol' tree was probably three feet across, seventy-five feet tall."

Uneasily I pictured the scene. I had been out in those woods already. I could see that old tree surrounded by wilderness palms, shadowy magnolia trees, sinkholes, decaying leaves, and grotesque-smelling cottonmouths.

"Then they fastened the chain to the man's other wrist. They left him there, naked, chained to that tree. The hunter that found his bones said you could still see where the man had tried to claw his way under that tree. He said it looked like he'd tried to dig the tree up. I imagine he did. The bark was skinned off where he'd tried to shimmy up the big tree, only to get to an unbreakable branch.

"That was cruel what them ol' boys did. We never did do anything like that." Eric's face was expressionless. He showed no emotion. I felt safe with him, but was this a lesson for me?

"Don't tell me anything I shouldn't know," I repeated.

The federal penitentiaries give inmates an opportunity to improve their minds, to learn things. Eric refused to waste his time. He took a computer class and discovered his mind operated with the same logic as the computer. Soon he was writing programs that organized system-wide meal plans for the food service division of the federal prison system. Eventually, Eric's program was used throughout America.

Once Eric had twelve million dollars in cash, holding it for the head man, the one who drove a green Rolls-Royce. The head man told Eric he was going to be a few days late landing his jet on the jungle-woods runway. "What I need you to do," the head man told Eric from his mansion in Miami, "is just hang out and watch the money till I get there."

At first it sounded like no big deal to Eric. He'd fill up a room in his house with the cash. He'd just sleep, watch ESPN, and wait.

Then the what if's came flooding into his mind. What if the house burned? What if the outside law came on a searching mission? What if one of his kids walked in and found it? What if?

So Eric loaded up his Chevy Blazer with twelve million dollars. Chevy designed the back seat of the Blazer to fold down so there'd be roomy storage space. But I doubt the engineers at General Motors ever thought of anyone's doing what Eric did, which was fill that space with millions of dollars in tens, twenties, fifties, and hundreds stacked from the front seat all the way to the back. If Eric took a turn too fast, the weight of all those millions threatened to tip over the vehicle. What if that happened on a windy day and the back window popped open and a million or so blew away?

"I drove everywhere," Eric told me. "Gosh, I went down Highway 19, down over across Highway 53 to Mayo and then back up. I drove for two days, almost never stopped. Went down to the beach, just constantly moving. Constantly driving.

"Starting off," he said, "I wasn't too uptight. I don't get uptight easy." But the more he thought about what could happen, the more freaked-out he became.

What if he was in a wreck, and the millions just spilled out into the middle of the road—money owed to Cuban-Americans and Colombians and the head man? He couldn't even lose a ten dollar bill because the head man's brother-in-law was a nerd-for-numbers accountant. Every single bill had to be accounted for. And up to now, there had never been a discrepancy. Eric was a man of his word. He would never steal from anyone. Eric might smuggle, but he would not steal. People with no honor stole.

"I had plenty of protection," said Eric, still remembering that nightmare ride with millions of dollars in the back seat. "I had an M-16. I had my 357, my Python. I had a nine-millimeter pistol and a shotgun. I hardly ate, bought a few things at the mini-market. Was too nerved up to stop. You could look in the back windows of the Blazer and see the mountain of money. Someone could break the window and grab all they could carry. And what could I do if they did? I couldn't very well report it to the police."

He said he kept having a vision of cash all over the road, loose, flying everywhere, the Florida Highway Patrol circling it, trying to herd it like a bunch of wild jungle-woods cows.

"Finally I decided to go into the woods. Then, after I got out on those rutted sandy roads the logging trucks used every few years, I thought, well, if I break down out here I'm forty miles from nowhere. If I get broke down, I get stuck, and then I can't walk out, can't leave the stuff. So it might be two or three days before anybody drives down this ol' road to pull me out. And then when they go to pull me out, they'd see the money. I thought well, I could hide it in the bushes or bury it and walk out."

But he couldn't do that either. The money was all bound in stacks, but he didn't have anything big enough to cover all those stacks. So Eric just drove and drove, his Chevy Blazer filled with cash, the proceeds from one medium-sized South American shrimp boat filled with marijuana.

Eric put hundreds of miles on his vehicle during those few days. Finally he pulled up at the appointed moment just as the small jet from South Florida touched down to pick up its cash cargo. By now Eric's clean-shaven face had a new beard. He hadn't washed in a couple days, and he smelled terrible, even to himself. He'd gone without sleep for so long that his eyes were burning and red. He must have looked like a madman to the pilots who'd just landed. Eric had never been so happy to see anyone.

After they loaded the twelve million in cash onto the plane, Eric picked up a couple of cold beers, drove home, and slept for twenty-four hours.

He still dreams sometimes of all that cash spilled out in the road, blowing in the hot wind, traffic stopped, everybody rushing madly to grab handfuls.

Bite

on an

Outboard Motor

ric's childhood was typical for a jungle-woods male of the time. There was a lot of fishing and hunting, especially deer hunting. The tangle of trees and thick, green undergrowth makes the land impenetrable in places, so people in the area usually hunt deer with dogs and pickup trucks. The dogs chase the deer and the hunters chase the sound of the dogs, driving like maniacs down roads of sand, listening to the hounds all the time, knowing what each sound means. Always the hope is they will catch a glimpse of the deer before it disappears again. A lot of deer leap the sand roads without touching them.

"The boys use Walkers, blue ticks, and black-and-tans. They've got to be tough dogs with great noses. You ride these roads and look for tracks. Find a fresh track and put the dogs out, carry the dog out in the woods where nobody can see his tracks. You don't want anybody else coming up behind you seeing those tracks.

"We just drove like wild people. As hard as you can run, you run your pickup. Sometimes you're going eighty miles an hour down them roads, more like lanes—just screaming. People run into each other on these little old curves. I mean, there's barely room for one truck, and they'll be one going this way and one going that way."

Just about everything around the jungle-woods is different from the rest of the country. They turn cows out to roam loose, and those cows get bad-mean. In the 1800s these woods cows could belong to anyone who had the horses, guns, ropes, and guts to catch them.

Could there be a better way to grow up than at the shore? Here at Cedar Island, Florida, Alex and Jesse Rice search for small fish, horseshoe crabs, anything they can catch.

Childhood in the jungle-woods was about doing things that were normal there and unheard-of to most kids. One of Eric and his friends' favorite pastimes was anything but usual American teenage fun in the sun.

"My favorite summer thing took place behind Grassy Island, between Grassy and the hill. (These people call the mainland "the hill.") You have a little grassy island about a mile off the coast. Behind this island you have this bay. During July, August, and September there's big bunches of sharks that get in the bay. I don't know if they're spawning or what.

"At high tide the water's only neck deep. At low tide there are places you can't go in your little boat. But those big ol' sharks will get in this shallow water. You can see a lot of them if it's calm. Anyway, we'd run the sharks down with our small boats. At first we'd try to run them into the real shallow water. Then we started shooting them with rifles and nine-millimeter automatic pistols. In there were bull sharks, hammerheads, black tips. They were anywhere from five feet to twelve feet plus. I mean there was some nice ones. We were out there in little old johnboats, and the sharks would be as big as the boat. It's a wonder any of us lived."

After they killed one, they'd haul it aboard, sometimes almost sinking the boat again, then haul it the twenty-plus miles to town and the local fish market. But the sharks were not at all easy to kill. Eric told me that a shark's brain isn't any bigger than a golf ball, and if you don't shoot him in the brain you're wasting your time. "You can shoot him twenty times with a rifle and not kill him. The water got real clear and pretty in August and

September. Real pretty. You'd ride it, and you'd see the fins sticking out of
the water. I mean, they couldn't go down; it was too shallow. But they
could burn through that water. So we'd run them. Sooner or later they'd
cut back. Some of us boys got thrown out of the boat. We'd be screaming
and hollering, 'Get me back in the boat!'

"We'd stand on the front of the boat, and we'd tie a rope on the front
of the boat and then tie it around one of our hands. We'd hold on just like
riding a horse. If you're throwed out, the boat ain't going to run over you.
You won't go back under the boat. You got to stand up on the bow on the
very front so you can shoot down and that's all it is. It's a blast.

"The shark we're chasing, he's starting to get agitated. He starts getting
real riled. So we have three or four boats trying to run down this one
shark, boats running into each other, flipping up, people getting thrown
out. And this shark gets cut off and turned around, and he runs right back
through the middle of us. It was crazy. I guess you could say it was our own
kind of rodeo."

The worst part of the whole thing—or the best part for these young
boys—was when the shark attacked the boat.

"They'll hit anything in the water when they get mad enough. You
can stick a stick in the water or a paddle in the water. They'll even hit the
motor. They'll bite on an outboard motor with the propeller still running.

"One time we had this boy from Tallahassee with us. He didn't believe
that a shark would really attack a boat. We were chasing a bull shark that
day. I shot him about two or three times and just made him mad. Directly
he turned around and came back and hit the boat. He hit the boat about
twice and grabbed ahold of the boat, and that city boy fell in the floorboard
and started screaming. We didn't have the motor cut off, and the next thing
you know the shark comes back again and grabs the motor. That shark
stopped the propeller."

After this much jungle-woods fun, these ol' young boys would often
take a powerful notion to cool off, kick back, and have some more fun.
Every community has the place where kids go to try to buy beer, but here
they never have much trouble doing it. Drinking has always been something most people did, unless they went to church a lot. The jungle-woods
has always been an easy place to make your own whiskey. People have been
moonshining around here forever—moonshine is part of their heritage. But
the people never did get into brewing their beer, so they went to the bar
down at the beach.

"If you were old enough to go in there with your money, you could
get you a beer. I mean, that's what everybody did during the summer. We
chased sharks, went to the beach, fished, crabbed, dug Indian artifacts, and

went to the bar at the beach. It was a great place to grow up. Everybody looked out for everyone else, made sure they didn't drown or wreck the pickup. Our people had no idea what drugs were then."

The Cooper *and I spent the night near
Turtle Key in the Ten Thousand Islands.
This tiny island began when a seed from a
mangrove took root here, and over the years
more and more mangroves took root. In
time, their root systems trapped seashells,
which were ground into a coarse sand. And
the island became larger, root by root, shell
by shell, and grain by grain.*

*Headed toward Yellow Shark Channel,
Keys lobsterman Kenny Hildebrant runs
his line. It is February, the time to pull his
homemade traps to be stored until next
year. It took us two hard days to gather all
his wooden traps. Several were ruined
beyond repair by the powerful beaks of
raiding sea turtles.*

On Windley Key, right off Overseas Highway, U.S. 1, perches Abel's Tackle Box. Run by Charlie Pritchard, it offers every kind of fishing hook, bait, sinker, wire leader, ice, and almost anything else you might need. A mounted tiger shark, barracuda, tarpon, sailfish, leopard ray, and dolphin on the front of the building attest to more of the same fish in the water not far from here.

The pastel pinks and purples that enchant the Keys thrill passengers on sunset cruises. This sailboat eases silently back to Islamorada from Florida Bay.

Larry Thompson mends his net while wearing the classic white rubber boots of a commercial fisherman. Although Larry has tried factory and construction work, all he's ever wanted to do is fish for a living. He must be an expert boatman, must think like the fish he seeks, must be able to build and repair all his equipment, must read the signs of the seas and sky, yet he barely gets by.

This red-gold winter sunlight makes the end of my South Florida day perfect as I enter the mouth of Jug Creek on Pine Island. I found a place to anchor for the night by a nameless mangrove island.

This is James Bloodworth, owner and operator of the most subtly outrageous drugstore in North America. His drugstore is on the courthouse square in Perry, Florida. Not only can you find classics like hand-dipped milkshakes, but also fifty-year-old dog and cat sedatives, thirty-year-old greeting cards, makeup with Twiggy's picture on it from the 1960s, and much more. Bloodworth's isn't a museum, it's just that stuff stays on the shelf until it sells.

The dark and deep spring-fed waters of one of the most enchanted and unknown rivers in America, the Steinhatchee, flow by the limestone banks and jungle of Dixie County.

My dad, Frederick Davis Jenkins, and me the second time he joined me on my voyage

As the sun says good night to Turkey Point Shoal, shore birds search for their last meal of the day at the end of Alligator Point, Florida.

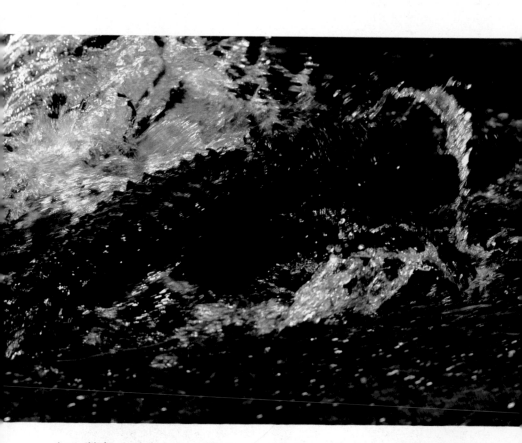

A second before I took this picture, this bull gator was as still as a rock as it sunned itself atop a mass of floating aquatic plants. I was about three feet from it in my Achilles inflatable boat, just below Wakulla Springs. It could have leapt into my lap.

Just after sunrise, Wakulla Springs comes to life. It was here that several Tarzan movies were made, starring Johnny Weissmuller.

The
Local
Drugstore

About the only place a jungle-woods person could hear youth music back in the '50s and '60s was at Bloodworth's Drugstore.

Bloodworth's is right across the street from the new Taylor County Courthouse in Perry, Florida. Perry is where the people of the jungle-woods go for doctors, groceries, welding supplies, cosmetics—anything they can't make, catch, or shoot.

Things don't change much in Taylor County, and they change even less at Bloodworth's Drugstore. At Bloodworth's, you can get a great egg and olive sandwich for $1.35 and an old-fashioned chocolate milkshake mixed in a stainless-steel canister for $1.15. You can also have a borderline otherworldly tour of the place given gleefully by Mr. James Bloodworth, proprietor.

Mr. Bloodworth, age seventy-two, has a soaring spirit. His smile lights up his whole face, and he moves like a much younger person. In the South people would say that Mr. Bloodworth is a sweet man and mean it as a compliment.

James wears plain gold-rimmed glasses. His skin is translucent, his hair still sandy red. He has big hands, which he uses delicately.

These days James does a lot of work with his Methodist Church, caring for the sick, the widowed, and the poor. James has never married. In his younger years he was quite a small-town character; in fact, he would have qualified as a character in any city in America in the '50s and '60s.

Bloodworth's Drugstore has been a gathering place for decades. Back in the days when young girls bought their makeup at the local drugstore, James used to give makeup lessons on the sly for girls whose mamas forbade it. (Even today, there are churches in the jungle-words that disapprove of makeup.) People who heard their first record here thirty or forty years ago still go back for nostalgic reunions with Mr. James. He has always loved music, even a lot of the latest stuff. He doesn't like rap music, though. He calls it vulgar.

The people of Taylor County all seem to love James Bloodworth. Visitors and customers sit on spinning white metal seats in front of a marble counter that was installed in 1936. They "visit" as they sip their delicious shakes.

My sister had told me about this place and about their old-time hand-scooped milkshakes. I came in one oppressive summer afternoon to have a chocolate one. At first things seemed more or less normal.

Inside Bloodworth's the light was soft and cooling. In the front of the store was an old weight machine that still tells your weight for a penny. On the wall to the left of the milkshake machine was a Johnson & Johnson baby poster so faded there was almost no color left. Above it was a sign for Toni Home Permanents; it must have been at least fifty years old. James told me the Toni people were the first ones to come out with a permanent you could do at home. At first the price was so reasonable that no one bought the perms. They didn't become popular until the Toni people raised the price, James mentioned.

"Can you believe they charge forty and fifty dollars for a perm in a parlor today?" Mr. Bloodworth fluttered his hands excitedly. "Goodness. Goodness," then he pointed out the window to the eternal flame that burned in the yard of the courthouse. "It goes out when it rains," he said.

Behind the weight machine was a Kodak sign advertising film. It was practically new—only about ten or fifteen years old. Behind the soda foun-tain counter hung a needlepoint slogan given to Mr. Bloodworth by his church: "When ye are in the service of your fellow beings, ye are in the service of your God." Next to it was a calendar from Citizens Bank. The calendar pictured a deer in the snow. James remembered that the last memorable snow in the area happened about 1957 or 1958. There were a few pipes and some Tampa Straights cigar boxes with a brick in the box that could be wet down to keep the cigars moist. But James quit selling cigars maybe twenty years ago, and pipes—well, there were a few pipes left over from the late '40s. They sat on the shelf next to the Zippo butane fuel for lighters. He didn't sell the lighters anymore, but customers could still buy the fuel, which had been on the shelf about fifteen years.

On display for free was Mr. Bloodworth's private bottle collection. He said that a man had told him it might be valued at five thousand dollars. There right in front of me was an Aunt Jemima pancake syrup bottle, maybe a year or two old. It was part of the collection. There was a jelly jar from Knott's Berry Farm, maybe a year old. All the bottles were on a pink shelf that ran the length of the store. Underneath was makeup, most of it made by Yardley in the 1960s. The eye shadow was in "mod" shades of pale blue, pale green, and pale purple. James told me that he had taken a tour of the Yardley factory in New Jersey and that everything had smelled wonderful.

I then spotted something on the shelves that looked really old. It was cough syrup, on sale for seventy-five cents. The label assured me that it did not contain any habit-forming drugs. Mr. Bloodworth said, "Today that would sell for at least four dollars, maybe four-fifty." He said that particular batch of cough syrup had been for sale here maybe fifty years. *Fifty* years!

Next to the cough syrup on the shelf, below Mr. Bloodworth's bottle collection, was antique Afro Sheen. Across the store in the card racks were yellowing greeting cards. One featured a buxom blonde woman gesturing like Uncle Sam and saying, "I want you." The card dated back to the sixties. James had crossed out the price on the back and raised it a few times.

Most amazing of all was the small cardboard box on the shelf, discolored with age, that announced, "Dr. LeGear's Nerve Sedative Tablets for Dogs, Puppies and Cats." The box held pet tranquilizers dating back to the 1930s and 1940s. According to the aged, yellow instructions that accompanied the sedative tablets, Dr. LeGear also made special tablets for dog constipation—doggie laxatives. One cause for doggie constipation, the ancient literature informed me, is too many bones in the dog's food.

I collect wacky Americana, so I offered to buy one of the remaining boxes of Nerve Sedative Tablets for Dogs, Puppies and Cats. James wouldn't take my money. He gave me a box.

Near the box of pet sedatives was a decongestant called, "666 Cold Preparation." James commented that some local people may have taken the 666 on the label to mean the product was associated with Satan. Maybe that was the reason there were still a couple of boxes for sale after thirty years or more!

There was eyeliner from the 1960s with Twiggy's picture on it. James showed it to me with an exclamation over the skinny model's beautiful eyes. There were also some five-year-old Q-tips and a couple of yo-yos from the thrilling time a Filipino yo-yo champion had come to town.

James fixed my chocolate shake, and we talked for a long time. He offered me one of his bumper stickers proclaiming, "Bump into Me at the

United Methodist Church." I thanked him and said that after the dog sedatives I couldn't accept another gift—unless he had a box of the doggie laxatives. He smiled and flicked his hand at me.

The only people in Bloodworth's Drugstore after my tour were two young girls drinking a fountain-style Dr Pepper. James whispered that their daddy was a preacher at one of the conservative churches in town. "Those girls sing like angels," he said.

The two girls had pale faces—a rarity here in sun-drenched Florida. They wore no makeup, and their hair hung straight and smooth—no hair spray or "big hair." They could not have been ready for what happened next.

The door opened to a blare of rock music, and a mysterious figure stood silhouetted in the bright sunlight that came through the door. Whoever it was seemed to glow with a hazy white halo. I was reminded of a dramatic entrance by Michael Jackson onto the concert stage. The figure seemed to be carrying something on its shoulder.

When my eyes adjusted to the brilliance surrounding this human form, I saw before me a small man carrying a huge radio-cassette deck. His hair was so black the color had to come from a bottle—no, he wore a black toupee. As he walked closer I saw a few gray hairs sticking out from under the toupee. He was about five-foot-three and weighed about 120 pounds.

"Oh, Bob," James said excitedly, "you always show up at the best time." He introduced his friend as Bob Prince.

"I try to be more like the Prince of Peace than Prince the rock star," Bob giggled in a low, chilling tone that seemed to make the preacher's daughters freeze to their stools.

As we talked, I learned that Bob was James's good friend. He had grown up in the jungle-woods on a farm where his family grew ferns for funeral parlors. Now he lived with his widowed mother just a few blocks away from the drugstore.

James wanted me to guess Bob's age. From a distance, his boyish body, face, and dark hair said mid-thirties. Up close, his gray hair under the toupee and his lined face said around fifty. I struggled to guess diplomatically.

Suddenly, without warning, Bob turned up his black plastic G.E. boom box, laid it down at his feet, and moved to the center of the floor. He grooved to a song from his rap tape. As the music pounded he hunkered, hunched, and twisted his body in a knot of gyrations and dance moves that a snake would have been proud of. The preacher's daughters seemed to be having trouble catching their breath. Another song came on, and he launched into a '60s-style twist.

"James and I don't never dance together, though," he shouted out from a twirl. "They'd run him out of town and me, too. They'd string us up and hang us by the treetops. This is redneck country," he added as he switched to the jerk.

"Someone once said to me that if you don't hunt or fish or play football, you don't belong in this county. I told that big boy that I didn't do any of those things and I belonged here as much as he did, so there. One of them tried to say I wasn't an American," Bob said with an expression that managed to be both dismayed and resigned.

Bob wore mirrored yellow wraparound sunglasses. His T-shirt was black and tight, and the short sleeves were rolled up high—he said he was going for the James Dean look. But his jeans were tight and white, and those were supposed to recall John Travolta. (Bob predicted that the styles from the disco-till-you-drop 1970s were coming back.) His black combat boots matched his shirt, his toupee, and boom box.

James said that he remembered when Bob was so shy he would have a hard time even talking to strangers, let alone begin dancing in a public place. "You're right, James, you know. I was such a shy person. But my dancing changed me. It freed me. It happened about fifteen years ago, when I was living in San Francisco for a while. I came in second in a dance contest. I've never been shy again." I guess not.

Bob broke into a series of moves in the middle of the floor, doing splits, full spins, claps, squeals—and laughing all the while. His was the eeriest laughter I've ever heard, a high, hollow sound that echoed out of his energized body. Bob could hire himself out to Hollywood as a laugher for vampire and Friday-the-Thirteenth movies.

By now one of the preacher's daughters had her hand over her mouth. James was clapping with the beat, keeping excellent rhythm. Then Bob suddenly switched off his boom box. He picked it up, glanced sadly at James, and walked out. The mood must have left him.

James said Bob had been coming in here regularly for ten years. The preacher's daughters began breathing normally again, and a few minutes later they left, too. There was color in their faces where none had been before.

I went to use the bathroom in the back of the store. On the walls was a collection of signs, handwritten by James, that he had asked me to read. They were pinned up in the bathroom alongside a picture of a little girl in a field of daisies: "Must we tolerate ugliness in speech when there are so many beautiful things to say?" "Don't let people say pollution is in the air only. It's in the minds and mouths of some." "Respect yourselves! Don't pollute. God hears and reads." I always read the writings on bathroom walls but I hadn't read any like these.

I had long since finished my milkshake, and it was almost closing time in the drugstore. So I bought a couple of James's '60s-vintage greeting cards, thanked him, and left. But during the several months I was around the jungle-woods, I went back as often as I could to have one of Bloodworth's hand-scooped milkshakes and to talk with James.

CHAPTER 25

Puff
the
Magic Dragon

Eric had been going to Bloodworth's Drugstore since his high-school days. He had missed the place when he was in Vietnam.

"After I graduated," he told me one afternoon, "I figured I better do something. I couldn't just hang around here. So I volunteered for Vietnam. A lot of boys from here volunteered. I had a lot of strong beliefs about this country and about our freedoms here."

Before Eric went overseas, he had no idea what marijuana was. But he soon learned.

"I was sitting on perimeter guard duty one night. There was a firefight in a little valley in front of us. 'Puff the Magic Dragon,' he was up in the sky. Puff was a giant gun mounted inside an old cargo airplane. It fired a solid red stream of blazing bullets from the plane to the ground. It was blasting out six thousand rounds a minute. Puff the Magic Dragon, we all called it. At night it puffed, it smoked, it flamed, it just roared.

"I had been in country about five or six days. I was sittin' with this old boy from Spokane, Washington. And this ol' boy, he says, 'Well, man, you want some of this?' I said, 'What?' He said, 'Some of this pot.' And I said, 'Well, I don't know, I ain't never smoked any.'

"So we got to smoking this stuff. We sat up there and smoked and got to watching this firefight. It got just psychedelic. We was laughing, saying how good the stuff was, saying how funny Puff the Dragon looked. Then something tripped a flare in our perimeter wire, and we never did see what it was. We got to laughing, and he said, 'Well, it's a monkey.' I said, 'No, it's a snake.' I was blasted. It's lucky there was no enemy in our perimeter wire. From then on, while I was in Nam, I got high every chance I got."

When Eric returned home from Vietnam, he didn't know what he wanted, where to turn. All he knew was that he had a terrible time settling down.

"The excitement of the war was so intense. Once I got back, things just didn't seem to fit. Normal life seemed so stupid—straining to work and barely survive at some really boring job. I could do just about anything with my hands or my head. After I got out of Nam, I did everything from selling mobile homes to iron work to going to college."

He was angered by the way he was treated one night after a football game soon after he returned home.

"Right after I got back from Nam I got thrown in jail. I was twenty, I'd been over there killing, escaping death, seeing stuff no one person should ever see, doing things no human should ever do. I got home to Taylor County, and I went to a high-school football game with some of my friends, and we were drinking beer. Coming back we got stopped by this cop, and he put me in jail for possession of beer. I hadn't even taken a sip for a couple hours.

"I says, 'Man, this is crazy. This is just plain crazy.'

"But that cop, he was a bristle-backed idiot. He didn't care where I'd been, that I'd been fightin' for my country. The concrete-block-headed cop sure didn't want some twenty-year-old saying nothin' to him. So he threw me in jail."

After that Eric became more rebellious and lost a lot more respect for the law. Eventually he bought a restaurant and lounge in Perry, putting a thousand dollars out for a down payment.

"I started building up a good business at the Skyview. Had some real, real good food. The lounge was doing great, and that's when I met the ol' boys. It was 1977. They wore fine cowboy boots and Levi's and a few thick gold bracelets around their wrists. They were clean-cut looking, just a bit flashy. Their Levi's were dry-cleaned and pressed. Their boots were Tony Lama or Nocona, probably snakeskin or ostrich.

"At first I had no idea what those boys were doing. They had a nice Chevy Blazer and a bass boat, and they were staying in the Holiday Inn and eating with me every night. Before I got the restaurant, I had gone and gotten my real estate license. So after about a week the boys told me they were here looking for some river property."

At first Eric figured they wanted their own fishing camp. That wasn't unusual in the area. Then they told him a secret. They said they represented

Almost all the shoreline of the Aucilla River looks as impregnable as this. In the early 1980s this river was one of the most active places in the United States for smuggling marijuana. Today it's probably the least seen river in the lower Forty-eight.

some Canadians who wanted to buy a river property. The only thing odd was that they wanted to buy the whole mouth of a river if they could.

After he thought about it, Eric figured that wasn't so odd. By buying the mouth of a river, they could keep anyone else from fishing anywhere near them. A lot of hunters do that when they lease hunting land, try to tie up as much as they can.

"For a long time we looked. I showed those guys every creek, every river. We went up and down every waterway on this coast. We fished and partied. After awhile I got a little bit suspicious, wondering what they really wanted. But I didn't really care. They were spending big bucks with me in my restaurant and lounge.

"The little one was redheaded, about five-seven, had a little belly on him—he was the real talker of the bunch. All the time yapping. The tall, thin one was quiet. He had a hawk nose. But they were funny. I mean these guys were really, really nice. They'd bring their families over, their wives and kids, and they'd stay with us. We did everything together. We all became really good friends.

"One night the little redheaded one says, 'We should tell you what we're really looking for.' I said, 'Well, I kind of figured what y'all are really looking for by now.' I said, 'If you'd told me that earlier, we could've saved a lot of time, not looked at some of those places.'

"They said that they had a guy in South Florida who needed a place to offload shrimp boats and a place to warehouse the cargo. They didn't say the word *pot*. I said, 'OK, that sounds fine to me.' I showed them all these different places and still hadn't talked about really working for them. But I was trying to find them the safest place to do it anyway."

There are several outback rivers on the jungle-woods coast. Eric showed them all of them. They had an eighty-mile stretch of lightly populated coastline to choose from.

Finally it came down to two of the least known, most untouched, most hidden rivers in America, the Econfina and the Aucilla. The Aucilla actually goes underground for several miles and resurfaces later. No more than a handful of people live along the banks of either river. The men chose the Aucilla.

One still morning when the air was smooth, I set out on the *Cooper* to explore the mouth of the Aucilla River. I had passed this area before on my manatee-finding expedition.

Because the bright green marsh extends well beyond the solid ground and creates a kind of vegetative maze, the actual river entrance is hard to find. When I realized how easily I could get lost in this isolated place, I decided there was no way I was going to risk taking the *Cooper* up the river. I anchored at the outer edge of the oyster bars, hoisted my Achilles inflatable boat into the water, and headed into the bay that bore no name on my chart.

For the first mile and a half through the bay and into the mouth of the river, there was marsh everywhere—high grass that took root underwater and grew like a green field above. Every so often I'd see a piece of high ground where a lone palm tree or salt cedar tree stood.

By the time the Aucilla narrowed into a real river I might have been hundreds of miles up the Amazon. The undulating growth and pressured quiet of this river jungle were overpowering. It made me feel lost in dinosaur times.

The riverbanks were loaded with old stumps and even entire washed-up trees, weathered and gray, stacked like giant bones. On the banks, plant life intertwined in an orgy of vines, tree trunks, and Spanish moss, which hung like a gray veil over everything. I could not see more than a few feet through the tangle of vegetation. The riverbank and surrounding swamp and jungle were a perfect environment for giant diamondback rattlers and the stinking, venomous cottonmouths. Locals said that some were as thick as boa constrictors, terrifying.

A small chameleon, its color a tropical green, floated by me on a golden-tan palm leaf. Alligator gars, prehistoric-looking fish with heads like alligators, rolled on the surface to gulp air, then slyly sunk from sight as soon as they saw me. I could see where gators had been slithering and crawling in and out of the river; the wild marsh grass trampled into narrow trails where they had dragged their heavy bodies. Never have I been on an American river so primeval, a place where plants and animals reigned as if the earth held no humans.

These jungle-woods and their rivers don't invite anyone in; everything grows in such a way as to keep people out. And then there are the house-sized rocks that come within inches of the top of the water, hiding and waiting, always ready to slash and sink the stranger's boat.

I headed my inflatable back downriver, back to the *Cooper*. Now I understood why Eric and the ol' boys had chosen the Aucilla.

CHAPTER 26

The
Head
Man

When the head man first came to meet Eric and see his new Aucilla River distribution center, he rode up from Miami in an emerald green Rolls-Royce. The man wore big diamonds and bright gold, and he had a deep suntan to show them off. Eric knew that kind of getup wouldn't do for conducting quiet business in the jungle-woods.

"I told them boys pretty quick, 'Hey, you can't be coming here dressed like that and driving something like that.' I said, 'If you want to do something up here, you got to get you a pickup truck and a hat.'"

By "hat" he meant the baseball-cap variety. That kind of hat is a big part of a man's wardrobe in the jungle-woods. It is necessary to have more than one, even a lot. Some jungle-woodsers collect them, hang them all over the walls of their dens.

It wasn't the hats or their colors that mattered so much; it was what they said. What was written on the front of your hat was very important. It had to be you. It had to make a statement.

The first hat messages I saw said, "Go Gators," referring to the University of Florida football team. A lot of the hats in the area stated athletic loyalties. There were a lot of Florida State University caps that proclaimed their wearers "Hundred Percent Seminole."

The next one I had to get close to read. It listed "Five Good Reasons a Beer Is Better Than a Woman: (1) Beer is never late. (2) Hangovers go away. (3) Beer Doesn't Demand Equality. (4) Beer doesn't get jealous when you grab another beer. (5) Beer never has a headache."

Another hat said, "I'll be sober tomorrow, but you'll still be ugly." Another warned, "Never underestimate the power of the USA." A green cap said, "Forget it—I'm going fishing." And another stated, "I may not be perfect, but I'm always me."

The last hat I read said, "The more I learn about women the more I like my truck."

The South Florida smugglers took Eric's advice, and soon the smuggling operation was proceeding smoothly.

"After the first load we worked on the Aucilla River," Eric told me, "everything went so good we knew that, hey, this is going to work. It can work for a long time. We can make a lot of money." It wasn't long before Eric was working full time as a drug smuggler. He hired his brother-in-law and wife to run the Skyview.

Everyone thought Eric had made the switch to real estate. Or if they thought otherwise, they didn't say so. It was true that no real estate agent in the jungle-woods prior to Eric had ever made the kind of money he was, but then everybody knew he was selling chunks of the jungle-woods to rich people from the outside. Surely that explained the Mercedes, the BMW, the beach house at Alligator Point. In that region it was not considered proper to ask a lot of questions when a tribe member prospered. When one of their own struck it rich—and there were very, very few ways to do that in the jungle-woods—people figured something good had happened. That was enough.

Jungle-woods people noticed fine horse barns built by local people who could never afford a horse before. People noticed when a bleached-blond high-school student started driving a new, cherry red Corvette. But that's all they did was notice. Nothing was said.

And Eric was far from the only jungle-woodser to be involved in drug traffic at the time. "In the mid to late '70s, when we were doing what we were doing, it was the norm. Almost everybody was in it around here. Everybody . . . if you wasn't directly in it, you were sure making some money off of it. The businesses, the local folks, the truck dealers, car dealerships, the washing-machine sellers, the boat builders, the telephone company, the banks, the lawyers—they all benefited from what we were doing. There was a lot of money brought in from all over the world, and a lot of it was spent right here because we were the local boys. A lot of that money stayed here."

This was trickle-down economics at work in one of its many illegal forms. During these years, all over Florida and the rest of the Gulf Coast wherever smuggling was happening, it was more like flood-down economics.

"Seems like everybody worked for us after awhile. I had a sixty-year-old man who had no idea what pot was, but he hauled thousands of bales of it. Sheriff's deputies, they made about eleven thousand a year back then. They could guard the end of the road or escort a truckload for us to the interstate and make twenty thousand in a night." If they worked four hours, they'd be making five thousand dollars an hour.

"If you had a small net boat (called a bird-dog boat) to offload the haul, we'd pay you ten thousand bucks for four or five hours of work. These people had been working like slaves for minimum wage."

I was glad I was never offered that kind of temptation. Could I have said no—at age eighteen, twenty-four, thirty-four, forty? I'm not sure, especially not if I lived in a separate world like the jungle-woods.

After my trip to the Aucilla, I understood why the smaller boats were valuable. The could run down the river, dodging submerged boulders, go out past the mouth of the Aucilla to the loaded shrimp boat, and haul in as many bales of marijuana as they could hold.

The mouth of this semitropical river was eventually used to smuggle more than a million pounds of marijuana. But only marijuana. Eric refused to smuggle any cocaine.

"One time, I get this call at about three in the morning. These boys, they wanted me to offload some yacht. They said the cargo was pot, but they wouldn't tell me much about it. It seemed weird that someone would be smuggling in a yacht."

Eric was leery of this situation, especially since the yacht came from Central America. The U.S. government had just begun surveillance flights over the Gulf to keep track of all boat movements. A million-dollar yacht coming to the jungle-woods coast from Central America would certainly raise some suspicion.

"When I heard about all these aerial watchdogs, I had decided I was going to get out of smuggling. But they said this yacht was holding forty thousand pounds of stuff, and that struck me as real odd. I wanted to find out whose yacht it was. Turned out it was General Noriega's. Back then, no one ever came out and said this dude from Panama was selling drugs to America, making millions and millions of dollars, using his country's yachts to run them, then turning around and buying weapons, whatever. But our government had to know his yacht was there off the coast. And I didn't think there was only pot in that load. So I said no, I'm not going to go do it. I didn't think anyone else in this area would do it either."

Gulls become a still life at the mouth of Ochlockonee Bay.

The Panamanian yacht cruised slowly back and forth between the Steinhatchee and Aucilla Rivers, protected by diplomatic immunity, awaiting word on which one of the jungle-woods organizations would offload it. But none of the boys along the jungle-woods coast would unload Manuel Noriega's drugs. They spend their lives hunting turkey, an extraordinarily cautious animal with heightened senses—incredible eyesight, phenomenal sense of smell. These ol' boys had learned a thing or two from the turkey. They sensed danger, a trap.

They said Noriega had forty thousand pounds aboard his yacht. If the cargo had been pot, it would have been worth nine million dollars. If it had been cocaine, as Eric suspected, you could add a bunch more zeros. Eric was sure it was coke because that was Noriega's specialty.

It wasn't long before Eric's organization began to fray. The weak link was the head man in Miami and his few people. They got out of control, a thing the jungle-woods people rarely do. You can't get out of control and thread a boat through a rock-lined river, or walk through the jungle constantly alert for the stink of the cottonmouth or the terrible sound of the leg-thick diamondback. You're always controlling your chainsaw or your gun or your mouth or your temper. You raise your voice at someone in the jungle-woods, he might just kill you for it. But the head man in Miami was always doing something silly.

"One time the boss man calls me. He's down in Miami at his mansion. I had been working with them for about a year, a year and a half. It was about two-thirty in the morning. The phone rings, and it's the man.

He's just in hysterics, crying, almost screaming, saying, 'Man, I need some help . . . I need some help.'

"I said, 'Well, what's the matter? What's going on?' And he says, 'Some guys kidnapped me, and they robbed me, and they're from the Mafia, and they're going to kill me.'

"I said, 'Well, send a plane up here and get me, and I'll come down and see what I can do.' So I got my M-16 and a bunch of little goodies together, shotguns and pistols and just one thing or another. About an hour later, a Lear jet comes whipping into our little airport. I get on the jet with this ol' pilot who used to haul us around a lot. I said, 'Well, buddy, what's happening?' He said, 'I don't know, but the man is sure acting crazy.'

"So we get down there and go to the house. What had happened, these guys had knocked on his door and flashed a badge and said they were policeman. Actually, they were muscle for these mob guys up in Detroit that the head man had stiffed.

"Well, the head man had been working, counting money, and they had several million dollars there in the house. They had two girls upstairs counting money. They had that much cash in their house, and there were no guards, no guard dogs, and they opened the door when some strangers knocked!

"These guys, they just busted on in. And so they got the head man and handcuffed him. Then they forced him upstairs. Upstairs are these girls with these big suitcases of money they're counting. So the robbers get the suitcases, then go back downstairs with our fearless leader. His brother-in-law, a squirrelly accountant—he was about to pee in his pants.

"You've got to understand—these guys that ran our operation were not the machine-gun-toting gangster types you saw on *Miami Vice*. The head man was more the hype artist, a slick-talking greedy type. His brother-in-law was a number-crunching wimp. The brother-in-law got so scared when the robbers were trying to get the head man out of the house with the money that he said, 'Excuse me guys, you're forgetting something.' Then he handed them another briefcase with three hundred thousand dollars in it.

"So the two Mafia guys put the head man and the money into their car and start off down the road. Well, the head man has always been a little crazy, right?" Eric said, grinning at the thought of it. "So these guys come to a red light and stop. Well, the head man, he opens the door and jumps out, handcuffed, right in the middle of a huge Miami intersection, a lot of traffic. He starts jumping around, hollering and screaming. Two cars back there's a cop. Lucky for him. I mean, without the cop, they'd have probably blistered him right there.

"This cop flips on his blue light and runs up there and grabs the head man. He's screaming, 'They stole my money, they stole my money!' I mean, this is drug money we're talking about—easy a couple million in cash."

Eric's expression turned to amusement at this point. I had come to expect good stories when I saw this expression on his often expressionless face.

"So the cops throw the head man in the back seat, a chase begins, and they run these two guys from Detroit down and stop them. They arrest those guys, carry them to jail."

Now the outrageous story began. Because of the amount of cash taken from the head man, the Internal Revenue Service got involved. The IRS questioned the strung-out head man, and he told them that the cash was for a real estate deal with him and a business partner of his, a Saudi Arabian.

What did the IRS do? They bought the story and gave him half his cash back! (They kept half of it in escrow.) Eric figured the head man was screaming at the IRS that they would have to pay him interest for all that "real estate deal" money they seized.

"Anyway, after all that, the man is freaked. He needs a guard. He knew I'd done Nam, so he asked me to do it."

Eric told the head man that his house in Miami was not secure. There were too many ways in—from the water, from next door, from the sky. So they could either go hide out on one of the isolated farms Eric owned in the jungle-woods or get them a boat and disappear for a while.

"The head man went and leased the *Cocoa Channel*, a 132-foot steel-hulled yacht, one of the most luxurious yachts anywhere. He hired five crew members and a cordon bleu chef. Also there was me, the accountant, and his wife. We spent about a month in the Caribbean till finally the head man got bored and felt safe again."

At that point, Eric had to get back to the jungle-woods. He was getting calls every day, more than once a day, telling him that things weren't running as smoothly as they had run when he was coordinating a lot of the action.

CHAPTER 27

Wilder
and
Crazier

I t took a loaded shrimp boat about a week to ten days to chug the approximately seventeen hundred miles from Colombia to the mouth of the Aucilla River. Usually the boat would be all rigged out for shrimping. The crew would even hang their nets in the water most of the day to look like they were shrimping. Sometimes they'd get in terrible weather, but they could not head for the safe haven of a port, even when a hurricane was upon them. Some of the boats and their South American crews were beat up pretty badly.

Eric and JWI (Jungle-Woods Incorporated) had the money to buy the best equipment available. Of course, they weren't legally incorporated, but they operated as efficiently as a well-run, legitimate business. They loved Sears trash compactors, which proved invaluable for packing the marijuana tightly. They had more money to spend than the government and were technologically way ahead of the feds.

"You would not believe the radio equipment we used," Eric told me. "We stayed in pretty close contact with the boats on their way up here, just to make sure everything was OK." Special crystals supercharged the radios so they could communicate from Taylor County to South America or anywhere in the Gulf. They also used sophisticated scanners for communicating. But never telephones. Eric, ever cautious, didn't believe in ever using a phone.

Like any salesman, Eric had different buyers for different varieties of the same product.

For the strongest stuff, there was a young guy out of New Jersey who would pay a bit more than everyone else—around $225 a pound—and buy fifty thousand pounds at a time, maybe enough to supply New York City for a couple days. To transport his purchase, the New Jersey buyer would hire college students and provide them with old cars and pop-top campers filled with bales of the stuff.

In addition, there was a buyer in Atlanta who bought all the sticks and stalks and seeds, what they called junk pot. And a woman in Orlando liked to buy all the bales of pot that had gotten wet below decks.

No matter what happened to the cargo en route to America, there was money to be made and, ultimately, people's lives to be trashed.

Eric took all sorts of precautions to avoid getting caught. "One thing, I always wore camouflage clothes when we were unloading at the mouth of the river. That way, if I got chased, I could run my boat aground and get out in the marsh. If the feds wanted me, they was going to have to run me down in the jungle. And I knew I could survive out there for a lot longer than those government boys. There's no dog in the world going to track you in that stuff. You cross the salt creeks and get into the swamp, and you can pretty well get along. Even at night I could get some general directions from stars maybe. But the best thing to do was just to hunker down, find me a spot, wait until daylight, then work my way out."

Eric quit the drug business before anyone could catch him. The head man down south was getting wilder and crazier, taking more and more risks, snorting too much cocaine and acting psychotic, like a cokehead will. At the same time, the government was getting more and more sophisticated in its surveillance. The National Security Agency had a way to monitor transoceanic calls, listening in for certain words and loran numbers that might indicate nighttime rendezvous.

Even some of the locals were getting a bit too rich, too loose. The old saying warns that "loose lips sink ships." And while loose lips almost never betray anyone in the jungle-woods, Eric was afraid they'd eventually sink their Aucilla River operations. He could feel the heat, and he felt no need to be greedy. By now he owned several farms, a couple of Corvettes, a BMW, a Mercedes 450SL, and lots of stuff. And he was having second thoughts about being involved with drugs.

"All the time the pressure was on me from people wanting our bunch to unload boats full of coke. But I've always believed there was a difference between pot and the hard stuff. Some of my buddies in Vietnam got on that coke and opium, and they got stupid. They got killed. Dead. Or the stuff hooked 'em, and that was a slow death."

Eric never broke under the multimillion-dollar temptation to handle cocaine. He never unloaded anything but marijuana, which at that time he believed was only illegal, not harmful.

Eric told the head man that he would not do any more business with him. "That head man, he became an idiot and a thief. He got crazy from money and power, and he wasn't worried about us at all. He was worried about himself, period. After we quit him, he kept trying to do loads. But they lost boats in the Carolinas, they lost boats off the Keys, off Louisiana. The government boys were catching 'em left and right."

When it all got too crazy, too hard to control, too many people on the edge, Eric stopped it all. At that point, he went into a laid-back mode, an inborn personality trait of the jungle-woods people. It was time to stop, retire, go fishing. He never expected his South Florida partners to turn him in. When the jungle-woods people become your friend, when they socialize with you and your kids, when they have you spend the night at their house and take you into their special places, they expect you to be there for them for life. After all, they plan to be there for you when you need their help. Friends don't turn on friends.

"I'll never forget what was happening the day they came and got me. I was at home. I hadn't done any drug smuggling for several years. It was 6:30 one morning, September 21, 1982. It was storming, raining bad, one of them ol' killer lightning storms. I had just finished building our new house that Saturday. I'd nailed down the stairs into the house on Saturday, had a wedding in the gazebo out there on the creek for my sister-in-law on Sunday, and then I got arrested that Tuesday. It was almost seven years before I spent a night in the house. Our daughter was two then."

Eric was in jail for six years and nine months. Because he very much wanted to come home someday, and because the jungle-woods is his home, he never told the authorities anything. Neither did the other eleven men who were a part of the Aucilla River bunch that the head man and his accountant turned over to the law. Even when they found out the head man only had to serve fourteen months of his twenty-year sentence because he had turned them in, they still were as silent as dead rats.

"There was five major snitches in the case. And then there was us silent boys from Taylor County." Right or wrong, legal or illegal, to the people of the jungle-woods there is nothing worse than a snitch.

At Eric's trial, the head man's accountant brother-in-law turned over all his records, records he was supposed to have destroyed. He had kept two sets of books, and the second set was enough to send Eric and his friends to jail. Eric's operation was charged with bringing in more than a million pounds of pot, with a street value of more than half a billion dollars.

Today, Eric assists law firms in utilizing his company's software to organize and access all their thousands of pages of information, depositions, and evidence. He assists the CIA in their classified applications. He comes across as an unconcerned, happy bear, even in the occasional suit he dons when he goes to New York on business. His feelings are mostly hidden, masked behind the banter. But his face shows occasional flashes of an unrelenting pain or sadness or anger or regret.

Before I left the jungle-woods, Eric borrowed a friend's boat, and we went wandering in the Aucilla River. He had many flashbacks, from diving here for dinosaur bones as a sixteen-year-old to smuggling bales of marijuana in the dark.

We stopped at the riverbank and tied up at the trailer home of a man who wore his white hair in a crewcut. He could have been sixty, maybe seventy. He, too, was one of the few who'd served his whole time in prison.

This man had been a fisherman all his life. Then he'd hauled bales of pot and made more in two nights than in two decent years of fishing. Then he was in prison. And now he's on parole.

All he'd ever known his whole life was the freedom of life on the primeval Aucilla River and the bays and the Gulf beyond, following the lead of the seasons while he tracked and caught fish. He knew well what the fish did, how unpredictable they were, how every year they moved to different places, showed up at different times. But now this man, this felon with his white crewcut and his fisherman's power-built body, cannot follow the fish. He has to get advance permission from his parole officer to leave his small area.

Eric can go to a computer convention in San Diego because he knows of these gatherings far in advance and can get the required permission. This old fisherman cannot predict his life that way. The fish don't schedule their "doings" in advance.

Eric can be locked in a room anywhere and go off for days, for weeks, for life into the world of computers and computer language. But the familiar life of the river and the sea is gone for the old man on parole. He is on a leash, a felon's leash, and it has almost killed him.

Smuggling marijuana has cost these men a great deal, but it cost the old fisherman more. As we sat together in the cramped living room of the older man's trailer, the air was heavy with regret, a shared sadness and silence. No small talk could overpower this silent sorrow. As we sat there together I knew they were as close as these jungle-woods men ever got to crying.

CHAPTER 28

Soft
White
Sand

Junior had on his "I Don't Dial 911" T-shirt when he presented me with a new cap that bore the name of his store in camouflage green and brown. Junior lived in a trailer behind his store, in a clearing next to where the Aucilla River crosses Highway 98. He was a friend of Eric's.

"You done qualified yourself to wear this thing," he told me.

I'm not sure what he meant, but I think this honor was due to the fact that I had listened to him and Eric and their friends.

Exploring the heart of a place and a people can be a dangerously vulnerable experience. I'd come to understand these strong, fierce people with their terminal need for freedom and self-sufficiency. I counted several of them as friends. I'd grown to love the jungle-woods, one of the most amazing and resilient ecosystems in our country. And it had meant a lot to me to get to know my sister now that we were both adults. It would hurt to leave here. I did not look forward to arriving somewhere else as a stranger again.

I did look forward to living on the *Cooper* again. The boat was my dear friend now, a fiberglass home that now had a deep, living connection to me. Navigating unfamiliar waters, searching on her for my next stop, sleeping below her decks offered me what small amounts of security I felt while I explored this crescent-shaped coastline. She was far more than just a chunk of fiberglass and metal. She was a steady presence in an unpredictable watery world.

I was no longer a radical stranger to the Gulf of Mexico. Some days, in fact, I felt full of confidence. But then would come a small-craft advisory or a new beach to land on or a swirling wind I'd not met yet. The never-diminishing need for concentration and the demands for instant decisions kept me alert.

I headed the *Cooper* west toward the Gulf's most beautiful and empty beaches—some have ranked them among the planet's most beautiful. A few were popular gathering places for sun lovers, but others were lonesome slashes of coastline or islands with far more shells and skimmers and resting turtles than people. Their dazzling stretch of white sand extended all the way from the Florida Panhandle to the Chandeleur Islands of Louisiana. Somewhere along here I might find the world's most perfect beach. And the place I intended to start looking was Dog Island, one of the many barrier islands that protect the coastline.

White sand surrounds Dog Island like a ruffle of ermine fur. The earth was overheated the afternoon I got there, but a moist inland wind promised a fine walk on the beach. I put the *Coops* into neutral to feel the movement of the current and the influence of the wind. This boat had become an extension of me from my feet up; I felt the way *it* felt. When the *Coops* was ready I switched the motor into forward and guided the bow gently to a sandbar.

I put down two anchors to hold the boat firmly and jumped off the bow into two feet of transparent saltwater, soothing as a warm hand. From the stern I could have dived into fifteen feet of clear, inky blue. These islands have no rock or coral to form a natural harbor, only sandbars pushing out from the land, easily visible when the tide is low. At high tide I could recognize the submerged sandbars by the almost colorless water that covered them.

Dog Island is no more than three-quarters of a mile wide and about six miles long. Some of its trees, usually pine, have been twisted into bonsai shapes by the constant wind. These barrier islands are nothing but sand, shifted by winds, currents, and tides. Hurricanes transform them radically, especially with smashing, direct hits. There is no rock anywhere to hold them in place, so they are always changing, always moving.

Each translucent grain of sand along this coastline once was rock, window-glass-clear quartz washed down from the Appalachian Mountains. For centuries, small pieces of these mountains have washed into streams, then into rivers, and drifted south. Finally, huge amounts ended up flowing out of the mouths of rivers into the Gulf. The Gulf's strong currents carried the grains of sand, and over much time these barrier islands and beaches were born.

*This rare beach, a **tangle** of washed-out trees and white sand, is about thirty miles south of Tallahassee. It's only a mile from The Oaks restaurant. This is how many beaches looked before "civilization" came to this continent.*

My plan was to take a half day to walk around the island. I worried that the *Cooper's* anchors might pull loose, sand not being the best holding material, and that the boat would be gone when I returned. If that happened I'd figure something out. All I cared about right now was getting on that beach. Or beaches, no matter how unknown. I felt immediately joyous and cleansed.

Walking alone on the soft white sand, I was in a state not far below ecstasy. I thought how my dog Cooper would have loved this place. He would have charged crazily into the shallows and run up and down the beach shaking off water like diamonds flying through the air.

On the Gulf side of the island, tiny, almost round fish flashed their silver sides and little yellow fins as hermit crabs looked for food in the knee-deep shallows inside the sandbar. Waves did not crash in this day but came ashore politely. Sand-colored minnows hit my wading feet.

The sandbar ended; I had to push ashore in chest-deep swirls of water. A gray fish about six feet long darted away. Probably a sand shark. Now I was on the six-mile-long Gulf shore of the island. Dunes loomed high up, overlooking me, facing into endless water soon fifty feet deep, soon two hundred feet deep, soon a thousand feet.

The bright white sand dunes west of Gulf Shores, Alabama, have healed themselves after many blasts from hurricanes. Here the sands have covered all of a refrigerator, except its wheels, blown out of a vacation home during a hurricane. Sand crabs have left the latest imprint on this sand, their delicate tracks.

I walked for miles and rounded the western end of the island. St. George Island was just across a deep-water pass to the west, separated from the mainland by the calm waters of Apalachicola Bay. It was from that bay that Warren had launched us into the dark Gulf on our shakedown cruise. That had been more than six months ago, but I could still taste the fear and excitement of that moment.

On the lee side of Dog Island, I came upon a creek that drained an interior marsh, but which was kept clean of decomposing matter by the flushing tidal currents. There I found my water hole, three and a half feet deep. Beer-bottle brown water from the marsh flowed into it over the white sands. I leaped in and lay back. The water, heated by the all-day September sun, served as my own private hot tub. The sundown winds created relaxing sounds, ssshing through the green pine needles. I could hear the slightest thud of a cone falling on sand, the far-off splash of a diving pelican, all rising in and out of the dominant water noise. My sun-warmed water was a pleasure, a gift.

The cool breeze blowing over the hot water made me twitch with delight. Everywhere the soft sand gave way to fit my body's contour. Could there be a more perfect beach ahead, farther west? Would I find it at Cape San Blas, Grayton Beach, Top Sail Beach, Santa Rosa Beach, or Gulf Shores? Not today, because I was here, and this place was perfect.

At twilight I headed back to my boat feeling restored to more-than-human strength. My muscles were loose, my footsteps weightless. Clothes felt like an imposition.

The feeling didn't last. I was yanked back to imperfection when hordes of biting flies attacked. These flies look like normal houseflies, but they inflict a painful, tormenting bite. They swarm on the interior side of the islands, and you can't swish them off fast enough. Now I had two things to worry about: being bitten into a state of crazy before I got to the boat, and being stranded by a rising tide that could carry the *Cooper* out to sea without me.

When I cut back to the Gulf side of the island, the wind swatted the flies away. I rounded the corner and was relieved to see my boat still at anchor, though the sandbar was now covered with water. I waded out and climbed aboard the *Cooper,* feeling a surge of something close to love.

You don't really hug a boat, or pat it, or kiss it, but I felt like doing that sometimes. The way I showed it affection was to shine it, work on it, maintain it, see that no one hurt it. I've never been one to shine anything, but I couldn't do enough for the *Cooper.*

After I'd hung out on Dog Island for a couple of days, I backtracked to Alligator Point. I got a ride to the eastern side of Ochlockonee Bay, where Highway 98 intersected with Surf Road. I could have gone north to a place called Sopchoppy or east to Panacea. Instead I stopped to eat at the Oaks Motel and Restaurant, which seemed to be an average kind of North Florida tourist place. I found the restaurant, sat down at my table, and idly glanced down at the place mat. Then I glanced again.

On the very top of the place mat was printed in red, "The Oaks family, their acorns, grand acorns, great grand acorns and the nuts they married—hope you enjoy yourself." Below this amazing slogan was a drawing of a large oak leaf with a family tree superimposed upon it. Each Oaks family member on the tree was symbolized by an acorn. Each person who had married into the family was represented by a nut.

I learned from the place mat that The Oaks was founded in 1953 by Alton and Ora Oaks. They are the mama and daddy, the oak tree from which many branches have sprung. The three biggest nuts belonged to their children, Clayton, Evalinda, and Sonja Lynn. From each of their three nuts came a line that stood for their families.

Clayton was the son of the founders. Next to his nut was a nut named "Genny." It was labeled "First Nut." Each of Clayton and Genny's four children had his or her own acorns.

Clayton and Genny must have been divorced, because closest to Clayton's big titled nut was another nut with the name "Anne" in it. Above that was the label, "Present Nut." So there were two nuts with female names attached to Clayton. Here was a family that was not ashamed of their past. I wondered what Clayton's past "nut" thought of his present "nut."

Both of Alton and Ora's daughters, Evalinda and Sonja Lynn, had their "first nuts" listed: Jerry and Buddy. Under their nuts were blank nuts labeled "Next Nut." I wasn't sure what that meant. Were the daughters divorced and not yet remarried, or did they have the blank nut there in case they might need another nut? Maybe they were husband shopping, and this was a bizarre way to advertise for one. Sonja Lynn had three little acorns. Each child had two names like she did; there was Jessica Star, Allana Moon, and Ben Eagle.

The bottom of the place mat assured me "We're glad you're here."

I wondered about my own family. If we had a restaurant, would we put our family tree on the place mat? It would be loaded with nuts. Nope, never. Dad believed in keeping the best face on everything involving family.

As I paid my check, I asked the woman at the cash register a question. She was a sultry-eyed, black-haired jungle-woods woman who looked like she had once been a wild child. Her body, once high and firm, was falling fast.

"Are you one of the Oak family I've been reading about?" I asked her.

"No," she sighed, her voice tired, as if she had been out until three in the morning for twenty years in a row.

"Are any of the Oaks here?" I wondered.

"No," she half groaned.

"Is this whole Oak family a bunch of characters or what?" I laughed.

All she could do was hand me my change and raise her eyebrows as far as they'd go.

Angels
Unaware

Impossible.

I could not have seen what I just saw on that beach. I swung the *Cooper* around, doing a fast power turn. Was it two people, in dark robes, one with—with antlers? Whatever it was, it was massive, haloed by the orange light of the summer evening.

I had to investigate. I stopped the motor. The creature turned a huge rump at me and ran. It seemed more than twice the size of a large whitetail deer.

I later learned that what I saw was a sambur deer. Once, before St. Vincent Island became a national wildlife refuge, an owner had stocked it with exotic animals. All had died out except for the sambur from India, which was able to adapt to the heat, humidity, and bugs and thrive on this protected barrier island.

I decided to change my route to explore the island and its mysterious resident. I often did this. All it took was a strange sight, a view around a new corner, a suspicion of something richly hidden. It was too dark now, but I'd be back to the island in the morning.

I motored through Indian Pass, a narrow waterway between the mainland and the island, and found a place to anchor in Indian Lagoon. I was lying in my cabin relaxing when something banged the side of the *Cooper*. Did someone throw something at us? I was just about to stick my head out the door when a man's voice yelled, "Is anyone on that boat?"

I stepped outside where the two people, a man and a woman, could see me. They were in a wooden oyster boat, small and open. The single, forty-horsepower motor was silent. They had come close, but now they were drifting away from me.

"Yeah," I answered. "I'm here."

"We need some help!"

On the sea, you always help. There's a shared knowledge that tomorrow it could be you who needs it. Few boats ever refuse an SOS from another.

"What do you need?" I called.

"Our motor broke down." The man rattled out the words fast. "And our anchor wouldn't hold—we didn't have enough rope for this channel."

They were caught in a powerful tide, drifting quickly out toward the Gulf, where their low-slung boat would have quickly been overcome by heavy waves. Though their condition was perilous, they didn't seem all that worried.

I pulled up my anchor and went after them. When I came abreast, I threw the woman a rope and towed them back to Indian Lagoon. After I anchored the *Cooper* near the place I'd just left, the man pulled their boat up to mine till they touched.

He told me they'd been out to catch some redfish for supper, out from the familiar part of the bay they usually worked.

"Me and the lady, one way we make a living is by tonging oysters. What living it is." He pointed to a pile of burlap sacks in the boat. I was curious about several long poles lying next to them. The man explained they used the poles, which had rakelike attachments, to pry the oysters off their beds.

"I used to be a full-time preacher," he told me. "But mainly now I help people with drug and alcohol problems."

His wife, a pretty woman with long brown hair, told me they had four children, all under eight years old. "We were gonna try to catch us a couple of redfish for dinner at Indian Cut when the motor quit. And you were here. The Lord was with us."

The man quoted, "'God is our refuge and strength, a very present help in trouble. Therefore we will not fear, though the earth should change, and though the mountains slip into the heart of the sea; though its waters roar and foam.'"

"That's Psalm 46," his wife added shyly as she smiled and pushed her hair away from her face.

"We didn't get to the part where the waters were roaring and foaming, but we would have if we'd gone into the Gulf." The man had an engaging grin that crinkled up his eyes and made his whole face glow. Their faith had obviously been tested many times and never faltered.

The man untied a burlap sack and filled a plastic bucket with oysters still in the shell. There was a shucking knife in his hand as he stepped into my boat carrying the bucket.

"Would it be all right if we shucked some oysters for you?" he asked. I said, "Of course." His wife came aboard, too. The three of us sat on the *Cooper* at the western edge of Indian Pass and ate raw oysters, salty and plump, that surpassed delicious.

After three or four dozen oysters, the preacher asked me what I was doing in Indian Lagoon. I told him. He asked me if I knew God. I told him I used to think I did, but I now realized I could never know all I wanted to know about Him. The man smiled. It was an understanding smile.

The preacher went to his boat to see if he could get his motor running again. He fiddled with his gas tank, unhooked the rubber line from the metal tank, blew into it, and reattached it. He tried to start his engine. It didn't. He messed with the sparkplug wire. Tried again. No response. He tried one more time. The engine coughed and began.

"We will leave now," he told me. "Thank you for helping us." Then he asked, "What is your name?"

"Peter," I said.

"What's your name?" I asked.

"My name is Peter, too," he answered. "Can we pray for you?"

The question sounded odd to me, yet it was strange that it sounded odd. At one time in my life, a lot of people had offered to pray for me. No one had offered in quite awhile.

I said yes, I'd be grateful for their prayers. "And if you would please say a prayer for my family?"

When I said the word *family* I was stunned with a sudden eruption of emotion. How much I missed them! Usually I tried to keep those feelings under control, even repressed.

The oysterman reached out his dark-tanned, oil-stained hands and held mine as he prayed for me and my family. We held our boats together for a few moments more. Then the preacher's wife let go of my boat, and they headed back in the direction of Apalachicola. She waved for a long time. Light gray smoke came from their engine and lay atop the warm water.

I watched till I couldn't see their boat anymore. I had been there at the right moment to help them. And they had been there for me, too.

The next morning my heart felt far more buoyant. I decided to row the quarter mile to St. Vincent Island to look for the mystery animal again. As I pulled my inflatable far up on shore, I saw many different tracks in the sand, signatures of the creatures who lived on this refuge island. I had been told that the interior jungle of this island sheltered all manner of animals usually considered dangerous. People said the largest black-backed gators in the wild lived in there. There were also plenty of the big diamondback rattlers and the heavy, aggressive, wild hogs.

I glanced toward the dark undergrowth, all green and tangled, where the beasts lived. I did not want to go in.

So I kept to the beach, following the weaving track of a raccoon that had dug under the gray and pitted driftwood. Large holes looking like small explosions were places where feral hogs had come to root.

Midway down the beach I saw four cow-sized hoof prints facing the Gulf and a disturbance in the sand where something had whirled and run. It was here where the antlered animal had stood. This island had a fearsome quality. Its interior was a tangled mash of vines and primeval palms where everything died and lay till it rotted. Could the immense deer feel the same as I did? Did it come to the open beach to look out at the open spaces above the ocean wishing for a way out?

My inflatable was waiting for me down the beach. I pushed it off into the water and left the island.

My wanderings along the rest of Florida's coastline felt aimless. The Florida coast would soon change to Alabama's coast and then Mississippi's. And although the days were still steamy in this semitropical climate, I knew autumn was on its way. But where was I going next? Where would I tie up again?

At home, when I felt this way, unsure of what to do, where to go, I would drive my pickup down a monotonous road or mow circles around and around a thirty-acre field on my tractor. There was something about pure, uninterrupted movement that soothed and centered my soul. Maybe riding the waves along the last of Florida's bright white coast would do the same.

There is an enchanted place, walled in by cotton-white sand dunes and bright teal-colored saltwater, just east of Grayton Beach. I was there one late summer morning. I walked halfway up one of the cool dunes and sat in the cleanest, purest sand I've ever known. Normally this moment would have been flawless, but it was not. Restless, I waded a bit and then swam back out to the *Cooper* and weighed anchor. I blew on down the beaches, searching, thinking, feeling, wondering what would surface next.

I rambled on down the coast, past more perfect places. They could not hold me. I passed Pensacola, where I had first picked up the *Cooper* with Warren. I marked the milestone with a certain satisfaction, but the restlessness wouldn't leave me.

It was near the coast of Alabama that I finally understood my odd, unsettled feelings. I'd seen thousands of large butterflies fluttering atop the endless water, heading always out to sea. Were they disoriented, blown out by a storm front? Were they committing butterfly suicide? No, they were migrating, drifting, flapping south all the way across the Gulf to a warm winter home.

I realized I needed to migrate, too. But not to warmth. I'd been through almost a year of endless summer, had all the warmth I could take. I'd seen enough of the endless green of plants and palms to last me a long time. I'd had all the sand in my pockets and between my toes and in my underwear I could stand. What I needed was winter—falling leaves, hard ground. I craved cold air, chilled enough to send me to a fire.

So now I decided I would go in the opposite direction of the butter-flies. I headed the *Cooper* into Mobile Bay, blasted north to the Mobile River, then headed up the Alabama River. In two days the *Cooper* and I had made it two hundred miles to a place called Wilcox County. And that's how I came to lose myself for the winter in a world where time has a com-pletely different meaning.

I took Daisy Durrant to the beloved home where she and her late husband, Rob, lived on the Furman place. The Furmans promised Daisy, who worked for them for decades, that if she would move into more comfortable and less isolated housing in town, that they would never again let anyone live in Daisy and Rob's home as long as they lived. The Furmans have kept their promise.

This old country store in Wilcox County is in front of the plantation home known as Liberty Hall.

A lone tree in the middle of the marsh below New Orleans filled with egrets

The Mississippi River still has almost a hundred miles to go after it rolls by New Orleans. Before it gets to the Gulf, in the area of Bastian Bay, stand some of the homes where Croatian oystermen and their families settled in America and created an entire community above the water.

Almost to the end of the Mississippi River, the river splits. Instead of a single massive stream of water it becomes many fingers (called passes) heading toward the Gulf. This place is called the Head of the Passes. A world-circling tanker passes the dock at Pilottown on it its way to Southwest Pass.

A block over from Jackson Square this
young woman plays some of the best
Dixieland jazz imaginable for free.

A mime decked out in Mardi Gras beads
entertains on Jackson Square.

In Cameron Parish a rare spoonbill ibis makes an elegant landing in a shallow marsh lake turned pink by the last light of this day.

Ralph Holmes, seventy-two years old and still a cowboy, on the Whitehead ranch. At one time Ralph was a champion calf roper on the black rodeo circuit. I rode hard with Ralph, trying to round up some seriously misbehaving cattle. We got 'em.

Diane Wilson sits on her shrimp net, mending it for tomorrow. She grew up on the bays surrounding Seadrift, Texas. Besides being a mother, shrimper, and wife of a crew boat captain, she is an environmentalist known around the world for her passionate effectiveness.

Sabine River

Mississippi River

Alabama R.

WILCOX
Camden
COUNTY

Baton
Rouge

Mobile

Gulfport

Lake
Pontchartrain

CAMERON
PARISH
Cameron

New Orleans

Holly Beach

Pilottown

PAUL M. BREEDEN

CHAPTER 30

Memories
Are
Long

I stood as if in a trance across the road from an antebellum mansion flanked by three moss-covered cedars, all battered by time. Not a speck of paint was left on its high columns; everything, including the forlorn rocking chair, was a weary Confederate gray. To the mansion's far left stood a lone, lightning-scarred oak tree; its branches cast crooked shadows on a small yard once carefully manicured, now tangled with weeds. To the right, crowding close to the yard fence, was a field of bright green winter wheat. There a flock of male peacocks spread their iridescent tails. They strutted about as if they wanted someone to notice.

I heard a loud *bang,* a shot, near my head. I ducked. I looked around. Was I trespassing? Was someone shooting at me? Shooting at the peacocks? But the birds had not ruffled a feather, and the opiating, humid air was as still as ever.

BANG. I flinched and ducked again, then raised my head to look for the source of the noise. Only then did I realize that I was in a grove of pecan trees. A pecan fell from a branch. My eye caught it dropping—bang!—onto the tin roof of an ancient corncrib I had stopped to photograph. Pecans were dropping everywhere onto the soft ground and crashing on the tin roofs of barns, smokehouses, and woodsheds.

The banging pecans woke me out of my dream world. I was just thirty-two miles south of Selma, Alabama, in sight of Highway 41. The *Cooper* was tied up at a dock on the river not more than five miles away.

If a mockingbird flew straight, it would have to flutter 125 miles from the old privet hedge where I was standing to hit the Gulf of Mexico. Here, though, I would find that almost nothing proceeded straight ahead. Everything curved around again to pick up the past, which was part of everyday life in Wilcox County, Alabama.

The fires of the Civil War missed this place: it was off route from the scorch-and-burn path of the Yankees marching from Atlanta to the sea. For this reason there are more antebellum homes stubbornly clinging to life in Wilcox County than in almost any other county of the South. Their dominating columns no longer speak of power, though. They rise up now, even if not straight and white, as memorials to a time when their owners reigned like kings and queens. The columns recall an era long past, a period that many want to remember and many want to forget.

Before the most important war that ever happened, before Abraham Lincoln was moved into his big white house near Maryland, most of the land here was owned in tracts of five hundred, three thousand, even five thousand acres. These plantations made their money by growing cotton. (Corn was for grits and cornmeal and to feed mules and hogs and milk cows.) The cotton was usually planted before Good Friday in the month of April after the land had lain bare for several months. The cottonseed was prepared for the planting in March, and the cotton was picked in the fall— by the slaves at first, then by sharecroppers, now by mechanical cotton pickers. But there is little cotton grown here anymore. What money there is comes mostly from lumber, cattle, and hunting leases.

Jobs are scarce in Wilcox County these days. You can tell because most of the newest living places are trailers. Few of the people who live in the once-dominating antebellum houses can afford to paint and repair them properly. I saw one new double-wide trailer set up in the front yard of a once-proud mansion, now sagging. Some of the old building's floors and beams had rotted from water damage. Honeysuckle had taken over the back porch, screens had long since rusted away, squirrels had gnawed holes here and there.

Why was the trailer put right in front of that sad remnant of a grand era? I think the old mansions stand like gravestones, huge decaying monuments to family pride. In Wilcox County the impulse to eulogize one's ancestors is a powerful force.

Memories are long in Wilcox County. Stories from 175 years ago are still told today as though they had just happened. Once when I was riding through downtown Camden with a southern gentlewoman of aristocratic bearing, she pointed to a man on the sidewalk. "That's a carpetbagger," she said. The man she had shown me was a descendant of a northerner who had come to the region *125 years ago!*

In Wilcox County, not far off Highway 28, this historic home awaits someone's attention. Wilcox County has the second most antebellum homes in the state of Alabama, some haunted, some lovingly cared for, many badly in need of maintenance, most still occupied.

That's not to say that everyone lives in the past, though. I was told about a seventy-five-year-old widow who lived alone in two backrooms of her antebellum home. A friend of mine saw her in the front yard with a shovel, planting two oak saplings about three feet high.

"Why are you planting those?" my friend asked, concerned that the old woman might overdo in the heat and injure herself.

The widow replied firmly, "I'm planting them for shade."

The family land is often the center of the universe in this part of the country. Land is what everything else grew from.

In the past, some members of land-rich families never married. An unwritten law has always been that one must marry a spouse who ideally had more land than one's people. Since many children of the largest plantations couldn't find the appropriate partners, they remained unmarried to keep the land in the family. Another way to keep the fence lines from changing was to marry a cousin, preferably far enough removed as to avoid genetic havoc. It is possible that one too many marriages between cousins has helped provide places like this with its characters. Genes that hit head-on can create some very entertaining people. On the other hand, people might just be more tolerant here. At any rate, behavior that would be considered bizarre in other places seems to be lovingly accepted.

There's a story of one prominent Wilcox County family. At one time they had hundreds of sharecroppers on their place, direct descendants of slaves. One of the owners had a black mistress, and both his wife and his mistress bore him daughters. The half-black daughter became the maid of the all-white daughter. Everyone said they looked just alike. Both daughters were tall and elegant looking, with thin arms and long legs. Each woman had a graceful, long neck and an aristocratic tilt to her face. The maid's skin was just a bit darker, but the difference was slight. Neither woman liked nor had much experience with the sun or sweat.

Heiress and maid lived together in the same house after their father died. In later years they did everything together. Both displayed a queenly

Excellent care has been lavished on the grand home known as Liberty Hall, where a descendant—a retired military officer—now lives.

manner in the little grocery store in Pine Hill where they stopped four or five times a day. One of them would get out of the car, breeze in, pick up a quart of milk or whatever, and breeze right out again, never stopping to pay. Nobody minded; they knew the bill would eventually be settled. The two women were much closer than employer and maid usually are. But if they knew just how close they really were, they kept that knowledge a secret.

One of the most ingenious characters I heard tales about in Wilcox County was Sheriff Lummie Jenkins. Here the sheriff has always been at least as important in the area as the president of the country, oftentimes more influential, and usually far more entertaining. But Lummie Jenkins was a standout in that exalted role. He has been dead for many years, but the people of Wilcox County have never been able to stop telling stories about him. Everyone in Wilcox County, white and black alike, has a Lummie Jenkins story. His life is a television series waiting to be made.

According to the stories, Lummie Jenkins was an exceedingly shrewd and dramatic man. His crime-solving abilities bordered on brilliant. But he never had to waste any taxpayer money going out and scouring this large county for his man (or woman). All he had to do was "put out the word." No matter how serious the crime or how much potential prison time the suspect faced, when Lummie sent for someone, the culprit always ambled into his office voluntarily. They knew they would be treated fairly if they

One of the oldest homes in Wilcox County

A once grand home, left alone

turned themselves in. And they knew that if they did not come when Lummie called, they would have to leave Alabama.

Of course, once the suspects reached Lummie's office, there was no guarantee that they'd 'fess up, tell the whole truth and nothing but the truth. Lummie never asked them to swear to God; that was too serious a matter. But he did say that if they wished to tell the truth right off, they would not have to drink several gulps of his truth serum. Lummie, a master of disinformation, had the majority of the county convinced of the effectiveness of his truth serum. Actually it was an awful-tasting mixture of vinegar, water, and something downright noxious. Legend has it that very few people ever actually took the serum; they just blurted out the truth. It was hard to lie to Lummie anyway, because chances were he knew you, your mama and daddy, your grandparents, and your reputation.

Wilcox Countians got accustomed to telling the truth while Lummie Jenkins was the law. There was a man who worked for Lummie on his big place, the old Jenkins family plantation in the Grampion Hills. This man came to Lummie one day, his brow crinkled in concern, wanting to ask his advice. It seemed he had gone home early the day before and found another man visiting with his wife. He told Lummie it seemed that every time he was away working for Lummie this man would come over to his house and visit his wife.

Every year Wilcox County, like so many southern places, has historic home tours, and ladies of the community dress up as it used to be and serve as guides. Jerry Burford models the dress she often wears.

The troubled man, a simple, sincere person, asked Lummie, "Sir, what should I do?"

Lummie shot from the lip. "Well, I'd just shoot 'im."

And that is exactly what the man did. He not only shot the visitor next time he found him with his wife, he killed him. At the murder trial, the earnest man's defense was nothing but the truth. "Yes sir. Mr. Lummie told me to do it," was about all he said, over and over, every time the lawyers asked him why he did it.

The jury found this sufficient justification, along with the dead man's low-down behavior. They acquitted Mr. Lummie's employee.

Lummie Jenkins could think fast when there was a crook around. There was a lot of moonshine made while Mr. Lummie was sheriff, especially in a place called Lower Peachtree. That was a doggone mean place inhabited by ornery, downright rebellious whites and blacks—knife-fighting, hard-cussing, thick-chested men and women. Lummie got wind that there was a big old still cooking down a bunch of moonshine in Lower Peachtree. He raided the operation one night as they worked, but the distillers evaporated into the dark woods.

One of the moonshiners dropped his hat in his flight. Lummie saw it and came up with a plan. He picked the old hat off the ground and shot three holes in it. He then walked out of the hollow onto the narrow road that wound up the hill to Lower Peachtree. He stopped at one of the houses and knocked. He had a suspicion.

An older woman came to the door of the tar-papered shack.

"Auntie," Lummie said, "I got a problem."

"Yes sir, Mr. Lummie Jenkins, what's that problem you got, sir?" she asked.

He said, "Well, I just shot and killed a man, and I need a wagon to haul his body out from down there by the creek."

She said, "Oh, yes sir, Mr. Lummie, we got wagons here. Who'd you shoot?"

Mr. Lummie held up the bullet-ventilated hat, and the woman became hysterical. "Oh my God, Mr. Lummie, you done shot my husband. Oh my Lord, you done shot him."

So Sheriff Lummie Jenkins caught his man. Again.

Ode
to
Uncle Esten

Marian Furman comes from one of the oldest families in Wilcox County. Her family tree features a 1930s Alabama governor; an exotic, cheese-loving, crossword-puzzle expert, never-married uncle; a ranching and farming matriarch called Mama Clyde; and many other potent characters.

Marian is the town photographer. Her husband, Herb, is the local surveyor. The Furmans have ten children from age twenty to thirty-four. I lived with the Furmans for several months in their large, white house, having first been invited for just one night. It was so fine to be part of a family again.

Today Wilcox County is 69 percent black and 31 percent white. All elected officials but two are black. The highly respected probate judge is black. The tax collector is a black woman; most town residents think she is as good as a politician gets. The tax assessor, also black, is liked and well respected by the townspeople. Of the six county commissioners, four are black and two white. Many people in Wilcox County, blacks and whites, no longer judge anyone by their color, but their character.

Jesse Beverly, age eighty-one, always sat in front of the Foodland store on a fine afternoon, and I sometimes stopped by to visit with him and hear his stories.

"I was borned on November 7 in 1910 right here in this county. Done seen plenty of change. I pretty much stuck right around here. I've been around Selma and Montgomery, but I haven't been no way out, you know." Jesse's skin was smooth as polished mahogany. He was thin, bright, and soft-spoken.

"I knows pretty well everyone in town here. Of them I knowed when I was growing up, all but a few of them done passed—dead, you know."

Almost every person who entered the small-town grocery spoke to Jesse, chatted a moment or just asked, "You all right?"

"I come around here, meet some friends, some of them I ain't seen in a good while, and chat with them, and then I go back home." Jesse lit up, his eyes shining with the appreciation of being known.

Jesse knew Uncle Esten, Marian Furman's late great-uncle. For that matter, everyone in Camden and in Wilcox County knew about Uncle Esten. He sometimes lit his cigars with dollar bills—my friend Daisy remembered that. She used to try to clean his room when he left the house every Saturday to go to town, and she'd find the partly burned dollar bills in the trash.

Jesse particularly remembered having to watch out for Uncle Esten's forgetful driving. Most of the time Uncle Esten had stayed in his room in Marian and Herb's house, the one I lived in now, but every day he had come out to drive the few miles into town to get his newspaper at Herman Ray's service station. The way he drove would have been a big, big problem (even a legal problem) most places, but here it was considered just another basically harmless personality trait of one of the local folk.

Uncle Esten never did have his brilliant mind on basic stuff like driving or business. When he was parking his 1955 Ford in front of the drugstore to get his niece a chocolate milkshake, he might be wondering if the word *xylene* would show up in one of his *New York Times* crossword puzzles. Then he might get his Ford in line but then forget to put on his brakes and bump into the car in back of him. Sometimes he might even reach for the brake and hit the gas. Then there would be a dent and another bill for his sister, Mama Clyde, to pay.

Uncle Esten's Ford was never repaired; after ten years and only twenty thousand miles it looked as if it had been hit all over with big hammers, little hammers, big rocks, and little rocks, scratched up and down and all around with a screwdriver. There was even a hole in the trunk, punctured by something higher than his big back chrome bumper.

Uncle Esten never drove fast enough to hurt or kill anyone. The main problem with his driving was that when he drove, he figured it was everyone *else's* responsibility to watch out for *him*. That's how his life had always been. His mama had looked out for him until she died. Then he had moved in with his powerful widowed sister, Mama Clyde, Marian's grandmother. She looked after him, too.

I stayed with the Furmans while I was in Wilcox County. Herb, a surveyor, and Marian (right), town photographer, are the parents of ten children and live in the family home that Marian's grandfather bought and lived in. Her mother, Minnie Leah Purdue (left), was born in the house.

Uncle Esten inherited a lot of land but could never stand to farm, and he couldn't even talk about business. Whenever Mama Clyde tried to speak with him about his affairs, he would begin to whistle and walk off. Much of the time, Uncle Esten just wanted to be left alone with his crossword puzzles. He did them with his fountain pen because he never missed a word.

Esten may have been in his own world, but he was not unsophisticated. He had fine tastes.

"Uncle ordered wonderful things out of the *New York Times* that the rest of the world here didn't even know existed," Marian told me. "He got our oldest son, John, a fancy telescope and all the information that went with it."

Uncle Esten wore out the index volume of the *Encyclopedia Britannica* and sent for all sorts of books from rare bookstores. He was big on mail order when most people in Wilcox County didn't know what it was. He ordered potent-smelling, exotic cheeses from all over the world and stacked them on his table. That cheese, along with his cigar smoke, gave his room an unforgettable ambience.

Uncle Esten stayed in his bedroom most of the time. Mama Clyde had a bell connected from the kitchen to his room, and she would ring that bell when it was time for him to join the family for a meal. Then, if somebody special was visiting, he'd speak to them agreeably and be very sociable.

Marian has a smile that lights up her deep brown eyes. Since her ten children and her fine relationship with her husband and mother give her plenty to smile about, she is almost always happy. She appears especially amused when she talks about the past.

"I wore pigtails," Marian told me one night as we all huddled around their smallish wood-and-coal-burning stove, the only source of heat in the house except for gas heaters in the bathrooms. At one time servants kept all the fires going in all the lofty mansions. Today, to live in one of these old southern homes in the winter is to be warm if you have a lot of money to burn or to be cold if you don't. At the Furmans' everyone wore as many coats inside as they did outside. There is no affordable way in our modern world to heat or cool rooms with ceilings that reach for the sky and are so large that ten waltzing couples could comfortably fit into them.

"I didn't like bows and frills and ruffles," Marian recalled, "and I went barefooted all the time. Spent a lot of time in the woods and down at the pond, paddling around, catching turtles and racing them, and catching snakes out of the trees. Often Uncle Esten went with me."

While they walked and wandered in the thousand acres of woods and fields, Uncle Esten would recite long poems from memory. One of his favorites was "The Cremation of Sam McGee." He would suddenly begin reciting poetry at the dinner table, anywhere, anytime. Practically everything reminded Uncle Esten of a poem.

"Uncle Esten could recognize all kinds of animals. He appreciated them for what they were, and he helped us look them up and understand them," Marian remembered, a tender tone coming over her voice.

"He's the one who told me that the box turtle was heading for extinction because of the highways that were built in the '40s. He told me that the people were going to squash the turtles, run them all over. He said that the turtles liked the highways because they were smoother to travel on. So I went on a personal crusade to save the box turtle from extinction. At one point I had seven of them. I kept those box turtles out there on the back porch for several years, all based on Uncle Esten's warning.

"Eventually everybody got sort of tired of the turtles all over the porch, so they prevailed on me to turn them loose. But still, to this day, I can't pass a turtle in the road. Can't do it. I have to stop and move it."

Marian's mother, Minnie Leah, remembered Uncle Esten with a protective fondness and a great admiration for his entertaining, sometimes erratic ways. Uncle Esten knew how much Minnie Leah loved chocolate milkshakes. Every Saturday he would take her to the drugstore soda fountain in Camden for her favorite treat. Minnie Leah's mother, Mama Clyde, didn't want her to have the milkshakes because they always upset Minnie Leah's delicate stomach. But Minnie Leah and Uncle Esten did their misbehaving anyway.

Minnie Leah recollected a lot about her Uncle Esten: "He was a great companion to my mother. They got along just beautifully because she was the one with the energy and the get-up-and-go and he was always there close by. You might say he was a recluse in a way, but everybody loved him."

A photograph of Uncle Esten showed nothing unusual. His hair was cut in the style of the '30s and '40s and was thinning on top. Wire-rim glasses rested atop his sharply angled nose. His feet were small, his body an average size. His bow tie was straight. His gaze was straight, too, right off into the distance. In all his pictures he looked faraway, as if he were somewhere else.

"Uncle Esten never married. He had only one true love, and he believed that she loved him as much as he loved her. He even bought a diamond ring to give to her. At the time, she was also going out with a young doctor, and she told this 'friend' of hers that if Uncle Esten had the doctor's looks or if the young doctor had Uncle Esten's money, she would marry either one or the other. Her friend told that around town, as some friends are prone to do, and naturally it got back to the men in question. They both dropped her.

"The reason Uncle Esten killed himself," Minnie Leah told me matter-of-factly, "was because Mama went to him one day and suggested—just suggested, mind you—that it might be best if he stopped driving for himself. He could get many different people to drive him anytime, Mama told him. What she didn't say to him was that she couldn't get car insurance for him because he'd had so many wrecks. Fixing all the cars he hit was costing a great deal of money." Minnie Leah took a quivering breath.

"Right away Uncle Esten went to his room, and soon there was a shot and he was gone."

Minnie Leah held out her hand for me to see. "I'm wearing the diamond ring he bought for his only love."

CHAPTER 32

Sweet
Daisy
Durante

Daisy Durante came to live on Mama Clyde's place before Marian, now fifty-five, was born. Daisy is eighty-two. People who know say she makes the best chicken pie in the world. Daisy normally doesn't make someone a chicken pie unless they're part of her family. She made me one after I'd known her a few weeks. Daisy and me, we were an item.

Daisy has lived an amazing life. She's loved and raised many children, her own three and a lot of white ones. What impressed me most was the attitude of irrepressible optimism she's kept through many years of struggle. Daisy's skin was unwrinkled, the color of coffee taffy. Everybody said Daisy loved to talk. She had several friends, most of them widows, and they talked every day on the phone, usually more than once. Daisy herself was not widowed, but she had recently had to put her husband, Rob, into a nursing home in Selma. It was a sad thing to take this powerful man away from the land and trees and fields he'd owned and farmed and still loves so much. Daisy still loves their place, too, though she doesn't live there anymore.

Daisy helped raise Marian and her brother, Miller. She worked for Mama Clyde for years upon years. But long before she came to Mama Clyde's place, when she was only eight years old, she was taken home by a white family to be their children's helper, their playmate. She learned to do the dishes the way Mrs. Meachum wanted them done, standing on a pot to reach the sink.

"My daddy was a railroad man all his life, but he always had a nice big garden. He grew the food for us. I never knowed what it was to work in the field or to hoe cotton. Then, after I got knee high to a duck, some white people got Mama to let me move in with them. I couldn't tote a baby or anything, but I could play with it.

"Those white people raised me. She dead now, and he dead, too. And they had five childrens, and I couldn't tote any of them when I started with them. They paid my mama some for me each week—I never knew what. So from the age of eight I was raised by white folks. I was raised by Mrs. Meachum and her husband named Johnny. He was a professor at the high school down in Conecuh County.

"I went to the colored school from there and everything. All my schoolmates say to me, 'She thinks she something.' Mrs. Meachum fix my clothes, sewed me pretty dresses. I was dressed better than anybody, and I just thought I was *it* at school." Daisy still dresses snappy. Today she had on a teal-colored sweatshirt adorned with a metallic silver poinsettia.

"This is funny . . . they had a milk cow, and I wanted to be real smart. I had a big old wagon out there, and so I put the babies up in the wagon, a girl and a boy, and I was going to milk the cow. I got my hands and washed them good and scalded my bucket out, and the old cow was real gentle. Oh, I was just a milking. Never had milked in my life, but I wanted to be smart so Mrs. Meachum, she'd brag on me. And the cow moved a leg, and oh, all the milk went out. When I look around, Mrs. Meachum was walking up. She said, 'Lawdy mercy, my children milking the cow!' And that was so funny for me."

Daisy's parents and many brothers and sisters lived in the railroad housing next to the tracks, so she could see her family anytime. Times were tough then, around 1918, and Daisy was proud that she was picked over everyone else in her family.

"Oh, they were lovely people. Ain't nobody in the world like them, look like to me. I thought so. They were nice. They didn't never whip me or anything. I had my own room. Sure did. I would keep my room clean. I was one of the family. I went everywhere they went, just anywhere. I didn't play with any black children, less I go home or to school. I had plenty of white friends. Mrs. Meachum's yard stayed full of white childrens. I was just brought up with white children." Daisy wrinkled her forehead as if she was agitated or confused or bothered.

"I could take the little children and just go all around the block with them and walk. When I go down and see my mother, when I see my sister and brothers and other friends, they talk to me, but they didn't want to play with me because they thought I thought I was white. They always say, 'She think she white.' And they walk off, and they whispering to theirselves. I just walk on off, too."

Today, Daisy's lady friends are both white and black. There's Amey, almost crippled with arthritis, and barefooted Sally Mae, the widow who lives on the hill above the sixty-five acres Daisy and her husband own and used to farm. There's Marian, my hostess, who was one of Daisy's white children, and a lot of others. The phone is these ladies' lifeline, since most of them can't move here and there as they once could.

"But I just try to do my uppity 'I'm nicer than you are.' That upset them. I remember once we were going to have a play in school, and they all got together talking about what they were going to wear. I knew what I was going to wear because Miss Meachum, she was in the bed sick, was making my dress. Peoples used to wear material, crepe de chine—real pretty. I knew my dress was out of that material because Miss Meachum had done showed it to me. But I wasn't telling them anything. So they was just talking. They going to wear this and that. And when I come in that night to go on the stage they didn't have a thing to do with me. But I still felt like a princess that night."

Daisy was married at age sixteen to Rob Durante, a very dark and handsome man from Wilcox County who had been working on a bridge-building crew in Conecuh County. He'd seen Daisy standing in the yard.

"That's the first boyfriend I ever had. And I just got married like something stupid. Daddy ought to have whipped me. But my daddy did tell me this when I married, 'If your bed gets too hard to lay on, turn over. Don't come back.' Every time it got hard, I couldn't go back. So I just stayed. And so I turn over many days."

Rob had several "outside children"—children born outside of wed-lock. To this day, Rob's outside children come see about Daisy, call her, visit all the time.

Daisy and Rob first sharecropped on a plantation near Pineapple. But the man who owned the place never shared any of the crop they had slaved to grow and harvest. He stole it all, a year's worth gone. Daisy and Rob had to look for another place.

There was then, and there is now, an underground of information about who were the best people to work for, who would actually give you your fair share. Mama Clyde, Marian's grandmother, was one of these—some say the best. Many black sharecroppers wanted to come and live on her place, rent some of her land and farm. Daisy and Rob moved to a house on one of Mama Clyde's farms, not far down from Whiskey Run, a road where a lot of land-owning blacks have always lived.

"I loved our place there," Daisy said to me so many times. They settled there in the early 1930s, during the Great Depression.

"Rob," Daisy said, "he was a good farmer. He wanted to work all his life in the fields. But I was working for white peoples, too. I kept white people in my mind."

Daisy went to work in Mama Clyde's house. She took care of Uncle Esten, helped raise Marian and her brother Miller. But she went home every day to her little blue house by the creek. It stood alone in the middle of a few hundred acres between Route 10 and Whiskey Run Road.

One of Daisy's favorite charges out of a long life of loving and caring for people was Miller Purdue, Marian's late brother. As a child he had a weak heart but a powerful spirit. He died at age forty-three of a fast spreading cancer.

"This family that begin with Mama Clyde, they the best. Around here, sure there were bad white people, some. One family I worked for I was supposed to call their little child Master William. Maybe he be only five year old, but if I didn't call him 'Master' he'd try and slap me. No one gonna slap me. I would not have it.

"Mama Clyde, she have a fish pond down behind their house. I used to say, 'Miller, let's go catch some fish for dinner.' He say, 'All right.' We got our hooks, went down to the pond, and every time I throw my hook in, I'd come up with one. Miller, he'd put his hook right there where mine's at, and it wouldn't do nothing. I catch another and he started crying. I said, 'Now, son, you caught these fish; I did not. And you don't say nothing, I'm not going to say nothing.' And so, we say, 'Oh, look what nice fish that Miller caught today.' We just had the nicest dinner. And Miller look at me, and I look at Miller, and it just tickle me. We never did tell.

"One time when he was about twelve, Miller had a little motor scooter. I'd do anything in the world he said do—didn't matter what. If he said, I want you to stay here tonight with me, then I'd stay. So this time he say he'd pay my way to the show that night. Rob was back at our house hauling corn. I know I ought to been down there helping him haul the corn and getting it out, but Miller'd been sick, and I didn't want to upset him. 'Well, let's go ask Rob can I go to the show first.'

"So I got on the little scooter with him, and we went on down there. Rob was throwing corn up into the wagon. Miller say, 'Rob, Day-Day's going to stay and go to the picture show with me tonight. OK?' Rob didn't say nothing, and I know he didn't like it because he didn't say nothing. Miller said, 'Day-Day, Rob's a mean man.' It tickled me, me and him on that little old motor scooter, going through Camden to the show."

It had been about two years since Daisy reluctantly moved from their wood-framed blue house on the narrow creek. She moved only after Rob suffered a couple of devastating heart attacks and finally had to be placed in the nursing home. Daisy couldn't look after the place by herself. But she missed it terribly, and she didn't like living in town.

Every week or so Rob would try to escape from the nursing home and go back home. I could understand why, after hearing Daisy describe their home so many times. Now she would show it to me. She'd asked me if I would take her out there, and of course I did. I knew how much someone could miss their piece of land, their place on earth.

"See this little branch, over yonder? See them big oak trees? Everything loves an oak tree. Little squirrels, turkey, deers. I was always telling Rob, don't you hunt my little animals." Daisy was as excited as a girl trying on her first prom dress.

She pointed to the creek. "My husband and myself been out there many times and caught catfish. We use a cane pole. When we lived here— oh, it looked so different. Everything was pretty and clean. This yard was clean. The crops were growing out here. It was pretty."

Marian had told me that she and the family had coaxed Daisy to move on into town because this house at the end of a long dirt road, potted with mud holes, was not a place for an eighty-year-old lady living alone. Daisy wouldn't agree to move until they promised that no one would ever again live in her house. No one ever will, as long as Daisy lives. That's how much the Furmans care about Daisy. Everyone in the family calls her Day-Day. They love her. She loves them.

"We had a cute little fence around the house, sure did. That's when I had my pretty flowers, had red roses and pink roses and white roses and big old lilies. I used to carry them to Mama Clyde all the time to set on the dinner table when they had company.

"I just enjoyed it so much down here. I love it. And I like to farm. I sure do. I'm a girl belong right out here in the country." Daisy held her cane like a feather. She stepped lightly. Her soft ebony eyes glowed with remembrance.

She pointed behind the house, recalling when everything was so neat, so groomed, so cared for. Now dried ragweed grew a few feet up the faded blue siding. "We used to have a corncrib there. It was a big old crib, and we'd load it up with corn. We had a nice pecan tree right there. Sure did. Still growing. I brought it from Miss Miller's house and set it out. It's not a great big one, but it's real good about givin' us pecans." She frowned at a branch whose leaves were mottled. Later she would ask Marian to come check it out. Daisy said when you love trees and you plant one from a baby, it becomes like one of your children.

"Oh, that house was so cute. I had it fixed up so nice then. It had a fireplace, and I love the fireplace. It had a cute little wood stove, and I loved it, too. We had a pump—we got our water out of the well. I loved to go pump water. I'd pump the water every evening right over there.

"Oh, that water was so pretty and good. That's the only kind of water we used. We took baths in a tin tub in the kitchen. I'd put a dishpan of water on the stove. Rob's water was on the stove to take his bath first. Then I'd put the children's dishpan of water and give them their baths, and then I'd put my dishpan of water and take my bath. That water felt so nice and warm. Sure did.

"Then we had a chicken yard over there, and a hog pen down there, and the milk cows over there. We grew everything. Peas, beans, peppers, eggplant, just everything. Butter beans, okra—we just had everything—corn, beets, watermelon, and cantaloupes. I'd plant everything I saw in the catalogs, even that bean that looks like a rattlesnake! Snap beans, about a foot long.

"Didn't have to worry about anything. Got ready to cook anything, we could do it. We had a smokehouse right in the back out there where we smoked our meat and our sausage. We had plenty of homemade sausage and great big old hams . . . just plenty of everything. We had our living. Had everything. I just enjoyed it so much here."

Sweet Daisy, a lady with the most irrepressibly joyous spirit, was ready to leave. Her arthritis was hurting her, and so was her foot where she'd had some toes amputated because of circulation problems. She reached for me and hugged me. "Thank you, Peter. You one of my childrens now, you know." I kissed her on the cheek.

As I closed the gate and got ready to drive her home, Daisy asked me if I would stop at McDonald's, a southern country store nearby. Shyly she asked if I would get her a beer. She said it would make her foot stop aching.

Her foot wasn't all that was aching. Daisy's wish was my command.

Happy Birthday, Everyone

At least every other week and usually more often, Marian's seventy-nine-year-old mother came over to spend a few days. Minnie Leah was frail now in body; she told me she always has had a delicate system. But in her youth, during the Roaring Twenties, she had been a vibrant but delicate flower, and people say she danced with an effortless, heavenly grace. The man she married, Marian's father, had been an artist, a musician, finally a farmer, inventor, and a "lovely" dancer. He had been dead for many years.

Minnie Leah has kept all her dance cards from all her parties when she was young. I told Minnie Leah that I too was quite a dancer in my day. If we had been together in high school, I would have tried to sign up for each and every dance with her. But since Minnie Leah and I couldn't dance, we talked and talked some more. I loved the massaging, sweet tones of her voice, which was slightly above a whisper. Every word was spoken with precision.

Maybe Minnie Leah picked up her exactness of speech from her mother, Mama Clyde, who had gone to Chicago in the 1920s to take elocution classes. Out of Mama Clyde came strength and courage, but she was just five-two. She used to say, 'I'm of the earth.' Minnie Leah was five-four in her dancing years, and 110 pounds. She was of the clouds and the perfect early summer days of afternoon dreams. Mother and daughter could not have been more different.

And yet it would never pay to underestimate Minnie Leah. She had the oddest mixture of painful shyness and quiet, unrelenting assertiveness. She was very independent, always had been in her silky kind of way.

Minnie Leah came to stay with Marian and Herb whenever she wished, even in the chilled winter. This home where Minnie Leah had been born was the heart of the family, as important as a living person. They could not desert it, though it was bitterly cold in winter. One of their cats and I fought each other for a red velvet chair nearest the coal-burning stove. One time I sat on the poor old cat in my zeal to feel a little heat.

Often Minnie Leah and I would sit around during the cold days and talk while Marian took pictures commissioned by various town associations and Herb was out surveying. Hers was the art of talking for the sake of a story told precisely.

"Daddy farmed. He had sharecroppers, and he was a better judge than he was a farmer. I can say that about him. He enjoyed the farm, but he didn't get too much money out of it. We had a good many black people living on the place, and then at his death, my mother carried on. She was really a better farmer than my father ever was.

"Billy, who lived down by the fish pond, worked here in the house. So did his wife, Virginia, and all of their children. Billy would bring the wood in every morning and build the fires before we would get up out of bed. Then he would build a fire in the kitchen wood stove and he'd put on the coffeepot. Then Billy and my father would sit at the kitchen table and drink coffee together. They did that every morning of the world.

"We were all Democrats; almost all southern people were then. *Republican* at that time was an ugly word. One time my father told my mother, he says, 'Clyde, look, you see that man over there?' Mama says yes. 'Well, he's a Republican.' And I looked to see what a Republican would look like.

"A lot of people had the attitude about Mama like they did about Roosevelt—that she would save us all. If any white person ever mistreated any one of the black people who lived on our place, she would go and storm at that person, warn him never to do that, never again. She just treated everyone fairly, and they could depend on her. If someone needed to go to the doctor or the hospital, she would take them and pay for it.

"Mama was one of two ladies who went to Europe with the Associated Women Farmers of America. She was an adventuresome woman.

"On their way to Europe in a big ship, crossing the Atlantic, a storm came up one night. All the ladies were scared to death, crying and praying. You know what Mama did? She went and put on a very expensive hand-

These Wilcox County ladies have played bridge together for almost fifty years, sharing with each other life's rewards, tragedies, and every days. They are, from left to right, Scottie Goodbold, Virginia Cook (seated), Mabel Lane, Hattie Riggs (seated), and Laure Johnson.

made blouse, said if she was going down on that ship, she was going down looking pretty. She brought that blouse home, and I still have it." Minnie Leah cherishes memories. She is the keeper of many of them for this family.

Mama Clyde farmed and managed a place of a thousand acres near Furman, in addition to nine hundred acres at G's Bend across the river, where she had a herd of cows. She also managed Uncle Esten's eight hundred inherited acres. She was eighty-four when she died, and until the last two years of her life she drove herself and ran the whole lot. Even when she became quite senile, she still met every day with Weston Brown, the man who managed her cattle herd. He would listen carefully to what she said, no matter how irrational, then go and do what he knew she would want him to do.

This is a strong line of women, the one of whom Marian, Minnie Leah, and Mama Clyde are a part. Marian and Minnie Leah often repeat a family story that has been passed from one woman to another for 150 years. It goes like this: "Our family came here from South Carolina on both my mother's side and my father's side. They were coming from South Carolina to Alabama, and they were going through Indian territory, and the father got very ill, so the wife bedded him down in the back of the wagon. She put on his clothes and put her hair up under her cap. Then she drove the wagon through Indian territory, pretending she was a man. And she made it. So that's one of our ancestors."

Minnie Leah told me, "We all have a little saying we use real often: Just keep on driving the wagon. Because that's what our ancestor did, and that's what we've all had to do."

The old concept of the fainting, fragile, magnolia-skinned southern belle who never raised a hand to work or made a tough decision is hard to realize in a place like Wilcox County. Many women here are strong yet beautiful, decisive, and in control. Even the few stereotypical "southern belles" aren't exactly as they appear. Often their whispery femininity disguises a will powered with sharp ambition.

The highlight of the week for some of the ladies of Minnie Leah's generation is playing bridge with their dearest friends. A group from Wilcox County who live close to Marian's house have played bridge together for fifty years. They have been through each other's lives together, like Minnie Leah and Marian and Uncle Esten and Daisy have.

"They saved a spot for me when I first came to live in Camden, when I married fifty-two years ago," said Miss Virginia, who lives nearby on Cooks Hill. Miss Virginia is a retired teacher. Minnie Leah's first boyfriend was Miss Virginia's husband's brother. "Our club is mainly an offspring from our mothers' original group. Now most of us are pretty old.

"We used to talk mostly of our children. But now we talk about grandchildren, too. We all have pretty houses and beautiful furniture. We used to talk about what we were going to do with this room or that room and all that sort of stuff years ago. Now we still have houses and furniture, but we don't care to talk about them anymore."

Miss Virginia had eyes that couldn't hold all the emotions she felt. Many of the ladies of this bridge club have lost their husbands, yet they still have each other. This continuity, these relationships that span generations, offer them much to hold on to in a rapidly changing world.

The card game was not so important now for these ladies when they met. Family history has taken on more importance. Some in the bridge club can trace their family lines back to the Magna Carta. Some belong to the Magna Carta Dames and also to the Daughters of the American Revolution. Probably the one organization that makes them feel strongest about their place in the world is the United Daughters of the Confederacy. To become a member, these women had to prove they were descended from a man who fought for the South during the War Between the States.

Miss Virginia wanted me to listen to a little essay written by a member of the club. It was titled, "Why I Am a Daughter of the Confederacy."

I am a daughter of the Confederacy because I was born a daughter of the Confederacy. A part of my heritage was that I came into this world with the blood of a soldier in my veins. A soldier who may have had nothing more to leave behind to me and to those who came after me, except the heritage. A heritage so rich in honor and glory that it far surpasses any material wealth that could be mine. But it is mine to cherish, to nurture, and to pass along to those yet to come. I am therefore a daughter of the Confederacy because it is my birthright. I am a daughter of the Confederacy because I can no more help being a daughter of the Confederacy than I can help being an American, and I feel I was greatly favored by inheriting a birthright for both.

In Wilcox County there is a bachelor who rides his bike ten miles into town, who has one light bulb in his house up in the Grampion Hills, where he lives all by himself. His name is Mack Parton.

Mack might be forty, he might be fifty. He still looks like a boy, they say. When people in town ask Mack how he's doing, he replies, "Fine and dandy, like sugar candy."

Mack is famous hereabouts because he knows almost everyone's birthday. No one has ever figured out how he knows—he just knows. And when your special day comes around, people here get their once-a-year call from Mack Parton.

One afternoon a few days before I left Wilcox County, the phone rang. Marian picked it up. Daisy had already made her daily call twice, and I had had a chance to say good-bye. She said I was one of her boys now. Minnie Leah was getting ready to eat her special cereal.

Ralph Ervin, the tax assessor, a man who seemed as tall as the door frame, had walked into the house, as usual, without knocking. He picked up a fresh-made biscuit in a chocolate brown hand and wished a good afternoon to Minnie Leah. He wore a silver gray suit, a smooth white shirt, and a loosened tie. While Marian talked on the phone, Ralph sat down with me at the kitchen table. He was waiting to discuss photography with Marian, his photographic mentor.

Just as Ralph reached for a second biscuit, Marian hung up. She had been talking to Mack, the bike-riding bachelor from Grampion Hill, who had called to wish her a happy birthday.

I could not believe I'd stayed so long in this lovely, drafty home where the Furmans had raised their ten children, where Minnie Leah had been born, where Uncle Esten's room was scented by exotic cheeses and stacked high with copies of the *New York Times*. I had been drawn into this world where one story led to another, where one discovery of a person's character followed another and another.

In tiny Wilcox County, Alabama, two hundred miles up the Alabama River from Mobile Bay, more than thirty miles from any city of more than twenty thousand residents, and more than nine hundred miles from Washington, D.C., I'd discovered a charming network of people who knew each other intimately and who accepted each other for all that they were, no matter how ordinary or extraordinary. There was a connection between the people here and to the land that was missing in so many other places I'd lived and known. I felt a powerful security in knowing these people's strengths and their flaws. I felt that we all had so much in common. And I realized that Wilcox County held something precious I often missed in my life—the time to be together, to listen, to care.

To break away and leave was very difficult. I could only imagine how it would be for someone born here, wrapped in the web of this place over the years. But the *Cooper* was lonely, and I missed her. I missed moving with her speed and power, the wind roaring past my face. It was time to go back to the sea, back to unseen things, and strangers waiting to become known to me.

Some
Seafaring
Rogue

I was suddenly thrown forward, smashing my right forearm and right cheek against the steering wheel and its fiberglass housing. The motors were screaming in full-revved shrillness, and yet I was stopped. The boat was straining against something that wouldn't let it move.

What happened? I tried to stand up. My eyes were clearing, my focus returned. My forearm hurt terribly; my jaw ached.

I pushed the control lever into neutral. It was early on the second day since I'd left Wilcox County, headed back downriver to Mobile and the Gulf. The water was high and the current was strong, carrying a load of debris downriver from the heavy spring rains.

Were my propellers entangled by underwater debris? Could that have thrown me for such a jolt, half knocking me out? I pulled myself up fully and looked around. The current had swung the rear of the boat around in a slow-motion move.

Was something slowing down the drift of the boat? Was the *Cooper* sinking—was there a gaping hole in the hull? I moved toward the back of the boat. Underwater, I saw what seemed like a submerged log, but it didn't seem to be blocking the engines. I shook my head, still dizzy, and went back to the controls. I pressed a button that should raise the motors out of the water. They would not rise together. I tried to raise the right motor. It came up out of the water. Then I tried the left motor. It would not move. Something was holding the left motor down.

I still felt groggy. The boat slammed into the brush-covered riverbank, again spinning the boat around. I got on my radio and called, asking anyone for help. There was no answer. I felt another, lighter bump; the *Cooper* had drifted into a floating tree or something. I called again on my radio. No response.

I heard the buzz of a light plane and I watched until it was gone. Then the *Cooper* and I were alone once more. Nothing came my way, only the green-brown river hurrying south. Vultures soared, searching for bloated, dead flesh. The water was ugly. I was annoyed, frustrated.

Then I heard something. It was a motor—an outboard motor coming upriver.

I waved my arms at two men in a flatboat. They never slowed down. They weren't going to stop. No rescue now. Who knew when?

Wait . . . yes—they were turning. They were coming back.

"Y'all havin' some trouble?" came the slow-flowing voice of a husky man wearing a red baseball cap. I saw a huge catfish, his tail still flapping, in the bottom of their boat.

"I've run into something. I was almost knocked out," I answered, rubbing my forehead. I had a skull-throbbing headache.

The man in the red cap and his partner tied up to the *Cooper,* and both came aboard.

"How come this motor's done raised up and the other'n's not?" the smaller man asked. He had an abundance of black hair on his arms and a co-op cap on his head. His teeth were stained yellow, probably from dipping or chewing.

"I have no idea," I answered. "The other one won't come up."

"I ain't seen a boat like this in this river before," the man with the red cap remarked. His eyebrows lifted as he shot a glance over at the other man. The glance was the fastest movement he'd made so far.

The red-capped man leaned over back by the motors and pushed my gaff down into the brown-green water. "Y'know, you done run into somethin' or another. It feels like somethin's stuck under this here boat."

"I heard *that,*" said his buddy. They seemed harmless.

"Yeah, that's what I think," I agreed. "But what is it?"

More vultures searched overhead. A few dead branches slapped against the bow of my boat. Then the man with the red cap moved to the stern of the boat and stepped off into the deep river! Just like that. But he was standing on something.

"Man, you done got some kind of tree or some such thing down below your boat," he drawled. "That's what's keepin' your left motor from raisin'."

From Mobile Bay, the Cooper and I curved back and forth for more than two hundred miles up the Alabama River until I came to Wilcox County. I was almost lost in a world where past and present are not separate. In Wilcox County the intimate details of your life are not only known but also known are the histories of your parents, grandparents, and great-grandparents as well. After several months here I headed back to the Gulf and a world where reality has a harder edge.

Then the smaller man, well balanced and muscular, followed his friend to the stern and stepped over. Now both of them stood knee deep on whatever it was that was holding me up.

"Somehow we got to get this here pole off a'here—"

The smaller one slipped and just missed getting caught in the rushing current.

"I expect we got the thing loose, buddy," the smaller man said to me.

Down below us in the river, two short telephone poles tied together with steel cable popped up, one longer than the other. Then they went back under, just out of sight again. Somehow the shaft of my left engine had slammed between the submerged poles, which had evidently washed away from some shoreline installation.

"Hey, guys, I thank you for helping me out." I reached out and shook their hands.

"Glad to help. Maybe someday you can help us on this river. Ain't that right, Leo?" the red-capped rescuer said. They eased back into their flatboat and whirred upriver again, as close to the east bank as they could get.

When I reached Mobile Bay, I was going to pick up Warren Norville again. I'd called him before I left Camden and asked if he would come with me for a long ride on the *Cooper*. Before, he had been the teacher, I the pupil. My respect for his knowledge and spirit had grown with every nautical mile of my journey. Now, I said, I wanted him to just sit back and enjoy.

I knew of no one who loved the sea more than Warren. He had the sea in his genes. His great-great-grandfather had been a master of sailing ships and a bar pilot, considered to be the best blockade runner of the Civil War. Captain Norville had waited for nightfall and just the right tides. Then he had sailed Rebel ships right past the watching Yankees. Once past them, he had rowed back through the Yankee lines again without being detected.

Like his seafaring ancestors, Warren is a true, hardcore sailor. The greater the wind, the higher the waves, the more both smashed at him, the better his hands and mind liked the challenge. His whole body seemed to light up when we got into the big sea, out of sight of the land. I couldn't wait to show him everything I'd learned.

Warren met me at the Port of Mobile. His white beard was still trimmed in the dapper maritime style. He looked me over carefully and said I had the look of a man of the sea. Once we were underway, Warren sat next to me as he'd done before. He appeared to be relaxed, but he was carefully observing my every movement. I felt like I'd guzzled ten cups of coffee. I so wanted to show Warren what I'd learned, yet I wanted to be smooth and precise in my movements that controlled the *Cooper*.

I roared off into the channel and headed almost straight south to the mouth of Fowl River, where Warren and Harriett have a summer home. Warren and I were going to spend the night down at their place.

More than once on our twenty-some-mile ride, Warren would start to say something, then stop himself. I guess he realized he didn't have to. I *saw* the supplemental green buoy. I *knew* which way to cut across the jaw-rattling wake of the loaded tanker. I *heard* that the motors were not exactly on the same RPM and made the adjustment. Sometimes Warren jutted his captain's jaw high, an unconscious gesture of approval. I believe he was proud that his teachings had not only been heard, but had become a part of me. When I passed that learning down to my daughters and my sons, they too would be a part of Warren and the Norville sea captains before him.

We got to the channel leading into the river, and I slowed to an idle. There was a long white dock stretching out from the land, where a blond man and his young son stood. I saw the man point out our boat to the boy. I remembered my dad doing the same, and I remembered wishing I could be on the boat, going wherever it was going.

The crisp winds allowed us to speak without straining. Warren put his right hand on my shoulder. "My boy, I do believe you've got this boating thing down. *Who* did you say taught you all you know?"

"I'm not sure, Warren," I answered, straight-faced, but beaming inside. "Some seafaring rogue, surely."

It wasn't far to Louisiana, even though I had a bit of Alabama coast and all of the Mississippi coast to cover. Getting to New Orleans on Interstate 10 would have been no problem, just 148 smooth miles west. But there were many islands, hundreds of miles of shallow marsh, mazes of canals and off-shore oil and gas rigs ahead for the *Cooper* and me as we traveled to the Big Easy. Warren told me to listen to some jazz and to eat some chilled oysters for him.

I stopped the first night on Cat Island off the Mississippi coast. For two days I camped here, catching everything I ate. But it's what I almost caught—or what almost caught me—that made the biggest impression.

I had waded out on a sandbar covered with a couple of feet of water about a hundred feet from where the *Cooper* was anchored. The tide seemed to be falling. I had a top-water lure that I was casting and reeling in, yanking it on top of the glassy morning sea so that it would make noise, a wake, like the movements made by small fleeing fish. Hopefully this lure would attract some bull reds. Bulls are arm-tiring, pole-breaking redfish that weigh more than twenty pounds. To hook one of these standing in this waist-deep water would mean a long battle between man and fish.

I saw a wake, a small V-shaped narrow wave atop the water, the kind made by redfish as they swam just under the surface. I cast right to it. Something huge whirled back around and gulped my lure down. I let it run five, ten yards and pulled back as forcefully as my pole and line could. It felt like I had a small car at the end of my twelve-pound line. I pulled back when the fish slowed; it took back any line I retrieved and took more as it swam.

I had on the funked-out Nikes that I used for fishing shoes. There were plenty of stingrays around. Getting one of their barbs in your foot or, God forbid, your leg was said to be one of the most painful experiences known to anyone. I did not lift my feet as I waded deeper. I shuffled, hoping that motion would more effectively move the stingrays away.

The fish and I fought each other for twenty minutes, maybe half an hour. My lower back ached with a shooting pain from trying to hold on to the line that was being strained, pulled, tugged on.

The fish seemed to make a mighty rush. Then there was no more fight; the line was slack. I was standing in water almost up to my chest now. Had the line broken? The fish come off? I pulled back the pole's tip and it went above my head. Something was still on the line, but what? Had the fish died? I reeled my line in, and the thing on the end of the line came toward me. What had happened?

All that was on the hook was the head of the redfish. It had been severed from the body with a cut as crisp as if made by a scalpel. That redfish had weighed at least thirty pounds. The only thing that could have bitten that much off and only left the head was a big shark. I could not imagine now the size of the shark's mouth that could take that kind of surgically precise bite. I can't walk on water, but I came close as I spun around and headed back to Cat Island.

That night I huddled by a fine fire of driftwood. The clouds stole the sunlight as the flames turned the sand orange. Next to the fire I'd hollowed out another deep place in the sand where I would soon scoop some hot coals. Then atop the coals, I would place driftwood soaked in the sea so that it would smoke. For a top, I would lay a couple of fencepost-sized poles that had washed ashore. (This end of Cat Island's beach had lots of things that had drifted up on it.) I'd soaked the redfish filets in saltwater for about an hour, then let them air dry, ready to smoke. For the moment, while the fire burned low, all I had to do was relax . . . and think.

Because of the life I've chosen to live, a life of traveling and then writing about my travels, I feel a constant pull between my love of exploring, discovering new places and new people, and my love of being home with my family in my gray house on the hill, sleeping in my own bed. I seem to crave the unknown and the known in about equal measure. Now with so many children, each so especially unusual, each with his or her own unique needs, it is so much harder to pull away. Yet it is necessary for me to do so. It is necessary to keep me the man I am.

I was grateful that Rita understood this. I desperately hoped my kids understood, too.

In a couple of months, maybe they would be able to understand a little better. In the summer, after school let out, I planned to have each one— Rebekah, Jed, Luke, Brooke, and Aaron—come down to spend time on the boat with me. This trip marked the first time I had ever been able to include my children in what I do. I looked forward to introducing them to my world of discovery.

There was so much we could do together—exploring islands, playing in the sand, talking around a campfire, fishing. After today, though, we would definitely not be wading and fishing. We wouldn't be wading, period.

I thought of seven-year-old, redheaded Luke. He was a thin boy, more prone to gaining freckles than weight.

He didn't weigh much more than that redfish.

CHAPTER 35

Uglesich's

These stupid radios with digital readouts always annoyed me when I was in a new city—as I was now—and didn't know the station numbers. The radio-tape player I had on my boat was great for cassette-tape jammin'. But it was terrible for trying to find a station, especially while trying to navigate the boat-crammed Industrial Canal near downtown "Noo Awlins." I had already passed two ships at least five hundred feet long, one from Italy, the other from Panama. I was like a swattable fly next to them. I was trying to get WWL, a station I had listened to a lot when I used to live in the New Orleans area. Instead I got WSMB-AM. Some guy with a young voice, a very slight New Orleans nasal tone and no Cajun accent at all, was talking passionately on his regular food show about a meal he'd just had. Within a half-hour of listening to him, I was a convert to this talking man, this Louisiana eating man named Tom Fitzmorris. Never have I heard anyone talk so effectively about food and eating. If he'd been an evangelist, the new converts would have been charging the stage he preached from.

On this afternoon Tom Fitzmorris was evangelizing about a place called Uglesich's.

"Yesterday I went to Uglesich's . . ." Tom's voice was breathy, full of excitement. "The meal I had there was so . . . I'll tell you what, if I go over there again soon and get a meal like I had there yesterday, I'm going to raise them to four stars, which is an unbelievable rating for a place that looks like it does, with concrete floors and bags of onions against the wall next to your table. It's just a dumpy, crammed place. If it's seen any paint in twenty years I'd be surprised. But what we ate there was incredible. I had a soft-shell crab that floated off the plate. That crab was so succulent; it probably came to that restaurant this morning. The barbecued shrimp alone was worth the whole trip. That shrimp had that magical combination of firmness and taste and was inundated with that fantastic barbecue heat. We had this delicious speckled-sea-trout dish that was sautéed in olive oil and garlic and herbs—incredible! I mean, this is the kind of food that you hope you get when you go out and spend thirty or forty dollars for a meal, and here it is being served for nine dollars."

Tom went on and on about Louisiana food, New Orleans food, Cajun food, and I was practically drooling as I maneuvered the *Cooper* between two more monster ships. I knew I would have to visit Uglesich's.

I was no stranger to New Orleans, but I had trouble finding Uglesich's. Then I had trouble believing it was the place Tom Fitzmorris had been talking about. To say the neighborhood was on its way down would be a gentle understatement. This area had crashed, and some of it had burned.

The restaurant's location at 1238 Baronne was not very close to the French Quarter and far from the tourist-beaten path. Uglesich's is only open for lunch—coming to this neighborhood after dark would be hazardous to one's health. There are cracks in the roads, cracked-apart sidewalks, cracked and crumbling foundations on some of the buildings, and crack cocaine sold openly on the street corners. None of this has stopped people such as the late billionaire Sam Walton, the mayor of New Orleans, Tulane students, and assorted tourists from around the country from finding it like I did.

The street in front of Uglesich's and the shell-paved parking lot next to it were full when I got there. The narrow, two-story wood building appeared to have been built in the mid-1800s. Faded, peeling paint and iron bars on the windows and front door may be chic now, but the Uglesiches don't care about what's hip. What Anthony Uglesich cares about is what's to eat inside his restaurant—soft-shell crabs caught yesterday, oysters dredged the day before, trout caught with hook and line from the lake bridges this morning. Freshness is one of the prime reasons southern Louisiana food can be so fantastic. Freshness, however, requires discipline—which Anthony Uglesich maintains assiduously. And once he gets the stuff fresh, Anthony knows just what to do with it—another prime requirement for great seafood.

The first thing I noticed once I got inside Uglesich's was the bags of produce lying against the walls of the place—Tom Fitzmorris had not been exaggerating. A middle-aged black woman wearing a white apron would walk through the tightly packed tables and grab a couple of potatoes to peel and cut. There were bags of onions, too, lying on the barren concrete floor. The small tables were surrounded with rigid metal chairs like the kind that used to be in ice cream parlors.

Never have I eaten such fabulous seafood as here at 1238 Baronne Street. I would have never gone to Uglesich's though—its being in a neighborhood not known for the secure feeling it gives you in broad daylight, not to mention its outward appearance—if I had not heard New Orleans food critic and food talk-show host Tom Fitzmorris rave about it.

A chalkboard listed the specials: Smothered Crawfish, Crawfish Yugo, Crawfish Delight (it was crawfish season), Shrimp Pasta. Also, Barbecued Oysters with New Potatoes. A slightly faded sign hand-lettered in black, red, and orange Magic Markers announced, "We do grilled and spicy grilled."

On a shelf I noticed some dusty packages of Wrigley's gum—Doublemint, Spearmint, and Juicy Fruit—and an open box of Band-Aids. The counter where people placed their orders and paid was stainless steel, circa 1950s. A plastic gallon jar of canola oil squatted on the counter along with many empty bottles of exotic and American-brewed beers. Barq's, the treasured local root beer, seemed to be the favored beverage of the wildly different kind of folks sitting around the tables.

I ordered the sautéed barbecued oysters and new potatoes. I ate and was transported to a state of elevated being I've been taken to by food only a couple of times before. My oysters were served on a plain, old, white china plate. Just a few minutes earlier, I'd watched Reuben, a young, thin man with the world's lowest bass voice, shuck my oysters. Here they even shuck the oysters fresh for po-boys. (The best po-boys, for those sadly deprived of our nation's most wonderful sandwich, are made on fresh and precisely heated French bread and must be filled to overflowing with fresh oysters, fresh shrimp, whatever. I've even had octopus po-boys.)

Empire, Louisiana, is on the lower Mississippi River and offers quick access for shrimp boats like these to the close-by bays and to the Gulf.

I didn't want to leave Uglesich's! I wished to soak up the place as my French bread had soaked up the garlic-exalted juices from my oyster dish. But I could hold no more. It would surely have made God angry for me to cover over the barbecued oysters with anything else. Plus, people wanted my table.

The next day, Uglesich's called me back. I decided to get there early, when the fresh seafood was delivered. I enjoyed watching the oystermen and fishermen and crawfish trappers bringing in their iced-down catch. I got to 1238 Baronne Street at fifteen after nine. Anthony Uglesich was there. So was Reuben.

Anthony Uglesich was a bespectacled man of about fifty. He had the soft, wise voice of a man who has seen everything a human can think of doing and was no longer surprised by any of it. He worked hard, but not frantically. He recognized me from the day before. I introduced myself and told him what I was doing. I also admitted I was a major convert to his food, his place.

I was sitting by the open door, enjoying the heavy sweet smell that ambled in like slow jazz from the outside, when Anthony brought me a dish of the day's special, called Sam's Trout after his late father and prepared with speckled trout that had come in less than an hour ago. I had noticed yesterday that he would just bring a dish to anyone who seemed adventurous about food.

Sam's Trout turned out to be smothered in garlic, olive oil, herbs, and spices. "My daddy never fixed this dish." Anthony told me. "I just named it after him because my daddy was such a garlic freak. When I came up as a little kid, he used to take garlic and wrap it between bread and stick it in my mouth and I ate it. And he believed in drinking a lot of olive oil. That's why we named it Sam's Trout."

While I savored my trout, I watched Anthony write the day's specials on the chalkboard. A trout sandwich fried or grilled would go for about $5.00, a trout plate $7.25. You could buy half a dozen raw oysters for $2.50 or a dozen for $4.00.

Anthony had an advantage when it came to oysters. He is Yugoslavian, and Yugoslavians basically control the oyster business. Anthony was brought the best and the freshest oysters by his people, who took care of their own first. Anthony said the best wild stuff—frog's legs, catfish, and crawfish— came from his Cajun fisherman west of here around Des Allemands.

Then George Fisher walked in. His gray hair wasn't cut exactly in a flattop, but in something closely resembling one. He was slim, not much taller than five-foot-eight, and dressed neatly.

George spotted me sitting alone and kind of latched onto me. He sat down at my table, but didn't say a word for about fifteen minutes. Anthony glanced over at him every few minutes. Finally, George told me he was sixty-five. He explained that he used to be the delivery man for this part of Noo Awlins. He said that he had delivered fresh French bread to this very place every day for thirty-one years. George told me that since he had retired and his wife had passed away, he just went around and visited his old friends at the restaurants he liked—the ones who appreciated him and his special talent.

It turned out that George not only delivered bread, he also sang. And though he might have retired from the bread business, he had definitely not retired from singing. He didn't really take requests. He'd been singing the same songs by Al Jolson, Engelbert Humperdinck, and Frank Sinatra for decades. And George didn't wait for diners, or Anthony, to ask for a song. He would just be moved to sing and out would come, "If we never meet again this side of heaven, I'll leave this world loving you."

George grabbed the microphone to my tape recorder so he could treat the restaurant to a song. My tape player did not magnify his voice, but

When this man retired after thirty years of delivering New Orleans-style French bread to Uglesich's, that did not mean that his service to the restaurant stopped. Now he comes in every so often to sing Tom Jones and Engelbert Humperdinck songs to the customers and workers. Only in New Orleans.

at least my microphone was big. He sang with passionate earnestness, his left fist clenched when he sang. And there were a lot of people to hear him, for by now the place was full, with five or six people standing in line.

The clientele at Uglesich's seemed to have come from all walks of life. There was a bear-sized man with tattoos, who looked like a Deadhead; he sat with two women friends in sandals and wafty lace blouses. Lexus-driving dealmakers sat across from retirees from Iowa, who sat next to the state's attorney general (who, along with his brother, owns the famous restaurant Antoine's). Anthony had told me the founder of Atlantic Records was a regular customer. He'd fly in a corporate jetload of people just for the gumbo loaded with crawfish tails.

The more people came in, the more the plates clanged, the bottles emptied, the dishes rattled into the sink, the louder George sang. George belted out, "There goes my only possession; there goes my everything." No one seemed especially amazed and stunned by George's crooning. But then we were in New Orleans, a place unlike any other in the United States of America. To the clients crowding Uglesich's, it just seemed natural. George had always been there when Uglesich's needed great, just-out-of-the-oven French bread. Now Uglesich's was here for George when he needed to sing his songs, the ones he'd been married to for most of his life.

The lunch rush was over. A huge man, each arm as big as an oar and covered in dark hair, his body filling up the door frame, toted in a burlap sack. He was the oysterman, Dave Cvitanovich. He was bigger than Hoss Cartwright from the television series *Bonanza,* but his face showed Hoss's same combination of sensitivity and grit. The burlap sacks he delivered were filled with perfectly plump oysters, the very best, dredged from down below New Orleans in bays settled by Yugoslavians.

Early in the century, many Yugoslavians—Sam Uglesich among them—leaped into the Mississippi River from their country's cargo ships and swam ashore to become Americans. Some built small wooden homes on stilts in Bastian Bay and other shallow bays downriver from New Orleans, near the mouth of the Mississippi. Eventually they built an intact Yugoslav community. At first they were called Tacos. They kept to themselves, spoke their own language, cooked with olive oil and garlic, and worked and worked the waters of the oyster-rich bays.

On either side of the banks of the Mississippi River, far below New Orleans, are a number of shallow bays that have been harvested and replanted with oysters. Most of the time these bays receive the ideal amount of freshwater from the river and just the right amount of saltwater from the Gulf to grow some of the plumpest, tastiest oysters in the world. And it was on these bays that the Yugoslav settlers built their communities and the oyster trade that would make them prosperous in the New World.

Anthony introduced me to Dave, and I asked him to sit down. Dave ordered a plate of barbecued oysters and new potatoes. I was stuffed with the trout, but my mouth still watered at the sight and memory of those oysters. They were easily the best oysters I had ever tasted.

"Yeah, oystering in this part of Louisiana is about all Croatians," big Dave said. "Actually, now that we're in this separatist mode of life, we're all Croatians. Many hate the word *Yugoslavia.* If you look at the names of some of the best seafood restaurants around New Orleans, they're run by Croats. There's this place, Uglesich's. You've got Drago's—that's Drago Sotonovich.

Two Croatian oystermen stand on deck after sorting another drag of oysters from Bastian Bay, down-river from New Orleans.

There's Bozo's, one of Tom Fitzmorris's favorites. *Bozo* is a Croat nickname . . . Bozo Vadonovich. The oystermen who control the oysters in southern Louisiana mostly have names that end with 'vich' or 'sich.'"

Dave got some more French bread and another Barq's; he ate even more than I did. He said his fellow Croats kept close ties with their European relatives. "My father went back to Yugoslavia and married my mother. That's the way the Croats were. They would go out in the world and work and then, once they did well for themselves, they would go back and marry somebody from their hometown. Well, what happened with daddy was that he fought for the United States in World War II, which ended in 1945. So he was forty-one years old when he finally did get to his homeland, and he married my mother. She was twenty-two, from the same hometown. His brother married her sister.

"Well, I was born here in Louisiana, but I couldn't speak English. We spoke Yugoslav at home.

"My first day of kindergarten in Buras, Louisiana, about seventy miles downriver from New Orleans (not far from the mouth of the Mississippi), the teacher says, 'Well, Johnny, what's this?' Johnny says, 'Oh this is a pig, and this is a horse.' Well, it came to my turn and she said, 'Well, Dave, what is this? What does the farmer have in his hand?' He had a rake, which I didn't know how to say in English, so I said *mutika*." Dave seemed to be dredging up some childhood feelings now.

"All the kids laughed, and it nearly killed me. I mean, I didn't want to speak Yugoslav anymore. I was ashamed, and whenever my family spoke Yugoslav I'd stay off to the side. But then my dad's brother came in the early '60s, and he didn't know a word of English. Me and him slept in the same bed, so that's where I started speaking Yugoslav again, and now I pride myself upon it. We have a very close community and a good family life. We stick together."

Dave said all his people were deeply disturbed about the war in their homeland and were doing all they could to help their people across the sea. Dave said he had nine cousins currently fighting against the Serbs.

After speaking of the present war, he lost his abundant appetite. He soon had to load up a truckload of oysters going to Chicago. Right now, he said, the best oysters were coming from Bay Adams.

After Dave left, I lingered and drank my root beer and reflected on how good it was to be back in Louisiana. I had missed her so much. She is so unique, so exotic compared to my world. And I had friends here, a history. It felt good not to be a stranger.

CHAPTER 36

Another
Big River
Day

Aman lay on the steps of St. Louis Cathedral. I couldn't tell if he was young or old, but his face looked as if it had been melted. A couple of fingers had been burned off his left hand, and two on his right hand seemed to have been fused together. He was smallish, curled in a partial fetal position, seemingly unable to move or even speak. An empty margarine container lay on the step in front of him with a few coins in it.

Standing next to the burned man on the steps was a tall, athletically trim black man in his mid-twenties. He wore light blue jeans and a designer T-shirt. A Sony Walkman hung on his Indian-beaded belt. He was belting out the gospel in a style totally alien to the Roman Catholic Church on whose steps he stood.

This man preached of the deadly wages of fornication, the sin of stealing, the desperate need for moral purity. Whenever black people walked by, he spoke to them, expressly, as his people. His haunting voice reached out as far as a voice could penetrate into the orgy of extremes that surrounded all of us around Jackson Square.

I was just two blocks from the Mississippi River, right in the heart of New Orleans's French Quarter. It was the kind of Louisiana day in April that made people break out in spontaneous laughter and dance.

The clown across from the preacher and the melted small man had drawn a large crowd. He chose a shy young woman from the circle around him. She had shoulder-length, dark brown hair and said that she was on her honeymoon.

The clown asked if he could put some balloons down her blouse. She shook her head no and nervously looked toward her new husband. He shook his head, too. If anyone had ever saved herself for marriage, this sweet young woman had. The clown, a master of manipulation, picked a teenage boy and a middle-aged tourist and stood them on either side of the newlyweds.

The clown begged and begged the young woman to let him put a handkerchief down her blouse, just a little ways. He implored the crowd. He begged her husband. He politely sweet-talked her. He begged the crowd some more, played them like a instrument. Finally she agreed.

Then the pink-wigged, white-faced clown very delicately pulled out a string of tied-together handkerchiefs and placed one just a few inches down her blouse, all the time talking loudly and joking crazily. He gave the end of the blue handkerchief to the boy and middle-aged man on either side of her and made a big deal of counting to five. Then he said, "Pull!"

They pulled and out popped the handkerchiefs. Tied to the middle of them was "her" bra. Everyone went wild. The young woman smiled quickly, then turned to her husband. Everyone clapped as they moved on. Or nearly everyone. One man, sitting on a park bench close by, was absorbed in combing the hair on his legs.

Some small tables were set out near the clown. Several young people dressed in medieval garb sat reading tarot cards. For five-dollar tips these readers promised probing wisdom to the curious.

At one table a man in purple tights and a purple scarf, with delicate silver chain mail covering the backs of his hands, dealt out cards with professional polish. On each finger were rings of turquoise and flashing stones. A few tarot decks were held down by violet-colored crystals. He was reading the fortune of a middle-aged woman, his bejeweled finger jabbing at a card.

At the table next to him was a red-haired, freckle-faced young woman dressed like a damsel in a medieval street fair. I noticed some brass dancing symbols holding down the damsel's cards. When I asked her about them, she told me she was a dancer. "Really," she insisted, "the dancing I do is traditional tribal dancing." With her cascading red hair and cool blue eyes, she looked like a Celtic princess, an Irish chieftain's daughter. She wore an evil-looking, snaking dagger in her belt. She said it was handy for cutting cheese.

I left the tarot readers and walked down a street of hand-laid stones that led to the levee. Once, long ago, these stones had been ballast rocks in the holds of oceangoing frigates. I saw a mime in a Scottish kilt jump up on a pillar nearby and, at the same moment, a tap dancer leap to the wooden walkway on top of the levee, his flashy feet flying, his shiny black shoes a blur. He kept beat for all the frantic fanatics, clowns, and jugglers below. It was just an average spring day in the French Quarter.

The levee separated the French Quarter from the gigantic Mississippi River. Down on the land, there was constant, uninhibited celebration. On the wide, brown river, all was muscle and metal and serious business.

This river, so impressive in New Orleans, has a humble birth. Actually, it is born in many places.

One place is high in the Colorado Rockies, where snowdrifts stand chest deep at ten thousand feet and bobcats leave their wide paw prints in the glittering whiteness. When spring brings a gradual thaw, the accumulation of each perfect snowflake begins to melt and trickle into a thousand rivulets racing each other downhill. The farther they go, the more force they gather, until the drops explode over boulders into powerful mountain streams. These feed river after river, always flowing downward, always seeking their ultimate outlet, until finally, they reach the great Mississippi. Their freshwater journey is not done until they pass New Orleans and merge with the Gulf.

At one of the many tables set up around Jackson Square someone wants to believe this tarot card reader.

The snow-energized mountain streams do not pick up much dirt as they rush east; there isn't much soil in the Rockies. But as the streams leave the high rock and enter the Platte River moving through the Great Plains, they begin to gather the topsoil that has eroded off the flat fields in Nebraska. Just north of Kansas City the Platte River gives all its water to the Missouri River. The Missouri is born farther north and is fed by melting glaciers at the Canadian border, near the Yellowstone River. It also collects the water of rivers that pass through North Dakota, South Dakota, Iowa, Missouri, and Kansas.

The Missouri meets the Mississippi just above St. Louis, pouring its western water in to join the water that started as far north as Minnesota's Lake Itasca. A little farther downstream, a little farther south, at Cairo, Illinois, the Pennsylvania-born Ohio River adds its eastern water to the mix.

The all-potent Mississippi I stood before now cuts across the northern half of the Western Hemisphere, taking into itself water from thirty-one states. Rain and snow that fall over a million square miles end up somehow, somewhere in the big river.

Water flows into Pennsylvania's Allegheny River from upper New York State to finally end up in the Mississippi. Water that has found its way into rock fissures bubbles up as springs in secluded hollows of the Great Smoky Mountains, then begins the long journey downhill into the Tennessee River and finally the Mississippi. From the Superior uplands of Wisconsin, from the lakes loved by the black wolves of Minnesota also comes water for the Mississippi. So does water from Indiana, Illinois, Ohio, Kentucky, Texas, Oklahoma, Kansas, North and South Dakota, Canada, West Virginia. Down gutters the rain goes into sewers, across parking lots, over fields, along valleys, into woods. It gently drizzles, it crashes in huge drops, it pours, it melts. And all of it ends up here, in this massive brown stream pushing hard toward the Gulf.

So many times have I stood in the open door of my hay barn and watched the rain run off the tin roof. I've wondered where it went after it ran down the hill to McCutchon Creek at the front of my farm. If it didn't end up in a cow's stomach or sink into the soil, then it kept going, joined the Duck River, eventually made it to the Tennessee River and then the Mississippi. Raindrops that had fallen on my roof, that had ripped off the leaves of the ancient red oak shading our family's house, were flowing past me now as I stood on the levee above the French Quarter in New Orleans. What force is carried in this mile-wide brown water. What power it has. No wonder it so easily overcomes mere humans.

Amazing and precise movements were happening out on the Mississippi right now. Diesel engines as big as small buildings were maneuvering their

There are many places below New Orleans with fascinating names. One of the most intriguing is Yscloskey, where many of the people's boats are worth more than their homes. Here a lineup of shrimp and oyster boats awaits the next trip to the bays or the open Gulf.

seagoing freighters. River pilots steered seven-hundred-foot steel ships from Italy or Jamaica or Russia up- or downriver to unload or pick up their tons and tons cargo. Many cultures coexist on this river, and each ship is like a separate nation.

This busy river-commerce world was hidden away, blocked by the levees that walled the river in. Down on land, you might never know it existed. But I became a part of that river world for a while. I went to work with some of the pilots who steered fifty-million-dollar ships down from New Orleans the ninety-plus miles to the Gulf, or up from the Gulf to New Orleans.

This night I was eight stories above the river in the control center of the *Stolt Surf,* a 556-foot-long American ship registered in Liberia. We were headed downriver through the fanning Mississippi Delta, toward the Gulf. Everything around us was a shiny black except for the lights of smaller ships moving far below us. Navigation signals, red and green lights, loomed up from the river on huge poles. We kept the green lights to our right and the reds ones to our left when we went down the Mississippi.

The stars hovered above, one or two breaking loose and streaking across the sky. When we got far enough downriver there were oil-rig lights too on both sides of the night. The moon lit up the silver-white waves of the ship's wake. We would be passing places strong with deep-Delta history, places where low-river people lived. Places named Pointe a la Hache,

Empire, Buras, Venice. We would end our voyage at Pilottown, the place where the river pilots and the bar pilots change places.

Every captain of every ship, no matter who it belongs to or where it came from, surrenders control of it to the river pilots before entering the Mississippi. Upriver vessels are boarded by a local bar pilot about a mile out in the Gulf. The bar pilots' responsibility is to get the ships into the mouth of the Mississippi, avoiding the ever-changing sandbars along the way. They pilot the ships to what is called the head of the passes, the point where the river, on the final leg of its seaward journey, splits off into a myriad of smaller passes. (The only pass used by the megaships is Southwest Pass.) Pilottown, the place where the pilots change, is just above the head of the passes.

The river pilots take command at Pilottown and take the ships the rest of the way to New Orleans. These same river pilots also return the ships once their business in the port is done. They board them in New Orleans and take them back to Pilottown.

I'd boarded this ship with a river pilot named Capt. Albert Short. He asked me to call him Shack. His grandfather had been a pilot; so had his father. He knew this eighty-odd-mile stretch of the Mississippi perhaps better than anyone in the world. (His only possible challengers would be his fellow pilots for this part of the river.) Knowing this part of the great river was Shack's life's work. He had to know her curves, her changing moods, her tricks.

On the high seas the *Stolt Surf* was captained by a German named Franz Weber. The vessel's chief engineer was a Norwegian, the first mate a Spaniard. Most of the rest of the crew were from the Philippines.

Captain Weber had cups of cappuccino and some exquisite goat cheese delivered to the wheel room for Shack and me.

We were only five miles from the French Quarter as the gull flies, but we'd gone about sixteen miles on the serpentine river when a voice came over the loudspeakers.

"Captain. Captain, sir. Pilot, we are presently without power."

The voice seemed normal in tone, but the situation seemed far from normal to me. Surely they did not float powerless in the current to save fuel! Maybe they did. Shack certainly didn't seem concerned.

A large tugboat the size of a hill was pushing at least ten barges, all tied together, and coming right at us. In the deepest black of night, only its hundreds of lights indicated its size. The whole thing, tug and barges together, seemed as long as a railway train. It could take a half-hour to make an evasive turn. Were we headed for each other? If we were, how could we avoid collision? And what would I do if we did collide? Our ship was loaded with highly flammable chemicals. The barges could be filled with oil or gasoline. A collision would almost certainly mean a huge fire and probably an explosion.

I thought about jumping overboard if the ship caught fire. But even if I were not injured in an explosion, I might not survive jumping into the chilled muddy brown river from this far up. Earlier that day, four stowaways from Central America had jumped into the river from a ship; two had drowned and two were missing.

I was not encouraged by the prospects. But if this oncoming barge was a potential difficulty, I couldn't discern it from Shack's behavior. He was totally calm, fully in control. If I had to land a jet on top of Mount Everest, I'd have him do it.

I asked him, "Shack, are we in some kind of situation or what?"

"What's a situation?" he asked me in return. If we were now in serious danger, surely he'd not be speaking to me in these calm tones.

On my last trip, another pilot had told me about the time he was captaining a tug to move an offshore rig when a hurricane hit him. He said it was no big deal. "All I did," he yawned, "was hold her into the wind."

Shack told Captain Weber to have his men stand by, to be ready to release the anchor at the bow. The bow was so far away from us it seemed to be in another time zone. A minute later I saw three crew members dash to the front of the ship.

Another moment passed, then diesel smoke surged out of the smoke-stacks behind us. There had been air in the fuel lines, they'd bled the lines, now fuel was again igniting in the massive engine. Everyone in the blacked-out control center breathed a deep sigh of relief. Only Shack seemed not relieved. But he had never seemed worried.

Shack told me that if the current had felt as if it were shoving us toward the bank or another ship, he would have released the anchor, hoping it would grab and swing the ship around on the anchor chain. But that had not been necessary.

Captain Weber, his strong arms crossed on his chest, walked over and stood next to Shack, his respect showing clearly in the gesture. It was for moments like this that river pilots like Shack were in control of these multimillion-dollar ships.

Per, the Norwegian chief engineer, came up to the bridge. His arms and jump suit were splashed with grease; in his hand was a German beer. It was he who had been responsible for getting the engine restarted. This man was only forty and had already been at sea for twenty years. Per said he was a *cigoeyner*, a gypsy. He told me in clipped English that his was a gypsy's soul, but in a body of undiluted Norwegian blood. Then he said that I should come down and see his "baby."

When a boat loaded with illegal drugs attempts to sneak through the treacherous Mississippi River Delta and runs into trouble, it doesn't call the Coast Guard for help. The crew either gets to where they are going or they abandon ship or sink. This one sank in Breton Sound west of the International Ship Channel. Today it is a hot fishing spot.

Per's baby was what had just caused us to be powerless—the ship's 10,500-horsepower, Swedish-built engine. We went to visit the room it lived in, four or five stories down. The huge chamber was hellishly hot and loud.

"Isn't she beautiful?" Per said proudly. "I don't need the book anymore to take her apart." He pointed around the engine room. "That's my life," he said. "I love engines. Anything mechanical. That's my life."

Per was truly in love; I could see it in the way he gazed at his gigantic charge. I'm no motors-and-engines junky, but even I was stunned by its presence. Per's baby was more than three stories tall and eighteen of my paces long. A spare piston hanging next to it was almost ten feet tall. The piston in my truck is maybe eighteen inches long.

In the engine room we had some coffee strong enough to make me feel like I could even take Per's motor apart. Then we made the climb back up to the bridge, where Shack was still calmly guiding the huge vessel through the dark Delta waters.

In a couple of hours the *Stolt Surf* would be in the Gulf, and Captain Weber would have her to himself till their next port of call. On this leg of their travels, the Gulf waters would stay with the ship all the way back to Europe. This is how Captain Weber explained it in his German-accented English as we finished our second round of goat cheese.

"The waters that come out of the Gulf of Mexico sweep around Florida and go up along the East Coast of America, then swing northeast and cross the Atlantic Ocean. Part of the Gulf current goes north to Norway. On beaches there you may find pieces of tropical wood that floated in the current all the way from Central America. When our ship crosses the Atlantic, we use our water temperature gauge to make sure we stay in the Gulf Stream. Staying in it pushes us faster, and we use less fuel. So you see the Gulf has a big effect on many places."

Captain Weber asked for my home address; he said he'd send me postcards from different ports. From what he told me, I could be receiving a lot of postcards. In the past year the *Stolt Surf* had sailed to Singapore and Malaysia, continued on to the Philippines, to Venezuela, then to Haiti. After Port-au-Prince there was New York, then Mexico, then Brownsville, Texas, then New Orleans, and through the Panama Canal again.

Now, with the help of Captain Short, there would soon be another port arrived at and departed, another port in waiting. Ships like these, the ones worth millions of dollars, can never stop for long.

Shack's work was over for the night. We had made the trip down from New Orleans to Pilottown, almost to the Gulf, on the *Stolt Surf*. Now he'd go home, and I'd catch a ride back upriver with another pilot. After waiting half a day in the river pilots' headquarters, built up on pilings by the side of the river, I climbed aboard a 732-foot Italian ship with a Captain Kline.

Captain Kline talked a lot more than Shack. He seemed to enjoy explaining his work.

"See, a lot of people think when the river is high, it's easier to get a ship up and down the river. But that's not what happens. When the river is high like it is now, it's bringing down a lot of silt. It's muddy, and it's real, real thick because of the silt. And as the silt runs downriver, it drops off. You have spots where the current is strong, and you get eddies. The silt just falls to the bottom and builds up, building sandbars at points in the curves of the river, at the mouth of the river, at the mouth of the delta. The channels coming up this river change daily. That's where the need for pilots arose.

"The pilot, he's an adviser to the master of the vessel. He's the local guy who has the local knowledge of this river. The first established pilots on the Mississippi were at the mouth in 1722."

Most captains are happy to hand over responsibility for their ships to the river pilots. But not always. One time, Captain Kline told me, a captain from India had refused to relinquish control of his vessel.

"What did you do?" I asked.

"Had to punch him out," Captain Kline answered. When it was time for Captain Kline and me to disembark in New Orleans, a crewman threw a ragged old rope ladder off the side of the ship. The crew boat floated far below, jammed up against the huge ship, both of them moving upriver, and waited for us to climb down the ladder. This for me was the most challenging portion of the journey.

At least five pilots over the years have fallen to their deaths from iced-over ladders or ladders that just broke as they climbed up or down. More than that number have fallen and lived. A river pilot does not have a mandatory age at which to retire, but he must be able to climb these ladders. (Captain Vogt was over seventy, I was told, and he still climbed.) Not being able to climb the ladder is usually what ends a pilot's career on this vast brown river. As I climbed down three stories, four stories, the hard steel decks of the crew boat unsteadily rocking below me, the ladder bouncing off the side of the huge ship, I could understand why.

Captain Kline had guided the ship to the point in the river, just below the French Quarter, where another pilot would take her on toward Baton Rouge. The ships never do stop, not even for a new river pilot. Neither does the river. This river stops for no one.

The French Quarter knows no stopping, either; it only slows down as the sun comes up. It was on such a cool morning that I noticed a strange creature. Only five minutes before, the young black man with the melted face and fused fingers—the one I'd seen the week before in a fetal position, immobile—had been running down the street, chattering and laughing, as active as a honeybee. Either he'd been healed or he'd been scamming.

But now my whole attention was focused on the strange figure pushing a grocery cart down the fresh-washed sidewalk of Royal Street. Probably just another street person, I guessed, perhaps turned away from a mental institution. But was this person a he or a she? I couldn't tell because he or she was wearing a papier-mâché gorilla mask. The person's rainbow-shimmering, ankle-length dress didn't tell me anything, either—around here you never could tell.

One of my heroes poses for me in the French Quarter.

"Hi," I said. The gorilla person stopped pushing the cart.

"Hello," came a polite, shy woman's voice. OK. Just what I thought. A female street person, with all her possessions in the cart.

"What's your name?" I asked.

"My name's Sunshine," she answered. Sunshine. Must be some old hippie who fried her brain on Sunshine LSD, maybe someone who never made it home from Woodstock.

"What do you do around here?" I asked.

"I make the children smile," she said, sounding so sincere. Her voice was seductive in a nonsexual way. Sort of hypnotic. But here you have to be suspicious of sincerity.

"You know," she continued, "I made this mask and my dress myself. I have a beautiful sun hat all covered with flowers, and I always like to have on either a silver or gold skirt."

She explained that she'd been doing this for four years. She told me she lived across the river in a middle-class place called Chalmette, where most yards are kept perfectly clipped and many have statues of Jesus. For many years she worked as a secretary at Avondale Shipyards. She had raised four fine children, had six grandchildren. But after she retired, she said, she was "just plain bored." So she put together a costume and became Gorilla Woman.

Sunshine said she dressed this way only on the weekends. During the week she did a lot of sewing. She went to a lot of grandchildren's baseball and football games. And, she said, the Council of Aging picked her up every weekday in their van, and she went to the senior citizen center for lunch. But no one in her neighborhood, no one she lunches with, has the faintest idea that on the weekends she changes into her mask and long dress and becomes Gorilla Woman. And that's fine with her. She's doing this purely for herself, purely for the smiles it brings. She said bright smiles washed away any sadness she might feel about living alone.

Every weekend Gorilla Woman looks forward to coming back to the Quarter. She sets up her seat and sits down. People take their pictures with her, and the children especially seem to love what she has become. After talking to her, I felt that way, too. Sunshine said it was harder to make grownups smile. But she made me smile all over. She also made me think. I hope I have the courage at her age to do something just because it made me happy and made other people happy as well.

Meeting Sunshine was a fine way to leave New Orleans. This lively, unconventional city always shocks me a little when I haven't been around her in a long time; she is so very different from places I know and live. But it seems I'm always smiling and singing when I leave Noo Awlins. I'm always glad I came.

It's Hard to Know
Your Life Is Threatened
If You're Asleep

I can usually feel danger coming right through my skin, but nothing warned me this time. Nothing on the horizon, no black clouds—everything was hot, wet, and dead still. The only danger of which I was aware was letting my mind melt in the already stifling heat of a Louisiana summer and becoming forgetful. It was easy to forget that rowboat-sized sharks could be lurking right under us, big enough to eat either of my boys as easily as I eat a peanut-butter cracker. I was determined to stay alert. But as far as I could see, everything was fine.

The *Cooper* was docked near the mouth of the Pearl River, not far outside New Orleans. After visits from Rebekah, Brooke, and Aaron, it was Jed and Luke's turn to spend a week with me on the boat. With my long-time friend George Dantin, we were going to do some exploring and fishing in the countless bays and inlets east of the Mississippi.

Tonight, two hours before sunset, we had arrived at an offshore oil rig in Breton Sound. George and I had spotted this rig before the boys came down, while he and I had been fishing. George is a Cajun, born and raised around the green maze of marshes and bays around New Orleans, so he was a good guide for the *Cooper* and me.

We rounded the rig. Four massive steel legs supported the superstructure, creating what oil-patch people call a production platform. We tied onto two algae-covered supports on the rig's east side.

We were here because of what happens as soon as night falls. When it gets dark around this rig, a sensor tells the generators to turn on its many

After coming in from a night of incredible fishing at an offshore oil rig, my friends George Dantin and Leon Audibert show off some of the best speckled trout we caught. We fished until our arms grew tired.

lights. The lights are meant to keep ships, fishing boats, and low-flying aircraft from hitting the rig and to give light to any workers who may be on her. But they also enticed outrageous amounts of marine life.

Darkness fell. The lights switched on. And suddenly the silky surface of the warm waters was swarming with life. Big shrimp were here, recklessly jumping because hundreds and thousands of fish were trying to eat them. And enormous predators were in turn gulping down the shrimp-eating fish. We could see hundreds of fish at a time darting through the light that penetrated a foot or two into the light green sea. They dashed or floated in and out. A stingray almost as wide as our boat flew through in slow motion.

The boys were blown away by the spectacle of it.

"Wow, Dad!"

"What was that, Dad, a shark?"

They ran from the front to the back of the boat. They leaned over the railing as if they wanted to get closer. They acted as if they wanted to jump into water with the fish and catch them by hand. And they made me as nervous as a first-time mother during her first week home with the baby. I tried to keep them within arm's length so that if one slipped I could grab the back of his pants.

But it was hard to keep up with two excited boys on a boat. As their confidence increased, they scampered around even more.

"Look! . . ."

"Wow! . . ."

"What kind is *that?* . . ."

Now George brought out the fishing tackle. I was still nervous. Some of those fish were strong enough to pull either boy overboard. I would never have done this kind of trip without someone like George along. So many terrible things can happen so quickly on the big water.

Jed and Luke pulled in fish together, both holding the pole. George and I helped. Some of the fish were so strong the boys could barely crank the reel. It was a fishing frenzy, a once-in-a-lifetime experience. We caught so many large trout, redfish, and drum that we were bored. For George and me, who had been fishing together for ten years, it was almost a sin to get bored while you're catching this many fish.

Jed bolted to the back of the boat to get a net. A ghostly white squid passed by just below the surface of the water. Finally, after a couple hours of following my boys around like an attentive guard dog, I had them come and sit beside me. I put my arms around them and pulled them close. They loved all this action. Concerned as I was about their safety, I was thrilled that they were finally old enough to join me. I'd been waiting a long time for this moment.

From somewhere, without warning, there were waves. The boat swayed enough to make anyone but a high-seas sailor feel awkward. And I was acutely aware of how easy it would be for a small boy to fall into this sea. All it would take would be one second out of my sight as the boys threaded their way back and forth between the front deck and the back deck. And once they were in the water, there would be little anyone would be able to do. The current would carry them away, life preserver and all. In the dark we couldn't see a thing. The rig had a persistent horn that was supposed to go off in a fog, but it went off all the time. Generator motors clanged constantly. We almost surely would never hear anything. I did not want to think these thoughts, but I had to.

I asked George the time—eleven. The boys were still running on high-octane excitement. I told them it was late and to get some sleep, we'd be getting up early, maybe going over to an island.

"Can we get out on the island, Dad?"

"Sure. But it's time for bed now."

They begged, the eternal-pleading of youth: "Please, can't we stay up a little longer?"

Then came my usual parental cave-in: "All right, a few more minutes."

Meanwhile, I got out a clean sheet for them to lie on in the cabin. I wet down a washcloth and rinsed off their sweaty, dirty faces, arms, legs, and bodies. Their T-shirts looked like they hadn't been washed after three weeks of food fights. There were fish scales on their arms and legs. I was amazed at how long those arms and legs had gotten. They were growing up so fast.

The boys were asleep before George could get his bedroll spread out on the steel floor of the rig. He hoped to catch some desperately needed breeze. I switched the radio to channel 3, wondering if there was any reason for the waves. The marine forecast said there was nothing coming.

I went below to join Jed and Luke, but the normally cozy cabin was like a sauna. I climbed back up on deck and lay there, trying to gather some coolness, some relief for my overheated body. Even in the open, there was no relief. It was like being suspended in a hot, invisible fog.

Earlier I'd asked George, one of the few people I trusted with my life, if we should stay here or head toward some protected waters. A lot of people and boats have been smashed apart around the rigs.

"I think we'll be safe here," George said. His face had that falling-asleep look all over it.

Up on deck I could feel the waves chopping at the boat. I was the only one awake. I had a worried feeling something was going to happen. I decided I should stay awake all night and keep watch.

"We got to get out here!" I dreamed that someone was yelling, telling me we needed to leave.

"Come on!" I opened my eyes. It was still dark.

"COME ON!" George was standing over me. The boat was banging, banging against the metal legs of the rig. I sat up. Where had *that* wind come from? No one had said anything about a fierce front coming through.

I shook my head to clear it. I was so drained and in need of rest. But what George said next jolted me wide awake.

"This weather is getting real bad. We need to leave. We could break loose, and the boat could get sucked under the rig."

The boat smashed against the rig again. I was knocked down just as I struggled to my feet.

"First, we need to get these ropes untied!" George instructed, stumbling toward the back of the boat. The *Cooper* had lines from its bow and stern tied to the rig. I went to get the bowline. It had slipped and fallen below the railing, where I could not reach it.

I could see that George was struggling to get his line loose. If either one of us fell in between the boat and the rig, we could easily be crushed to death.

"Pete, this is going to get a lot worse before it gets any—" George almost fell in, "—better," he finished.

I pushed against the rig, expecting that superhuman strength I'd heard parents get when they are rescuing their children. I still could not reach the rope. I decided to get my gaff from the back deck and try to hook the rope. I fell on the narrow walkway alongside the cabin. A wave crashed against the bow, pushing me forward; only the railing kept me in the boat. My shin had to be badly bruised. I got the gaff.

George had just then gotten his rope untied. Now he would have to hold on to the rig with his own brute strength until I got the bowline untied. If he let go of the stern, we could be washed under the unmovable steel of the rig.

George is a very strong man. But no one could hold on for long under those conditions.

I reached for the rope again. I could not grab it. The boat fell off a wave and lunged toward the rig. A five-thousand-pound boat was about to collide with what seemed like a million pounds of steel—and my arm was in-between. I yanked it up. I got it out in time.

"Pete, I can't hold this . . ." George was silent, then continued, "much longer." I wondered if George ever lost his composure.

I finally got the rope untied.

George had been watching. "Pete, now, on the count of three, push us off . . . then you go to the controls. I'll stay here and keep us from getting under this rig." He had already started the engines. I'd never even heard them running.

We both pushed off. It felt like the motor-end of the boat might get pulled under the rig. I could not hesitate. I ran to the controls, pushed them into forward. I felt the wind and waves to figure which way to steer. The boat jerked forward too hard. Where was George?

Where was he? I looked left and right. Nowhere. He was not where he had been a second before.

Something touched my shoulder. It was George.

"Pete, you do have a spotlight on board, don't you?" he asked. Now we were adrift, blinded, in a brutal sea dotted with rigs, some with lights, some without. I remembered a story George told me about a guy who had run into one and killed his passenger.

"I *had* a spotlight. I think it's in this compartment under my seat." But I had recently cleaned out the *Coops*. Knowing me, maybe I'd left it out somewhere.

I thought I heard one of the boys calling out. Luke was known to walk in his sleep—just take off, even run. I listened closely. It was neither

Jed nor Luke. It was Don Henley singing the song "Sad Cafe" from The Eagles' greatest hits tape, on low. I'd been listening to it earlier and never turned it off.

George found the spotlight immediately. He hooked it up to one of the batteries and walked out onto the bow with it. The sea was almost as dark as death, dark as only the sea can be on a moonless night.

"Pete!" George yelled. "Didn't I see you using that hand-held compass today?"

"Yeah," I answered back over the sound of waves beating against the boat.

"Did you take a reading off that island that was behind us, Gosier Island?" George wanted to know badly.

Another wave hit us. George, holding on with one arm, almost lost his balance. Another wave smashed against the bow and partially drenched him. Could the spotlight lens explode if hit by water?

"Yeah," I repeated. I *had* taken a reading on that island.

"What was the reading?" George knew how my memory worked. When I got stressed, sometimes I couldn't remember anything.

"It was 105 degrees," I shouted.

"Well, head for it," George said sternly. "Are you sure that was the reading?"

"Yes," I said. I hoped I was right.

George swung the spotlight hungrily, searching for rigs and steel well-heads. If we hit one of those, could it explode, cover us with clouds of natural gas?

I put the compass dead-on 105 degrees, almost due east. Now I was almost sure I heard Jed. "Dad . . . Dad . . ." He was such a soft-spoken, thoughtful child. I took my eyes off the compass and looked down to where the boys were sleeping, or had been sleeping.

"What are we doing, Dad?" Jed asked politely.

"We're moving, buddy. A storm's coming in. You can go on back to sleep if you want."

"Do you need any help?" he asked.

"Pete, what are you—!" George shouted. "We're going to run into a—"

I jerked my head up to see we were about to run into a wellhead—no lights on it, no bell. I steered hard to the right.

I got back on 105 degrees and looked back down at Jed. "You just relax for right now, son. If I need you, I'll wake you up, OK?"

"All right, Dad," he answered. Luke would probably sleep through a hurricane.

Why didn't the marine forecasters warn us about this front? How did they miss this thing?

"Pete, there . . . do you see that?" George asked. Normally, George would have been enjoying this, harassing me about the danger, telling me we were about to sink. Usually he delighted in messing with me. But having the boys with us had turned him serious, too.

I looked out where he was pointing the light. I didn't see a thing but aggravated whitecaps, angry waters. My friend kept swinging the light back and forth across a short area. I thought I saw some green, marsh-grass green. I did see it! It was Gosier Island. George said that we'd get in behind it, put down our anchor, and ride out the storm. Hopefully the bad weather would be over by morning.

The island offered a shield of protection. The boys never awoke again that night. I went down and lay with them, listened to their breathing, recognized the usual positions they slept in, heard Luke talking in his sleep. I kissed both of their faces and never knew how long it took me to be gone into sleep. George slept on the deck. There was no rain.

Morning came, and as usual Jed was the first one awake. When I opened my eyes, the first thing I saw was him looking at me, still lying there, probably wondering where breakfast was. I told George I was going to buy him and the boys the best breakfast we could find along the banks of the Mississippi River.

I'd just had a review lesson in what I'd already learned over and over in a year and a half of exploring these Gulf of Mexico waters. These waters, the skies over the Gulf, the winds—they all did whatever, whenever they wanted. And we humans basically have two choices when it comes to the sea.

We can either stay away from it all.

Or we can be ready for anything.

CHAPTER 38

Big
Bashing
Waves

I was in one of those rare slammin' and jammin' moods, as strong as the ones that blew through me at age eighteen. Go for the wild side. Take the megarisk. Today I wanted to go as fast as I could to the worst part of the storm, feel its fury, shake my fist at its threats. I felt like one of those invincible folks who throw parties instead of evacuating when a hurricane's storming down on them.

I was south of the heart of the Cajun country in the Intracoastal Waterway. It had taken me a couple of days since leaving New Orleans to get this far. I'd just gassed up in Intracoastal City, not far from Abbeville. But the Intracoastal felt too tame now. There were no waves; no thought was required to run down its center. The mood I was in, I needed a challenge, maybe even danger.

I could not decide which way to go. I could continue on the Intracoastal across most of southern Louisiana. Or I could burn south and take the Four Mile Cutoff. From there it was a straight blast to Vermilion Bay. I could bang through the bay and take the pass by Marsh Island, past Lighthouse Point, and westward into the Gulf.

Maybe I'd been in this southern Louisiana land of passion and daring long enough to absorb some of the local people's character. Or maybe I was truly confident in my ability to run the *Cooper*. I decided to go for the open Gulf.

I'd be moving along the coast of Cameron Parish, keeping the land in view. Louisiana is divided into parishes rather than counties, and Cameron

Parish is known to have more alligators, otters, cottonmouths, muskrats, and mosquitoes than any other place in all the bayou country. Its human residents have their most significant beauty pageant in the fall. All the young dark-eyed Cajun women strut their sultry bodies on stage in sequined evening gowns—but they share the stage with the muskrat-skinning contest. Subtlety is not a big part of these people's lives.

After an hour in the unobstructed Gulf I saw a curtain of black blocking my path. It reminded me of the front Scott and I had faced in the Keys. The front looked like electrified fence filled with thunder and lightning, and it extended from the coastline at a ninety-degree angle, stretching far out into the Gulf. There would be no going south and around it—even if I had wanted to.

This was the kind of thunder-infested cloud bank that suddenly darkened earth and sky. Its lightning was supercharged because the saltwaters were so warm, the air so humid, and the sky so cool and dense. Whatever it hit it could hurt or kill. I had never been able to get a satisfactory answer about what happened when a boat was struck by lightning. But I was going to risk finding out.

The front first touched me with a caressing gray mist. It was coming toward me. I was going toward it. Come on, hit me!

The temperature dropped; the change was dramatic, like stepping into a room-sized refrigerator. A bad sign. In front of me were defiantly larger waves. I thought briefly about turning around. I would not.

At first I thought I would head right into the waves. That was a mistake. One or two came over the bow and broke some snaps on the zippered vinyl windshield. My breathing became short and fast.

Something transformed me right after that wave. I liked what was happening. These rugged, big-bashing waves were a fine thrill. I think the same look must have come over me that I saw in Warren and Scott when they faced heavy seas. Before, these conditions had frightened me, even when someone else was at the helm. Not anymore.

But then again, this was only the beginning. Already I could barely see anything in front of me. The curtain of rain blocked out the horizon, blocked everything but about fifty feet on all sides. And the waves were still breaking over my bow. I realized bow-first wouldn't work, so I angled offshore and rode along the sides of the waves. I was relaxed, which surprised me. The energy of excitement surged through my body, yet I was in control.

I knew exactly how much power to give my engines, I knew just how the *Cooper* would ride the curve of the wave. That was the difference now. I could feel how to use the force of these waves, this wind, and my

Here in western Louisiana there is so much undeveloped coastline and so few people that even cows have their own beach.

engines—not fight them, fear them, give in to them. The *Cooper* was an extension of me, guided by my experience, my knowledge.

A double lightning bolt struck so close I thought I could smell electricity in the air. We were about five miles off the coast, about even with the Rockefeller National Wildlife Refuge.

The wind and rain were loud outside the cabin, but I popped in a cassette Scott Bannerot had given me—Bob Marley and the Wailers. They sang "Buffalo Soldier" and "Get Up, Stand Up"; my body began to flow and bounce with the Jamaican beat. The *Coops* and I moved through the waves as if we were dancing with them. I sang out loud.

When I finally pulled into the port of Cameron, about 235 road miles west of New Orleans, I couldn't keep the grin off my face.

In the lowlands of Louisiana, you grow up accustomed to danger. Fearlessness about slithering reptiles, brutalizing storms, and dark, eerie endless waters must be passed on to babies in their mothers' milk. The people of this Louisiana coastline are radically different from any others I've ever met. The fear and frustration that normally come from living in a place like this have somehow been replaced with an irrepressible joy and hilarity.

Here it's nothing to see canoe-sized, black-backed gators blocking one of the few roads that crosses the marshland, especially in September when the bull gators are traveling, looking for females. Their eyes gleam demon-red at night when a headlight shines on them. To some, living around the gators would be like living with dinosaurs or monsters. But the people of Cameron Parish don't worry about such things. If you're going to live surrounded by the river, marsh, and swamp waters, you're going to worry about different things than the rest of America.

Here in Cameron Parish, they turn big black-horned Brahma cattle into the marsh from pull-off places on Highway 82. Sometimes these cattle are lucky to find a dry place to stand. The heat and the marsh make them bad-mean; stockyard professionals hate to see "them Luu-zee-ana swamp cows" come through the auction. These cattle will jump over six-foot fences to get at you; they *want* to hurt you. It's as if they know that humans are the ones who turned them loose in the heated, humid furnace of a summer marsh void of shade. Sometimes the mosquitoes get so thick they swarm a cow's nose and smother it to death. And clouds of mosquitoes offer no shade.

The sea is always here, making waves, taking land, stealing it a grain at a time, a couple feet a year—or taking away big chunks through the not-so-rare hurricane hits. Thunder-bangers that would make most people hide in their basements are just a faint inconvenience here. Besides, no one has a basement; the water table is too high.

Every year there is the same old hurricane season. Radar now tracks the storms all the way from African waters, across the Atlantic, and along the Caribbean. Will the hurricane enter the Gulf? Will it roar up the Atlantic Coast? If it gets into the Gulf, which coast will it hit? Who can worry so much? If they worried about all that, these people would have moved off a long time ago.

They remember, though. Hurricane stories are part of the folklore of the region.

In 1957, for example, Hurricane Audrey came ashore at Cameron in a terrible frontal assault. No one who lived through her will ever forget that date—June 27. No one was ready when Audrey blew in, and the winds and high water came close to killing everyone who stayed in their homes. More than 550 dead were counted. Many, many more were never found—or their bloated bodies could not be identified.

When I came to Cameron Parish in 1992, a television reporter from Lake Charles was interviewing a tough-looking rice farmer at his family reunion. Everyone was cracking crabs, peeling crawfish, laughing. Then the reporter asked this sixty-year-old man about Hurricane Audrey, and tears suddenly dripped down his creased, tan face. He said he had lost his mother, his two aunts, his grandmother, his . . . He couldn't go on.

In just about every room in Cameron Parish, under every mimosa tree, on practically every boat, at about every gathering of two or more, there will be people there who lived through Audrey's killing spree or people who are descended from survivors. I'm sure that tears have been shed by someone every day that has passed since Audrey hit—every day for the past thirty-five years.

Many people fled to the courthouse in Cameron to escape Audrey. Berton Daigle was clerk of the court in those days. I asked Berton, now retired, his hair still mostly black, if he knew about the man who had been stuck up in his attic with his family. Someone had told me the story. This particular man had brought a shotgun with him and a box of shells. When the water rose and was about to get into his attic, he had to blow a hole in the roof.

Berton smiled, his dancing eyes flashed a second. "Yeah, I know him. That was me."

Berton Daigle, as pure a Cajun as you get, was once crowned king of the fur and wildlife festival here. That year he presided over the beauty contest and muskrat-skinning competition. Whoever is the fastest muskrat skinner at this annual festival is usually the fastest in the world. The best skinner from Cameron Parish can skin a muskrat in under ten seconds. Before oil was discovered, trapping muskrats, nutria, and gators was one of the few ways the people could get cash. (Nutria are beaver-size rodents.)

I'd met Berton through his friend, Charlie Hebert, who owned the dock where I had tied up the *Cooper*. At my request, Berton recounted his story about surviving Audrey. "You know how you tell when the weather getting bad 'round here? From my house here on the Creole Road, if it's really, really bad, you can hear the Gulf roar. In fact, whenever I was a kid, my grandmother used to sit on the front porch and listen, tell us what it getting ready to do." Berton speaks with a definite Acadian accent. His grandparents almost never spoke English.

"If it was roaring real hard from the east, that meant stormy weather was coming. Then if the roaring was coming from the west, that meant a norther was coming—you knew the wind was going to turn and come out the north. That's some of the predictions we had in those days. Not much."

They didn't have much more warning when Audrey came. Their house is about five miles from Cameron and a mile and a half from the Gulf. The land between them and the Gulf is all marsh, save for a little ridge and a built-up road. Their land is about three feet above sea level.

"The afternoon before the hurricane, it start raining by gush. The wind kind of gushed in. My wife's people came here from Johnson's Bayou. The only way over here from there is by ferry, and that would be wiped out if a storm hit. They came to my house for refuge. At about ten o'clock that night it was raining and blowing pretty hard.

"I called Sheriff O. B. Carter and ask him if he knew any news about the storm. 'Should we leave in the middle of the night?' I ask him. He say, 'Whenever you come to work tomorrow morning, we'll talk about whether we should evacuate or not.' So we all went to bed and slept. About six the next morning, a few people got here and said, 'Well, we can't go to Cameron. The water is over the road.' That was real early.

"So I got in my truck, and I went over to my daddy's. He lived just a quarter mile from here in the old house. I said, 'You want to try to make it to the courthouse in Cameron?' We could have taken a boat over there. 'No,' he said, 'we've been through hurricanes before. We were here before this old storm, weren't we?'

"My daddy said he didn't believe it was going to be that bad. Anyway, by the time I got back to my house, that quarter mile, I looked down the field and I could see a wall of water coming, rolling about two feet high. That wall was tiny compared to what would come.

"We found out afterwards that my wife's grandma had already drowned. It was two or three in the morning whenever the water went over their place. Her daughter saved herself by grabbing hold of an old icebox, but my wife's grandma, she was eighty then, she drowned. Nearly every house between here and Cameron was washed away but a few."

"Anyway, I was running across the field trying to get to the house in two, three feet of water. When I got back, well, the water had just kept a-coming up, and all these logs and pieces of houses that had already broke up on that front ridge were coming at my house."

Everyone here lives on the narrow ridges that rise above the marsh. The ridges are ancient beaches maybe a quarter-mile wide. The front ridge, the one closest to the Gulf, was where a lot of the local black people lived. Hundreds were killed when the storm first hit.

"When it got to where it was coming in the house, well, I told them, 'Looks like we have to crawl up in the attic.' So we started hauling ourselves up in the attic. There was nine of us up there."

A lot of families were clambering into their attics on that day. A couple of families had members too overweight to fit through the entryway into the attic. They drowned as the rest of the family stood helplessly watching.

"The water, it finally come up right up to the ceiling just below us. I figured it was going to keep coming and coming. I had my shotgun and had a box of shells I took up there with me. So, what I did, I took the gun, and I shot in-between the rafters to break a hole in the roof."

There was all kinds of praying and screaming and crying in that attic and many other attics, but the wind was so terrible that no one could hear much. People say it sounded like three freight trains coming through. In another attic without a shotgun—this one out on the front ridge, twenty-nine people drowned.

"I had taken five life preservers up there with me, and a rope. I had my plan made up that I'd make me some knots in the rope—you know, some little handholds, real close together. Like I said, we were nine of us up there. We had two boys that were about twelve or thirteen. Our little girl, she was only ten years old."

At that point Berton had to stop and collect himself. Recalling the tormented hours of Audrey still seemed to short-circuit Berton's memory, and emotion often overpowered orderly recollection.

"In case we have to take to the water, I thought, well, we'll put five of the life preservers on the children and older women and the other four will just hang on to the rope, you know, kind of in a tight circle. That's what I had planned on.

"During the day, every now and then, I'd stick my head out through the hole in the roof, and I could see pieces of houses and logs go past. I saw one go by with a little black fellow on it—going by fast.

"An old cow, I don't know if it was ours, she rubbed against the house floating there in that ten feet of water. She was looking for a way to get on top of the house or something to save herself. But anyway, our seventy-two head we had in the pasture, they disappeared. We found three or four after the hurricane on high land in the Big Lick area."

Before the hurricane, Cameron Parish had about fifty-five thousand head of cattle, and almost twenty thousand of them drowned. They lay rotting everywhere afterward. But Berton said that cows do well when high water comes. If they didn't, all of them would have been lost.

"About two in the afternoon I looked out the east eaves of the attic and I couldn't see my daddy's house. I said, well, the house is gone. All that time, our house shifted around on its cinder blocks, and we had only a single floor at that time. The blocks went through the floor, and the house sank. Probably if we had a two-story floor, it would have been like a boat. In fact, my neighbor's house went and floated off just like a boat; it didn't break up till it was somewhere in the marsh.

"The water was about up to the eaves, and the waves were just like in the Gulf when they are ten feet tall. Every hour I'd look at my watch, and only five minutes had passed."

Berton's neighbor and his wife, just a quarter mile away, crawled onto the roof of their house, but it broke apart. They tried to survive by floating on what was left of it. But they had to fight off all manner of snakes, hogs gone crazy, cattle thrashing to get on what was left of the roof with them. The neighbor's wife was bitten by a poisonous snake and died. Her husband clung to her till they were rescued, miles from where their home once was.

"Finally it stopped," remembered Berton. "So I decided to go towards my daddy's house and see if they'd been able to live through it. I just knew they were drowned. The water was still over waist high, so I took my oldest boy and I put life preservers on us. In places the water was so deep that only our heads were sticking out. We walked down to my daddy's house, and when I got close I could see the old house was still standing." When Berton told me of this discovery he began to cry.

"When I got close, I hollered real loud and nobody answered. I walked a little farther and hollered. Nobody answered. When I got to the front porch and hollered again, I heard my daddy say 'Whoo!' I felt better then." Berton's emotion washed over me.

"Yeah, my mother was there, and her granddaughter and my daddy. You know those old people, they didn't believe in banks. Instead of having their money in the house my mother had a money jar. It was tacked up under a rail of the fence. That was in case the house caught on fire, so the money wouldn't burn. She waded out first thing and got that jar, stepped on a piece of glass and cut her foot wide open. I never did find out how much was in that jar."

I Hug Her
and
Hug Her

Berton Daigle lives today in the same house where he rode out Hurricane Audrey. The hole he shot in his roof was repaired, as was the rest of his flooded home. He doesn't live far from Debbie Therriot, his handpicked successor as clerk of the court and the first woman ever elected to a major office in the parish. Berton was clerk from 1948 to 1976. Debbie has been clerk ever since.

Cameron Parish is imposing in size but small in population; less than ten thousand people live here. Debbie is the kind of natural politician who visited every home in the parish on her way to victory. Her eyes quickly analyze any situation, and she can be anything that is needed, making the transition from tender to testy in a second.

Debbie told me her story in her office, which was decorated in a style borrowed from the pages of *Country Living* magazine. After a couple of minutes she transported herself back to being eighteen again. But first she got up and closed both her office doors.

Debbie was eighteen when Audrey came within a minute of wiping her, her husband, and her parents off the earth. People only had minutes to make up their minds as to how they would try to survive.

Debbie's maiden name was Broussard. Her daddy was slim and wiry and energized like Debbie. He was a professional duck hunting guide, alligator hunter, and muskrat and nutria trapper. She is of the first generation in her family to make a living from a full-time job rather than from the marsh. Her daddy only took outside work when he had to, doing carpentry or taking seasonal jobs at the refineries or in construction.

Debbie was the son her daddy never had and went everywhere he went in the marsh, did everything he did. When he went to capture gators by sticking poles with hooks on the end down the holes where they lived and snagging them, she grabbed hold and pulled, too. She became one of the fastest muskrat skinners in the world, competing at the world championships for muskrat and nutria skinning in Maryland. Her childhood on Little Chenier (*chenier* being the French word for ridge), roaming the hundreds of thousands of acres of marsh that surrounded them on all sides, definitely helped her live through the panic and horror of Audrey.

"We were just sittin' in my mama and daddy's house talking about the storm, not expecting anything real bad, when Daddy said, 'Look, them houses in Creole sure are close.'"

Those houses her daddy saw, usually about five miles across the marsh, were riding atop a twenty-foot tidal wave coming right at their narrow little ridge.

"We never worried about storms until Hurricane Audrey hit here. And since then, it's been watch out for the storms and run from the storms when they come in." A dullness came over her usually sparkling Cajun eyes.

"My husband was working in New Orleans for Crane Brothers then, and he had just come in around four in the morning. We were very fortunate that he did, because he probably saved our lives. I was staying at my mom and dad's house. He told us that they had been sent home because there was a hurricane coming in and we said, 'A what?' And so we started listening on the radio, and before we even heard too much about it, the tidal wave hit."

Debbie's husband, Jerry, is from a place called Grand Chenier. His brother is a member of the internationally famous Cajun band, The Hackberry Ramblers. Debbie and Jerry met at a high-school 4-H exhibition when she modeled an apron trimmed in red that she'd made as a project.

"In Little Chenier we had twenty foot of water, and it all came at one time on a big wave. In that wave were houses, drowned people, animals, snakes, fish, trees, everything. It hit here about seven in the morning." At that point Debbie got up again and told her assistant to hold her calls. She knew what was coming.

"Some of the Creole houses that rode that wave got caught right there on the high side of our one-and-only road that dead ends on Little Chenier, where our house was. Me, my mama, daddy and granddaddy, and

Debbie Therriot, clerk of the court, is the first elected woman in Cameron Parish. She stands with the sheriff everyone calls "Sun-o." Both have survived some wicked storms, but none worse than Hurricane Audrey.

our kids all grew up there." Once, the only way to Little Chenier had been by boat. Debbie had to take one to go to school.

"Then all of a sudden, when that biggest wave came over the road, our house fell apart. We ran and got into one of our marsh boats. We were lucky. We stored all the boats in a boathouse right behind our house. We had only a couple of minutes to do something. All four of us got into a boat, but we couldn't get it started. So we just tied it onto the boathouse until the boathouse blew away, and then we just rode the waves all day in that boat." Now the slow-motion, all-day terror would begin.

"Well, our boat was just a little flatboat about eighteen or twenty feet long and about three feet wide. Jerry and I and my parents were in that boat all day. Actually, we were in and out of the boat. You know, we'd get blown or thrown out, but then we'd catch ahold of the boat and get back in. I don't know how we survived, but it was just like fighting for your life for the next twelve hours, because we were rescued about seven that night.

"The winds were real strong. They would pick up the whole boat. At times we were airborne because the winds were so strong.

"Sometimes we could see around us, sometimes we couldn't. You'd see people you knew all your life blowing by you on some board, a piece of tree. One time we saw a horse standing on top of the side of a barn, surfing by, literally standing atop that wood. All the animals, everything still alive, were trying to find something to crawl on, and they'd crawl into the side of our boat and turn our boat over. We were turned over a whole bunch of times. But we always managed, the four of us, to get back in the boat. Most of the time, I was tied to the boat or tied to Jerry because I was so tiny at that time that the wind would lift me up and try to take me with it.

"My mother, she was just hanging on. And dad, before he got his eyes injured, he would help her. He was a terrific swimmer, even though he was a little fellow. But he had some eye damage during that storm—all that stuff blowing in his eyes. By the end of the hurricane he couldn't see anymore.

"My grandpa and relatives were living next door to us, and we saw their house take off while we were tied to the boathouse. So we thought, well, that's the end of them. During the day, we could see grandpa's house at a distance, floating like a boat. A couple of times we came close enough to shout to them through the windows. Their house floated all day long and didn't take on enough water even to ruin the furniture. Jerry even tried one time when they were close to get out of the boat and swim to the house. But there was no way. The waves were immense, the undertow terrible.

"Before this, about the only thing I'd ever been afraid of was snakes, but not that day. We shared our boat with them. They'd be curled up right next to us. It seemed like every living thing knew we were all just trying to live.

"Finally after twelve hours we ended up in the Intracoastal Canal, which was about twelve miles through the marsh from our house. We had to have been going around and around in circles that whole time. We saw a tugboat anchored there, waiting out the storm. They took us aboard."

As soon as they went aboard they told the captain about all the other people that must have been washed onto the banks of the Intracoastal.

Debbie wanted to go looking for her grandpa's house, the one they'd seen bobbing like a cork.

"They got the tug running, and we found people and animals all up and down the levee of the canal. There was one woman we found, she'd had all her clothes blown off her. She was standing there in shock, surrounded by soaking wet cattle, hundreds of snakes, mad nutria. It was terrible. She had been on a piece of wood with her mother, but her mom drowned. She was the only one in her family who survived."

"We knew for sure that there were people all along this levee, so we ran that tug until dark and picked up people. The first thing we came to was grandpa's. And they were all in there waiting for somebody to come pick them up. The house was just leaning on that levee. Later on they got a tugboat and a barge and went out there and barged it back to where it had been on Little Chenier."

Certain of Debbie's memories of the storm time were coming back to her, ones she did not want to remember. She bowed her head. She was about to get to what for her was the most devastating event of the whole nightmare. But first she told me this story.

"There was a lady from the Grand Chenier ridge that was found east of here in the marshes on a tiny piece of high ground. She was an older lady. They figured she'd probably survived about two or three weeks after the hurricane. They could see where she had walked around and where she had made herself a place to sleep and stuff like that." She died before the rescuers got to her.

I know that Debbie wonders if the same fate befell her best friend. Her eyes glazed over and her complexion turned a white shade of gray when she told me about Belva Boudoin. "Well, my very best friend through all of school was Belva. We had just graduated from high school, and Belva was going to be married in three weeks. She was so happy. She was to marry this fine, good-looking, strapping young man. I was going to be her maid of honor. We had bought all the clothes. We had already been to church in Creole to rehearse for the wedding and everything.

"Belva was tall and thin, had long, curly black hair. She was a real beautiful girl, a Cajun beauty. If she had been born in a later time, she could have gone to New York and been a model.

"Now Belva had always been scared of the water. We'd go swimming, and Belva would just sit as far from the water as she could because she was scared of it." Being afraid of the water in southern Louisiana is a bad fear to have, because water is about all there is.

"I'm sure she panicked when that tidal wave came up. She was at my godmother's house spending the night when it hit us all. They lived on

The narrow road that goes down Little Chenier, an islandlike ridge surrounded by marsh, where Debbie Therriot lives. When Debbie was a little girl this place was reachable only by boat. Cajun families have lived here for generations, surviving in the circling marshes by fishing, running a few cows, and hunting alligators, ducks, and muskrats.

Little Chenier, too. My godmother drowned, her two kids drowned, and so did Belva, they say." Debbie picked up a pen and tapped it on top of her desk. "The only one that survived was my godmother's husband. He climbed up in a tree. He said he put the others on a mattress, and that was the last he saw of them." She released a long, painful sigh.

"We never found Belva. She may have been found and not identified. They said you couldn't tell who anyone was; you couldn't even tell black from white. I'm forever having dreams about being on vacation somewheres and seeing Belva on the side of the road or in a crowd in a mall. She is just there." Debbie's had this same dream for thirty-five years.

"In my dream, Belva's been hit on the head and she has amnesia. She doesn't know who she is. When I find her, she doesn't know who she is, and she doesn't know who I am. I go running to her and hug her and hug her."

She Got Up
and
Shook It All

Less than a mile down the road from the Cameron Parish Court-house and Debbie's office, on the concrete building by the ferry that goes to Monkey Island, someone has painted a mural. Billy and Red used to shrimp a lot off Cameron Parish. If they tore their nets up, they had told me, they would come into port to C. J. Kiffe's Net Shop, near the mural, and get them repaired.

Framing one side of the mural is a leaping tarpon. Framing the other side is a jumping largemouth bass. In the center, large letters spell out: WELCOME TO CAMERON—No pollution, no traffic light, no big city life, no city police, no trains, just boats.

The mural features a hand-lettered list: "Things to see in Cameron: The Louisiana Fur & Wildlife Festival. The Southwest Louisiana Deep Sea and Inland Fishing Rodeo. Fish, ducks, alligators, muskrats, nutria, birds, shrimp, and deer." Also, it says, "There are 2,500 public-spirited citizens." The very last bit of writing on the mural says, "Don't blink twice or you'll miss the time of your life."

"Don't blink or you'll miss the *party* of your life!" should be lit up in neon on a blimp every Fourth of July, when thousands head for Holly Beach, the rustic center of the Cajun Riviera. *Every* Fourth of July weekend people come to the Cajun Riviera for one of the most outrageous human spectacles in the nation. It's a time of endless revelry I would not have believed if I'd not been there.

Why has this annual Cajun Woodstock never been covered live by MTV or CMT or *Nightline?* The only reason, surely, is that they haven't heard about it yet.

To get to Holly Beach, one has to make a pilgrimage through miles of uninterrupted marsh. The marsh goes on for hundreds of square miles, surrounding Holly Beach on three sides. And yet thousands of people congregate every year on this isolated spot. And this happens in the southern third of Louisiana, where the word *inhibitions* has a totally different meaning than it does in the top two-thirds of the state.

Most people on their way to the Cajun Riviera from Cameron cross the Calcasieu River by ferry. Once across the river, they take Highway 82, the southernmost road in the parish, west to Holly Beach.

On either side of the road, small drainage ditches are crowded with water hyacinth, their light purple flowers giving the marsh and swamp a rest from endless green. Turtles with duckweed drying on their black shells sit on anything that will hold them out of the water, even the skeleton of a cow. Squashed armadillos lie on the road in various states of decomposition, dreaded fire ants feeding on them. But the stream of people from every Cajun town in Louisiana does not really notice. These adventurers, traveling down Route 82 at seventy-five or eighty-five miles per hour, have only one thing on their minds. It's time for a major blowout, the kind that full-blooded, full-time southern Louisiana natives can handle with ease.

Whole families come to blast off here, year after year, from rice- and crawfish-growing towns like Mermentau, Jennings, Crowley, and Gueydan. They also flow in from larger cities like Lafayette, Lake Charles, and even New Orleans. Once at Holly Beach, it's about fifteen miles of hot, stinking, muddy marsh in every direction to any kind of a place with a name. The surrounding marsh keeps the people herded in.

After a day or two at the Riviera a lot of the people forget for hours at a time where they are, even forgetting what planet they're on. For me it was a little like being on another planet, except that the aliens looked pretty much like me. Actually, I was the alien here.

In most of America you have to go to the big city or far away from home to break loose, dance, sing, shout, and "act a fool." Not in southern Louisiana. And when a lot of folks in America cut the ties that bind them, loosen their collars to jump and shout, they tend to do it with their own age group. Not in southern Louisiana. When these Luu-zee-ana people come together on the Cajun Riviera to frolic, they do it all together. A six-year-old will be laughing and whooping it up with a sixty-eight-year-old. There will be thirty-year-olds shaking it with seventy-seven-year-olds, and fifteen-year-olds hanging out with their parents.

Holly Beach consists of just a few streets, some sand, some paved; the main one runs just off the beach for a bit more than a mile. The water in the Gulf here is very muddy, but compared to the brown swamp and canal water it does have a sea-greenish tint. The native people say it's pretty. There are several rough-built cottages that look a little like Louisiana hunting camps. Only a handful of people live on the Cajun Riviera year-round. Those that do place aluminum foil in their windows to keep the blasting sun away.

I'd been invited to this Cajun blowout by the former Miss Sweet Potato of Louisiana, Shannon Suire. Actually, her official title a few years back was Miss Yambilee, referring to the better-sounding local word for the sweet potato. Shannon's daddy flies a crop-dusting plane and owns a flying service out of the big rice-growing town of Gueydan.

Shannon and I met when we were both judges of a crab cook-off up the road in Hackberry. (Two guys in their thirties won with a fabulous grilled blue crab.) During the judging, Shannon told me what went on at the Cajun Riviera. She said that her boyfriend and her parents and other family were all there, staying in her aunt's house right on the main sand road. She also said proudly that her daddy, Lloyd, cooked the best speckled-belly goose and that the view from their deck was amazing.

I went, I saw, I cruised. I was amazed.

The focal point of all the celebration, the place where everyone centers their jumping and playing, is the main sand road right off the beach. This road is jammed with masses of people and cars. They all walk and ride at about two miles an hour. They go up the road and then down it, then up it, down it, again and again, on and on for days. The procession never stops, it only slows down a bit between three and seven in the morning.

At first I found myself judgmental, uptight. There were so many pickup trucks, so many thousands of people so much rowdier than I. And I wasn't twenty-two anymore. But how could I feel that way? I drive a pickup, too—a super cab. I handled Woodstock. Come on, Peter, chill out.

I jumped into the back of some stranger's pickup. Four Louisiana State University students were already in it. They had no idea who was driving. Three of them seemed to know what year it was; the other one was gone, out, numb. They all had super squirt guns, and they handed me the one that belonged to their "sleeping" friend.

Those guns shoot a long way, more than a hundred feet. Everyone was drenching everyone else. One guy tried to shoot me at point-blank range. He missed.

Two ladies, around sixty-five, sat in folding lawn chairs in a small yard right off the sand road. Next to them were multicolored piles of water balloons that they threw at anyone they pleased. Behind them, for backup, was a man about their age with a high-pressure hose. He was drenching anyone who dared attack them, or was he just saturating everyone in range? Just about everyone who drove by shot squirt guns at the ladies; their red shorts were soaked. Hysterical laughter followed people everywhere as they ducked down or ran for cover.

The bottle-blonde person driving the flamingo pink custom-lowered IROC-Z Camaro behind us had pulled her wiper blades out so she could place empty beer cans on them. When she turned on the wipers, the cans rattled back and forth and back and forth, hypnotizing the car's occupants and making it easier to endure going one or two miles per hour all day long.

Behind the pink Camaro, a canary yellow Toyota truck had picked up another passenger. She was young, bikini-clad, and weighed at least 250 pounds. Her black eyebrows were very thick and grew together in the middle. She had the words *Wild Thing* painted on the widest part of a very wide, white body. It appeared that until today her body had never before been touched by the sun. If she heard a song she loved on some truck's jammin', bammin' speakers, she got up and shook it all. She had a lot that shook.

The song "Achy Breaky Heart" seemed to be playing in every fifth truck or car. That hit competed with blasting heavy-metal tunes by Metallica. Once I heard the Spin Doctors. It was crushing hot, but no one was in an ornery mood. The train of people driving on the sand road never moved faster than a creep, always bumper to bumper. A coal black Camaro had its hatchback open and four or five college types crammed in it. A rap song was pounding out of the car, the point of the song being "big butts."

Some ingenious type had painted a big white X in his yard and dared everyone to drive by and hit it or him with their empty cans. His yard was at least two feet deep with aluminum cans, which he would surely take to a recycler. Stunning, deeply tanned Cajun ladies, some in Day-Glo pink and purple thong bikinis sauntered by.

The sheriff, a man everyone called Sun-o, had all his deputies here, but *they* were from southern Louisiana, too. This is a rite of their people. They were here just to make sure that everyone kept on having a good time and no one got too wild or got really stupid. Southern Louisiana's definitions of "too wild" and "really stupid" are not the same as the rest of the United States. Still, if there were any fights, I never saw one.

Right before I left to go back to my boat, a slim young woman in her twenties ambled by with a four-foot-long, bright green lizard gripping hold of her chest. I thought it was a tattoo until I saw it move.

The Suires fed me baked wild goose and invited me to stay another day, but I wasn't ready for another day of going up and down and up and down the sand road. I could see that even I would take awhile to feel at home on the Cajun Riviera on the Fourth of July.

When I got back to my security blanket, the *Cooper,* I turned on the radio so I could sing while I cleaned. I wanted to get the boat shining because tomorrow I'd be in Texas.

A preacher was shouting and praising the Lord at a camp meeting nearby; he said he was in Iota, Louisiana. He sounded young and energetic. He shouted that the praise, the laughing, the miracles were in abundance.

"Will you clap your hands and shout to the Lord for what he has done? Would you worship him? Hallelujah!" The preacher yelled as loud as anyone I'd ever heard on the radio.

"Listen to me now, people!" he kept on. "I've just gotten a word from the Lord. WOW! Hallelujah!" He paused.

"People, you people, and people within the sound of my voice, *right now,*" he shouted louder for emphasis, "*right now* you are being healed, even though you weren't going to get your disease for six months. Cancer, right now! Healed before it ever even begins!"

The preacher breathed out his intensity like it was fire. This was the first time I'd heard of people being healed six months before the disease began.

"Right now! You are healed of that ulcer you were going to develop! AMEN!

"If you have been healed by the Lord tonight, and you know that you have been healed, would you put your hands up and wave them? I see that hand. Yes, I see that hand. Thank GOD! This is in America! It's happening for us here tonight!"

A lot of amazing stuff was happening in Louisiana this weekend among all God's people.

But then, a lot is always happening in Louisiana.

Straight
and
True

I rumbled out of the port of Cameron along with the pogy boats, which were headed out for their day of fishing. Their spotter planes flew overhead looking for schools of pogies, or menhaden, small fish rich in oil. The winds were nice to all of us in the Gulf today.

I was heading west, the last bit of Louisiana coast off to my right. Texas, the next (and last) state whose coast I would explore, was about thirty miles away. This journey began slowly, with its year of preparation, but now the end seemed to be approaching quickly. My anxiety with running and navigating the boat had been replaced long ago with the thrill of discovery. I'd become lost in the stories of people I'd been meeting.

This trip had revitalized me, reaffirmed that at age forty I could still take on substantial challenges. My spirit of adventure was not imprisoned in my imagination or my memory.

But this voyage was still far from over. It would end when I got to the Rio Grande River on the Mexican border, and that was 450 miles of shoreline farther away.

When I left places on my walk across America, they disappeared from view so slowly. In the wide-open West, I could look back for days and still see what I'd left. Now I could blow away from my last stop and it was gone in minutes. Because of the speed and power of my boat, I had to look ahead, not back.

The speed and power of the *Cooper* and the freedom it gave me to keep moving, to escape, to never be vulnerable was addictive. Why ever stop, anywhere? Why not just blow by every place? Stopping could be such a hassle—reaching out to strangers, being vulnerable, finding a new place to keep the *Cooper* and me. But stopping, opening up to others, was exactly where the richness was.

I could not have done this particular boat trip when I was twenty-two. I had to do the walk first, to learn to slow down, to be vulnerable, to understand both how different and how alike people can be. I had been exploring the Gulf for about a year and a half so far. When I was twenty, I probably would have come from the Keys to here in two weeks.

The way for me to get into Texas was through Sabine Pass. (The Sabine River forms the boundary between Texas and Louisiana.) If the waves and wind were in a gentle mood, I would stay in the Gulf till I got to Galveston and the Bolivar Peninsula. But if the cotton-shaped cumulus clouds coming in from the south started looming dark gray and threatening thunder, then I'd pull in through Sabine Pass and head down into Texas in the Intracoastal Waterway.

The afternoon sky turned a gray black. Today I was not in a mood to challenge nature. I headed for the Sabine.

The Intracoastal Canal was beautifully smooth. Cattle grazed near its eroded edge, and muscular Braford bulls immersed themselves in the water to escape the Texas summer sun. The bulls looked like hippos.

I was spacing out. The heaviness of the humid heat and the blinding sunlight were taking control of my eyelids and shutting them. It had been hot and humid like this when Luke and Jed had joined me back in Louisiana. That first day I had let them steer the *Cooper* on the Intracoastal, and they were far too excited to be sleepy.

I had let Jed steer the boat first, then taught him to accelerate from zero to thirty-five miles per hour, then taught him how to go in circles by putting one motor in forward, the other in reverse.

Of course, seven-year-old Luke had to do exactly what Jed did, and if possible *before* he did it. But when it was his turn, Luke seemed to have trouble steering the *Cooper.* He kept veering off to the left, then he'd veer off to the right, headed straight for the canal bank.

I stood next to my redheaded son and watched. He held the stainless-steel steering wheel so proudly, so strongly in his long, narrow, freckled fingers. He so wanted to please me, to show me he could do whatever I wanted him to, to do at least as well as his big brother, Jed. But again he veered left, then right.

What was wrong? It was so easy for Jed and me to keep the *Cooper* in the middle of the canal. The water was perfectly smooth, like a long mirror. But Luke couldn't seem to steer in a straight line.

After ten minutes of gently correcting Luke, I was getting irritated. I struggled to overcome my annoyance. Patience had never been my strong suit. I try to make a special effort to be patient with my children, even though I want all of them to be able to do many things well—and do them almost immediately. I knew Luke was the kind of child who had to do things exactly as I did them. If I sat in the captain's seat and swung my legs while I drove, he did that. If I stood a certain way, my hands on my hips, he stood that way.

Again, Luke almost ran into the bank of the canal. "Luke, why can't you keep the boat in the middle of the canal?" I did not like my tone of voice, tension connected each word.

He was obviously hurt. I bent down on one knee and put my arm around his slight but pugnacious shoulder. I looked forward. And I saw nothing but the console, the wheel. I couldn't see the canal or anything else in front of us.

No wonder. Now I really felt like an idiot. I kissed Luke on his cheek. He squirmed into my affection, relieved.

"Luke."

"Yes, Dad."

"How can you steer the boat if you can't see at all?"

"I don't know, Dad." His jaw was firmly set. "I was just doing it just like you did, that's all."

"Well, buddy. Let's get you a couple of life-preserver cushions so you can sit on the chair and see, too."

"OK, Dad."

From then on Luke held a course as straight and true as an arrow in flight.

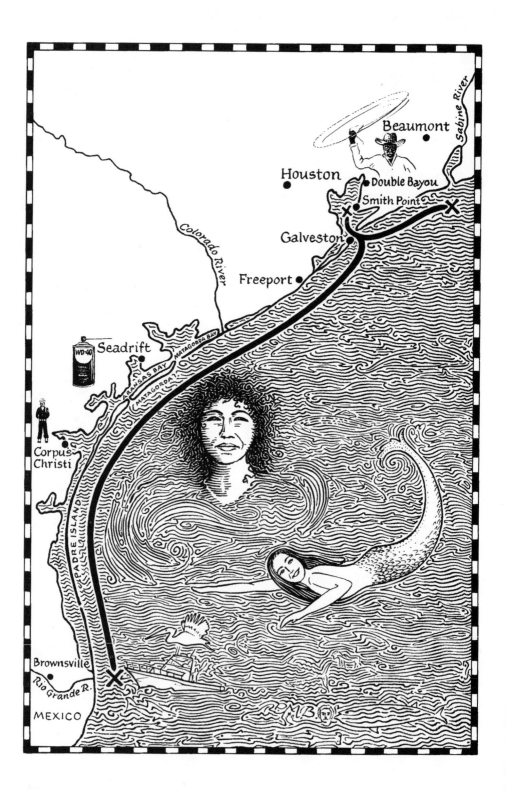

Beaumont

Houston

Double Bayou

Smith Point

Galveston

Freeport

Seadrift

WD-40

ARANSAS BAY

MATAGORDA BAY

(MATAGORDA I.)

Colorado River

Sabine River

Corpus
Christi

PADRE ISLAND

Brownsville

Rio Grande R.

MEXICO

CHAPTER 42

Judge Jackson
and the
Wedding

his Texas judge uses an abandoned school for his office. He holds court every so often in the old cafeteria. Usually the crime is nothing too serious—stealing oysters off a private reef in the bay, taking someone else's calf (intending to eat it), occasionally a bit of bodily harm. Or having six people on a boat with only four life preservers. That was my offense. Somewhere I'd lost two of the life preservers from the *Cooper*. The wildlife officer, out protecting the wildlife, had pulled me over and given me a ticket. That's how I came to meet the local judge, Quinten Jackson. I had to go before him at the old school and pay my ticket.

Quinten Jackson comes from a prominent Chambers County family. His great-great-granddaddy, Humphrey Jackson, came to the area in 1823 as one of the first white Texans. Quinten wears tight-fitting jeans and scuffed Nocona boots dusted with dry dirt. He always carries a handgun, and his spurs are polished by years of wear. A person in this part of Texas, the coastal-plains cow country I call the sand-land, never knows when he'll need his spurs, and Jackson's spurs have spoken to many a high-spirited horse.

The judge wears a wide-brimmed hat but usually takes it off in his office. He sits with his feet up on his desk next to a framed picture of his handsome son in a football uniform.

Everything in this part of Texas has a lot of space around it. Early land-grant ranches once were more than a hundred miles across. They're not quite as never-ending anymore, but five, twenty, sixty thousand acres of land

I went before Judge Jackson, justice of the peace, to pay a ticket.

isn't small either. "Big" in Texas can be, and should be, a birthright, not something to pay a lot of attention to.

Quinten, age sixty-two, is justice of the peace for District 3, a part of Chambers County, Texas. District 3 extends out into Galveston Bay; it has almost as much water as it does land. The land is sand-land, and it juts out into the brackish bay like a thumb. On the south side of this thumb of land is East Bay; on the north side, Trinity Bay. Looking west is Galveston Bay, and it's only forty miles to the center of Houston. But although the sand-land and the sprawling city are geographically close, they remain about a hundred years apart. And there's no doubt among the sand-land people as to which place is the better world to live in.

Long before any Texans settled here, sailing ships used to know when they were near the sand-land because the Gulf waters would darken with oil slicks, natural seepage from oil deposits near the surface. But when the Jacksons were granted much of this land, long before Texas was a state, no one had any idea that the greasy black stuff would eventually make some of the settlers fabulously wealthy and leave others with none at all.

Judge Jackson's district stretches east to the Barrows Ranch, and takes in the communities of Double Bayou, Smith Point, and Oak Island. If someone drowns in the bay, Judge Jackson presides over the inquest. If there is shooting, Judge Jackson is there. If some lovesick couple "done been fussin' and fightin'" and the relatives are worried maybe they might hurt each other, Quinten goes over and tries to calm everyone down. He calls them by their first names and usually has the angriest one sit down with him while gently suggesting to the other to ease off into the yard and walk around.

Judge Jackson knows about everyone here and what they do. Usually he has a good idea why they misbehave—because Ron lost his job at the auto parts store, because Lucille's not been taking her medication, because Joselle's back to drinkin', and because every couple of years Ricky just has to hit somebody.

Performing occasional marriage ceremonies is one of Quinten's more joyous duties. Late one Friday afternoon a couple of years ago, when Quinten was getting ready to go home for the day, two men and a woman came into his office. The men were freshly shaven; they had on clean slacks and button-down shirts. The woman was average-pretty, probably in her late twenties.

"Hey," the three addressed Quinten. Because of his cowboy dress, they assumed he was here to see the judge, too.

"Howdy," Quinten answered.

"You seen the judge?" they asked.

"Sure have. You're looking at him." They seemed relieved to see that he was dressed like a rancher-cowboy.

"Judge," said the older man, gesturing toward his companions, "these two lovebirds got plans to get married in a couple weeks. They wanted to come out here and have the ceremony. It'd be a good chance for them to get away from Houston, with all them niggers and Mexicans and chinks and Jews."

The reference silenced Quinten a minute. He didn't appreciate their attitude. There were plenty of blacks out here amongst the ranches—people he'd known his whole life, many that had cowboyed on his family's ranch. Double Bayou was a mostly black country community of some fifty or seventy-five families. There were plenty of whites, too, and Mexican cowboys and oyster workers.

He knew his three visitors weren't from around here because he knew everyone who was. He suspected they might be members of the Ku Klux Klan. He was well aware that the Klan was using a local ranch as a paramilitary training base.

Quinten asked them straight, a Texas tradition, "You boys part of that bunch out at the ranch, doing that training with the automatic weapons and all?"

"We sure are." The KKK lovebirds were holding hands. "We like this here country of yours. All we want is to have a quiet family-style weddin'. Would you perform it for us?"

Quinten was quiet for a long time, considering. He did not want to marry them, but he was elected to serve the people regardless of their race or creed. And Quinten, he's a sly old country boy, he couldn't help what else he was thinking. They probably didn't know that his brain was racing a thousand miles an hour, debating, feeling so many things. They probably just thought these old country boys out in the depths of Chambers County think slow. But Quinten had other reasons as to why he might just go ahead and marry the KKK members.

"All right," Quinten finally said obligingly. "I'll help y'all out."

That young couple seemed so happy they'd be able to have the wedding where the air was clean and the people were "good," far away from "that nasty Houston." They told Quinten the date, time, and about a pretty spot where they'd like to have the ceremony—on the banks of a bayou, by a green field filled with wildflowers and widespreading live oak trees. It was on the ranch where they were training for race warfare. The older man slapped Quinten on the back as they left, a show of affection.

Time passed, the Saturday of the wedding came. Fluffy white clouds flew overhead, blowing like sheets on a clothesline. A bunch of cars bounced down the gravel road to the wedding site, carrying the guests and the marriage party. None of the cars were from Chambers County. None of the guests knew Quinten and his family.

Quinten figured the man getting married must have been a high-ranking Dragon in the Klan. A couple of Grand Dragons were in attendance. But nobody wore white sheets. Quinten wore the same suit he would wear for any wedding.

It was the kind of warm, easy day when people naturally put their arms around each other. Kids were everywhere, running and giggling. The kids seemed to take a liking to Quinten. They followed him everywhere he went; they wanted him to hold their hands, lead them around.

Quinten had no idea if there was some kind of special ceremony KKK members used. Did they pledge allegiance to their Dragons, swear that they would uphold certain beliefs? This worried Quinten, even though they'd assured him he would just follow the normal, legal wedding ceremony and pronounce them man and wife.

The ceremony was uneventful. Afterward, the couple kissed and gave Quinten a big hug. The lady kissed his cheek. Everybody went off to celebrate, and Quinten went on home.

Quinten often wonders if the KKK lovebirds he married have ever learned that he is part black. He often smiles thinking about it.

Sand-land Texans are a distinctly different breed than their southern-Louisiana neighbors. They react differently to living where hurricanes rule, where the ground is often not ground at all, but a shallow lake. They don't laugh and dance and lay back as much as the people of southern Louisiana. But most of these coastal Texans react to the eruptions of heat and humidity and violent tornadoes and hurricanes a little more philosophically than Mr. Martin, who moved to the edge of the marsh by the Whitehead ranch when Joe Whitehead was a boy.

During my time on the sand-land, I stayed on the Whitehead's ranch with Joe and his wife, Annette. Joe, a veterinarian as well as a full-time rancher, explained the people of the sand-land to me. He told me about Mr. Martin and his small ranch next to a grove of live oaks.

"Mr. Martin, he came here from Kansas," Joe told me one twilight evening when we were checking out part of his cow herd. "He wouldn't do much work; he'd just sit on the porch and rock. He figured if he built anything, a hurricane was going to come by and wash it away and destroy it. I guess he probably lived through four or five little hurricanes over the years, but nothing really major. His house burned down after he died.

"Eventually," said Joe, "you're going to lose most everything you build around here. It may be fifty years. It may be ten years, or maybe next month, but your barns and everything else are going to go one of these days. Then you just build all over again."

We came to the edge of a large pasture, maybe seventy-five acres. "You see how there is a lane between those two barbed-wire fences?" The gap wasn't wide enough to drive down, so I had figured it was used to run cattle through. But Joe told me there was another reason for it. That gap was a direct result of pure spite.

Joe Whitehead was a laughing man. He joked a lot about his bald head and his once-flat stomach, about the floods and the fire ants. But those who don't laugh enough—those who let the brutality of the environment in this part of Texas get to them—easily get mean. It happens to cows, and it happens to people.

Joe explained the reason for the fence. "Yeah, some neighbors here who didn't get along with each other would build their fence four feet back into their property line. That way nobody could tie into their fence. The other landowner would have to build a totally separate fence if he wanted to fence his cattle in, or he'd be trespassing. And trespassing can be dangerous around here—a reason to use a gun."

Like a lot of places where just about everybody knows your name, the sand-land had some prominent families. Joe listed them for me. There were the Jacksons—the white Jacksons and the black Jacksons. There were the Whites—the black Whites and the white Whites. And there were the white Whiteheads. There were no black Whiteheads, at least not that Joe knew of.

I just had to ask if there were any black Blacks or white Blacks. There weren't.

It wasn't easy keeping the families of the sand-land straight. There were the black Jacksons who look white, like Quinten. There were also white Jacksons who had been tinted dark by the sun. There were some really ebony-skinned Whites.

Joe and Annette Whitehead were related to the white Jacksons and the black Jacksons because Joe's great-grandmother was John Jackson's aunt. John Jackson was Quinten's grandfather. The Jackson who started it all was Humphrey Jackson, born in 1784 in Belfast, Ireland. His father owned flour and linen mills and was a member of the Irish Parliament. Humphrey first settled in New Orleans, then bought a sugar plantation up the Mississippi. There he married Sara and they had four children; their eldest son was Quinten's great-great-grandfather. The Jacksons left Louisiana with Stephen F. Austin's three hundred original white colonists of Texas. (To be descended from one of Austin's three hundred original pioneers is thought by many Texans to be superior to being the first man on the moon.)

Quinten's grandfather, John Jackson, was the wealthiest man in Chambers County. A local newspaper article, written in 1927, described the old man this way:

> He had to be drawn out before he would talk of the hard times when there wasn't a fence between Trinity Bay and Beaumont. He rode in one of American's finest automobiles. A great 8 cylinder, which made the dirt road sometimes non bumpy. He was a thin man, not too thin, but healthily slim and as straight as a poker. One would take him for 65. (He was 80+ at the time.) He is rated to be the wealthiest man in Chambers County and he doesn't deny the charge. He wore a cow-man's great hat and a soft, and expensive flannel shirt. His old vest, the mark of the boss rancher, was open. On his face was a light gray beard but the outstanding thing about this man was his smile that came from his mouth and eyes.

Quinten must have inherited this trait because when he smiles his whole face lights up.

In those days, in that part of Texas, people measured worldly wealth by how many cows a man had and how much land he owned. But some people around here also measured a man's worth in the sand-land by how well he took care of his children, and they judged John Jackson wealthy in that respect as well. John never married, although he had five children with a woman of color named Charlotte Lewis. Charlotte was born in 1859; she was eleven years younger than John. Quinten told me his grandmother was light skinned, a gentle woman whom he thought was probably part Cajun, part black, maybe some Native American. "She was all mixed together like a lot of us Americans," he said.

John and Charlotte's family was no secret in Chambers County; everyone knew about it. Their children's names were Lena, Felix, Arthur, Mavis, and Ocie. John saw to it that they all went to college if they wished; he spent a lot of time with them and his grandchildren to come. Quinten remembers his slim, white-bearded granddaddy stooping far down to play with his toy trucks in the dry dirt at his Grandmother Charlotte's house.

When John Jackson died in 1934, he left twenty thousand of his driest and highest acres to a white nephew. He left the rest, more than ten thousand acres, to the three sons he had with Charlotte. At the time, decades before integration, this was a radical thing to do. Still, the twenty thousand acres that went to the white side was considered the best land, because then the most valuable land was where cattle could be raised. The ten thousand acres willed to the part-black sons was closest to the marsh and often too wet to run cattle on.

When the will was written, John Jackson surely did not know that oil
and gas would soon be found in lands like these, that some of America's
biggest fortunes would flow from this sand-land where few wanted to live.
And so it came to pass that one of the most productive oil fields in Texas
history would be found on those ten thousand acres left to John's three
boys. One of them was Arthur, Quinten's father. Almost no oil was found
on the twenty thousand acres of high ground left to the white nephew.

The Jacksons' oil field was called Oyster Bayou. At times that field has
generated more than ten thousand dollars a day from its thirty-nine wells.
But all those riches never corrupted John Jackson's sons. Felix, Arthur, and
Ocie spent their lives on the family land, kept on raising cattle, gave away a
lot of money to black colleges, and loaned a fair amount of it to their
neighbors (white and black). Everyone says they did their giving and loan-
ing in the Bible way, "without letting your right hand know what your left
hand was doing."

Shaped
by a
Horse

The Whitehead ranch headquarters was a large, comfortable, yet austere home surrounded with low-built barns for storing hay, tractors, welders, and tools. It was a hundred yards off Highway 562, just a couple of miles from Smith Point, on the very tip of the peninsula. Smith Point has a little store where Joe gets his *Houston Post* every day.

In front of Joe and Annette's home was a shallow pond surrounded by haunting cypress trees that had been planted by Joe's father. The trees' brown-red trunks contrasted brightly with the blinding green of the duck-weed that covered most of the pond's surface. In the afternoons, heifers wandered here to drink the water.

The corrals at the Whitehead ranch were state of the art. Joe's squeeze chutes were capable of holding the wildest stock. And the stock in this area could be extremely wild. Some of Joe's neighbors' cows were truly savage, eager for the opportunity to spear any human with their wicked horns.

One of the main things that made the cattle mean around here is the environment. The pressure-cooker humidity, earth-sweeping hurricanes, and flesh-eating fire ants combined to make this area one of the most brutal in the state.

The cows and bulls roaming this place require cowboys and horses as rough-tough as could be found. There used to be plenty of both, but when I visited there weren't many left. That was why Ralph Holmes, age seventy-

A cypress pond near the Whitehead ranch headquarters.

two, still cowboyed for one ranch and another. He worked for Joe Whitehead a lot.

Ralph had been a professional cowboy since he was twelve years old—and there are few anywhere in the world who could claim that they had been cowboying for sixty years. That's cowboying on a working ranch, not show-biz rodeoing. Ralph, who was once a champion rodeo calf roper, knows the difference well.

The first time I saw Ralph was from behind. He'd pulled his new gray Dodge pickup truck and horse trailer into the yard of Joe's ranch headquarters. He was walking back toward the truck, leading his slim-built, white-faced horse. And I could see that the space between Ralph's legs had been permanently formed in the exact shape of a horse's midsection. Like a Chinese woman's foot that has been bound to become small, Ralph's bone structure had been permanently altered by many decades in the saddle.

Ralph's leather chaps had been etched by thorns that slap and gouge; he wore them because he had to. His hat had deep, saturated stains from hundreds of unforgiving roundups. Ralph wore gold-rim glasses now. His gray moustache was carefully trimmed. He moved like a Zen master. His arms didn't swing. He kept them poised at his side, always ready to yank back on the reins, reach for his rope, pull his hat down harder in a wind, or brace for a charging cow.

Working cattle on the Whitehead ranch. Most cattle are part Brahma, bred to survive the brutal heat and humidity and ceaseless cold winter rains, not to mention hurricanes, clouds of mosquitoes, fire ants, and rustlers. What kind of people thrive here? Most that I met were hard-headed, unrelenting individualists.

Ralph stepped strong, yet his boots did not move fast. In this dead-on summer heat, nothing moved fast unless it thought it was running for its life.

Ralph's horse, whom he called Bald, was rangy and long-legged. Ralph told me he was mostly quarter horse but part thoroughbred, a combination Ralph liked on the stretched-out sand-land where there can be miles between fences. Most cattle on the Texas coast are crossbred, too—part Brahma. They have the long Brahma legs, and some can run like elk.

I soon started riding regularly with Ralph. I felt that just being near him would make me a better horseman. He seemed to be able to communicate intuitively with a horse. He wasn't much of a talker, though. He was a kind man and seemed happy to answer my questions as we rode. But if I hadn't kept on asking, he might have said one word an hour—and that word would have been directed to a granite-brained cow.

"Yes, sir, whenever they need me I'm here," Ralph said when we had a moment to talk by a clump of tallow trees. "Anymore though, I just work horseback. I don't wrestle the calves now, but I can do the branding and such. My old legs and my knees are getting bad; I can't do a lot of work walking anymore. But on horseback . . . when I'm horseback I can give a man a pretty good day's work."

Since late that morning we had been riding hard, trying to bring in some of Lionel's cows. Lionel, his skin the color of dark walnut, ran cattle on the several-thousand-acre ranch owned by his people, the Mayes, right across from the Whitehead place. (People said the Mayes were related in some way to the white Whites.)

We wanted to get the cows to a gate across the road from the Whitehead ranch, herd them down Highway 562 and into Joe's pasture, and then work them at Joe's pens. But Lionel's unruly cattle despised being herded. They broke off in small bunches and went off in every direction like popcorn popping. And they could probably run ten miles in certain places without slowing down much. Lionel's cows were mostly Brahma, and they weren't used to seeing people and horses. They were inclined to run, then hide in thick bunches of impregnable trees. The worst of them would try to hook a horse with its horns and tear its stomach out.

"Ever since I was six years old and started going to school, I've been riding a horse. You either walked or rode a horse to school. My own first horse, the one that I raised when I was a kid, I called her Pearl. She was a mare. And after I got grown, my favorite roping horse was a big sorrel horse I bought from one of the Jackson brothers. His name was Dude. He was so tall, you could have trouble getting on him. But once you got on him, you were horseback."

"You were horseback" was one of Ralph's favorite phrases. In this excessive, extreme environment, dealing with cattle that can be as ferocious as wild animals on the African plains—well, just *being horseback* and staying there is a much more profound statement than it first seemed.

I asked Ralph how often he and his wife, a highly respected retired schoolteacher, went to Houston. "No, sir, I really don't go there very often.

"You couldn't hardly pay me enough to live in the city. I like to go there every once in a while and visit, but to live in the city, I'd have no part of it. First thing, it's too cramped up. You're too close together, and people are not friendly like we are down here. I guess you've noticed everybody who passes, they'll wave at us, and everybody knows everybody, and if you need a favor, they're only too glad to help you. But in the city, you could be lying out there choking to death, and they'll walk by you.

"No, sir, I don't get to the city much. I'm just a country boy."

Ralph and I were working a group of cows that had young calves, some less than a week old. They were lagging back. We'd press the cows hard, and the calves would group up and take off on their own. I'd go back and get them, and Ralph would stay to hold the mother cows. But some of the mothers would break off and come back at me, thinking maybe I was hurting their babies. What a mess.

We stopped to let the cows cool down and mop our own streaming foreheads. We'd started too late in the morning. The combination of heat and humidity here was the most intense I'd ever felt.

Lionel's herd got a lot hotter—and much more belligerent—before we got them back to Joe's. They were totally unimpressed with humans and horses and preferred to stay as far away from human habitation as possible. But not all cows in the area felt that way. The Whiteheads, in fact, had one cow that yearned to live in the house.

Rosemary was a longhorn, white with big reddish brown spots. She had been adopted by the Whitehead kids the morning her mother gave birth to her, then just walked off and left her.

There were plenty of pictures of Rosemary in the family album. "She lived in the yard," Joe told me, "and she was raised with the dogs. As she grew on up, she began acting peculiar, and we realized she thought she *was* a dog."

Most of the dogs on the Whitehead farm were herding dogs. When they weren't working cattle, they spent their days lying in their shaded yard, and Rosemary lay with them. When Joe needed his horses, he would just point at them and the dogs would round them up. Rosemary would go with them, herding the horses just like the dogs. She rabbit hunted with the dogs. They'd jump a rabbit, and she'd jump in there with them and run that rabbit. She'd even crawl under the fences like they did until she got too big.

Even after Rosemary started getting cow-sized, she kept trying to sleep inside the house. She could open the door, and if the dogs came in she'd follow. She never would leave her dogs, and they wouldn't leave her.

"You know, it was kind of amazing," Joe remembered. "That first winter we turned her in with the young heifers, the dogs stayed with her. They slept with her. The *real* dogs would come home in the heat of the day, but then they would go back in the field at night, and they'd all sleep together. Yeah, when we fed the other heifers, the dogs didn't let any other heifer eat till Rosemary got through eating. They'd stand guard around the feed trough; they'd fight those cattle off."

Rosemary was nine years old when I met her and had only had one calf—by that time, other cows her age had borne six or seven. Maybe she didn't relate to bulls. She still lives at the Whiteheads, still confused as to whether she's a dog or a cow, still looking to be pampered.

Ralph and I came to a low, semiswampy place. A calf that did not follow its wise mama ran back into the black, muddy hole and got stuck, but it yanked itself out after the mother cow gave it an agitated call.

There is a very odd geological feature here on the sand-land. Quite often you'll find a perfectly shaped round or oblong pond. They are shaped so perfectly that some early settlers, figuring the whole area was all once ocean, thought these indentations were old whale nests. I hoped no more calves decided to get bogged down in one.

Somebody with not a lot of sense brought an oriental tree to these parts for fast-growing shade. It's been a disaster; the tallow trees are taking over the sand prairie. They can grow into almost impregnable mazes, great for the cows, which were refusing to mind us, but bad for the natural grasslands the cows need.

We split up and rode through the outside edge of an acre-sized bunch of tallow trees, hollering, beating the branches. I was screaming and telling these cows how dumb they were. Ralph smiled and said, "You know what cowboyin' is, don't you? It's a lazy man's job. He's too lazy to work and too proud to steal, so he works cattle."

We finally got most of our bunch of thirty-five cows and twenty to thirty calves out of the trees, moving across a barren patch that looked like a salt flat. But there was one Brahma cow that would not come out. She started to roar, not a good sign. The interpretation of her roar is that she's had about all she's going to take and she's ready to fight.

"Better leave her," Ralph said. She was one of those gray Brahmas with the black circles around her eyes, and Ralph told me that type would just as soon hurt you as do your will. Besides, Ralph added, she may be just about ready to calve, or just has, and has her calf hid out in a clump of grass. Sure enough, as soon as we took out after the others, she doubled back, covering the ground fast, till she made it back to her just-born, wobbly legged calf.

We finally drove our cattle to where Joe and Lionel were waiting with the rest of the herd, who were in no mood for waiting. Lionel hurried to open his gate. A cow, her tall horns curving high up to the sun, lunged at him and kept going through the open gate onto the main paved road. The herd followed. The few people who came upon us pushing the herd, which covered the whole road, just drove through us slowly. Finally, we got Lionel's herd, unaccustomed to people and pens and horses, enclosed across the road in Joe Whitehead's pens. Many of the cows were breathing heavy, a hot, angry panting.

It was a custom for the ranch to provide the noon meal for everybody working cattle on the premises. Even though that day they were working *Lionel's* cattle, two days before Lionel had come in with Ralph and another hand to work *Joe's* herd. So Annette played hostess. A lazy Susan at the center of her table was loaded with black-eyed peas, creamed corn, boiled blue crab (pulled out of Joe's traps by him and me last night), fried shrimp (caught by Joe in his cast-net last night), some fresh redfish, and some home-grown beef. The supply of iced tea was endless. I spun the lazy Susan first and stopped the shrimp in front of me.

In another time and another place, all of us would not have sat down at the ranch owner's table spinning the lazy Susan together. Ralph, Lionel, and the other hand—being black, or part black, or just not all white—would have had their food in the kitchen. But not anymore. Ever since Joe took over the ranch, their lazy Susan has spun for everyone, black or white or mixed, related or not.

Lunch was over. There was some branding to do, some shots to be given, some cows and calves to be cut out and sold. Ralph and I got back in the middle of the action after he moved Bald into a deeper patch of oak shade. A few days later I left the Whiteheads and moved on against the wind, pressing on farther down the Texas coast.

Up There
Is My
Country

T hey shouldn't have been fighting so close to Swan Lake. Two men, probably welders from a local ship-yard, were trading punches, their baseball caps turned backward and their bare fists flapping as their tempers flew out of control. They were hacking at each other right there on the edge of the canal I was traveling on, not far from Freeport, Texas. Then one threw the other into the water. I'd seen it coming.

Near the Freeport harbor channel I passed a low cinder-block building whose windows were coated with white dust. The parking lot and the building glared white in the passion-bursting sun. Some of the pickup trucks in the parking lot were half rusted out, and there were a couple of shrimp boats tied up at the bulkhead next to the building lot. Taking up the last space at the bulkhead was a sailboat, its fiberglass faded dull. A small black dog stood under a tarp that covered the rear deck, barking furiously at an unsteady shrimper wobbling toward his boat. It wasn't even lunchtime, and the man was drunk. The July sun on the Texas coast drives some people to drink, some to fight, and many more inside to escape it.

I'd had no breakfast, so I idled the *Coops* over to see if this place sold food as well as beer. There were plenty of Cajuns in this part of Texas. And if Texas Cajuns owned the place, any food they offered would be guaran-teed fine. Maybe boiled shrimp. It was shrimping season right now.

All I could see was a Lone Star Beer sign in the dust-caked window—no outside clue about food. And there didn't seem to be a place to dock.

"Hey, you need a place to tie up?" A voice came from somewhere on the sailboat. "Yeah, you."

"Sure do," I answered.

"You want to tie your boat up, you can throw me a couple lines and tie up on my starboard side, no problem." The voice was coming from under the tarp, where the little black dog was.

A thin man emerged from the tarp and held out a hand. I threw him my bowline and put out two rubber fenders that would keep our boats from scratching each other. He was extremely tan, with hair past his shoulders. At first I assumed the word RICE on his T-shirt referred to Rice University in Houston. As I drew closer, I saw two smaller words written above it. His shirt proclaimed "Eat More RICE." His ancient-looking Top-Siders had dried saltwater stains all over them.

"Nice boat you got there," he said.

"Thank you. She's been good to me."

"Where you headed?" he wondered.

I told him. Then we talked about how different the coast of Texas was from the rest of the state. He'd been raised in Fort Worth; I'd walked across Texas from Lufkin to the Panhandle.

He said that inside the concrete-block, sunburnt building I could find some fine fresh-boiled shrimp and saltines. Why didn't we go inside and have some, he half-asked, half-wondered. He told me his name was Alexander.

A 1950s bomb shelter would have had 100 percent more curb appeal than this joint. On the bar there was one revolving gold plastic Budweiser sign in the shape of a globe. A fluorescent tube glowed over a pool table that looked like it had been used as a wrestling mat. A piece of shrimp net hung limply on the wall, kept from falling to the damp floor by a couple of plaster lobsters.

"Where you headed in your boat?" I asked him. He looked at me with brown eyes that held a hint of suspicion.

"I'll be somewhere east of here whenever I get there." He ordered himself an ice water and two pounds of boiled shrimp for the two of us. I've never seen anyone dehead, peel, and eat shrimp faster. He had to have a supercharged metabolism to be that thin and eat as much as he did in the next couple of hours.

Alexander explained how he'd graduated from the Naval Academy and served his time on an aircraft carrier. He told me how he felt detached from the sea and the world while circling the globe, running the carrier with computers and buttons, seldom feeling the wind or sea.

I ordered three more pounds of the boiled shrimp, which had come out of Matagorda Bay just yesterday. The shrimp was flawlessly cool and firm, yet packed with a zesty spicyness. They just had to be using Zatarain's seasoning when they boiled it.

Some man with black hair and a prematurely old body opened the door and let the blinding light in. He told a man at the bar that his wife was calling him at the outside pay phone.

"After the navy I sold commercial real estate in Dallas and made a lot of money—made enough on one deal to buy my boat. Never did occur to me that I could use her anytime other than the weekends. That is until four years ago when I decided to spend at least five years traveling around the world." He brought with him only five thousand dollars in twenties, in case, but he'd only spent about nine hundred in four years. He earned money here and there as he went.

He pulled his chair up tight to our table.

"Four years ago I was never planning on coming back." He told me about how he'd come to resent being so controlled by a government out of control, out of touch. Alexander despised the octopus arms of "Big Brother" out of Washington, mentioning that while the Soviet Union was splitting up and freeing up, Americans were becoming more controlled, less free.

"Why did you come back? You just visiting or are you back for good?" I wanted to know. I shared his feelings about our outrageously wasteful, detached government. I too felt again like I had before I began my walk in 1973—that my country was in a dreadful condition, seemingly unwilling to do anything about it. At one time, prior to my walk across America, I had thought it was the people who were at fault, who made the country the negative force it was. But it wasn't. I believe now that it's mostly the government that is driving the country recklessly, toward a terrible crash, unwilling to make the tough decisions to correct the errors of the past.

Alexander and I both grew quiet then. Hal Ketchum was singing a song about a small-town Saturday night. Alexander had yet to answer my question about why he'd come back to the States. He picked up his quart-sized glass of iced tea. He started to say something, but stopped, then started again.

"You know, the reason I came back is that, after living in a bunch of other countries, some that first seemed like paradise, I couldn't make myself stop being an American. After living in Belize for six months, I told myself I'd never go any farther north. But I was sailing back down to South America when I said, Up there is my country. It's my parents' country, it's my grandparents' country and their grandparents' before them. They didn't give up or leave when it got bad or unfair. Well, neither am I."

The next day, he turned around and sailed for Texas. Now he was searching for the place he would tie up his boat. He said he was thinking about running for political office.

I'd been struggling lately with similar feelings of disgust and frustration with the way things were run in this country. I was weary of hearing myself spout off and complain about what was wrong. It was time for me to get involved where I lived. It was time for me to speak out and fight back. I would not sit back and leave things to other people.

Right before I got up from our table, which was almost totally covered with shrimp heads and shells and empty saltine wrappers, I reached out my hand and he grabbed mine and we both squeezed.

Running
from
Andrew

I needed to move a lot faster.

Any day now I might be running for my life.

All along the Intracoastal Waterway there was anxious, almost hyper movement. Boats were everywhere. Radios were squawking.

The past week Hurricane Andrew had roared out of the Atlantic and annihilated a big piece of southeastern Florida. Soon it would be back in the Gulf, and the weather people said it *might* come and hit land again right here in Texas. It was definitely heading to this end of the Gulf Coast.

Had my friends in the Keys and Marker 7 been hit? I stopped at a marina and tried to call Scott Bannerot and his friend, Kenny the lobsterman. The phone beeped fast, ba-ba-ba, that out-of-order tone. I started to dial Goodland, then hung up. Right now the eye of Hurricane Andrew was projected to be directly over Marker 7 Fish House. No, I should try to call. I dialed again. It rang and rang. I figured it was out of order, but ringing. Someone answered. It was Barb.

Barb, maybe because she was used to creating tattoos and riding Harleys and working with mullet fisherman, didn't seem to be breathing any faster than usual. She said that right then it was blowing about a hundred miles an hour, and they were ready for the worst. She and Bob had decided to ride the storm out there. They didn't have any way to move their "children"—the pit bulls, the parrots, and the Harleys. She said that she didn't know where Billy and Red and their families were.

I heard some wind noise. There was a crashing sound. Barb explained that the massive ice-making machine had blown off the roof above the walk-in fish cooler. The water, normally just covering the mangrove roots on the island, had not flooded them yet, but it probably would. Barb expected the high water to do most of the damage. The parrots squawked frantically in the background. I told her I hoped they'd all be OK. There were more sounds of metal crashing. Then the line went dead.

My worry about my friends in Florida was overrun with a more immediate concern for myself and the *Cooper*. I had just had firsthand evidence of the storm's destructive power, and soon Andrew would be rejuvenating itself in the Gulf. Where could the *Cooper* and I go to escape its destruction if it came to this part of the Texas coast?

The Gulf was hot, more than eighty degrees. The weather bureau scientists said that hot water would supercharge any hurricane that passed over. Some said that as warm as the Gulf was now, the hurricane could possibly become even stronger than when it had first hit Florida.

At this point, the experts were projecting Andrew would hit land again and maim and destroy anywhere from northern Florida to south Texas. It would take a day or two to track the storm's movements and predict its hellish course more accurately.

Was Andrew coming to get me? Everyone on the coast was consumed with that question. Every so often on the Gulf, some of the people and much of their property have to be sacrificed to one of these monster storms. Now everyone was on edge, waiting to find out who the victims would be.

Living on the Gulf during those days was a little like living in a war zone where battles could be expected to erupt somewhere—but no one knew exactly where. The warring force (the hurricane) marched so slowly and its course was so unpredictable that millions of people were kept watching, wondering, expecting. It was a fearful time, but also strangely exciting. Long-time Gulf Coast natives seemed to get a rush from all the attention and the aura of danger that a hurricane watch brought.

Gulf Coast residents were well aware of the terrible destruction that a hurricane can inflict. They remained tense and alert, making what preparations they could while they waited to find out exactly where it was coming ashore. Children picked up on the anxious focus of the adults. Even the animals and birds seemed to act differently. Fear hung in the sultry air. Several hundred miles of coastline were in wait, listening, watching, hoping the hurricane would die out in the water, knowing better. Andrew was becoming stronger with every hour.

In a way all this anxiety seemed silly because only a small bunch of us on the Gulf would bear the brunt of the hurricane's fury. But not to prepare was even more stupid—especially after seeing on television what Andrew had already done to boats, homes, animals, and people in Homestead, Florida. I had to decide what action to take if Andrew came closer. I had to find a place that would be safe for the *Cooper* and me.

All around me in the Intracoastal, tugboats were pushing long lines of barges toward hoped-for safety. Sailboats were cruising at their fastest twelve knots. I passed several million-dollar yachts moving to shelter. Every captain had an idea of the best way to survive a hurricane. Some steel-hulled megatugs and tankers choose to go out into the Gulf to fight the storm away from the confines of rivers and canals. But barges would be swamped by the waves on the open water; the tugs pushing barges would either have to ride the hurricane out in the canal or turn upriver. The captains of some craft believed in going upriver and tying as many lines as they could to as many trees as they could find. No one thought it was wise to stay tied up at the dock, though.

I saw no small boats; they'd all been hauled out of the water and put on trailers. But the *Cooper* needed a big truck, a stout trailer, and I had no access to either. The *Cooper* and I would have to stay in the water and handle what came.

If I kept running down the Intracoastal Waterway, I could keep going all the way to Mexico. But going up some river probably would be the best for the *Cooper* and me. If I went up a river I would have some protection. But the confined space of a river offered danger as well, should Andrew decided to come on a search-and-destroy mission. In a river my chances of being smashed against banks, docks, or other boats would be greater. And of course we could only go so far up any river before being blocked by a dam or a bridge.

But there was no point in paralyzing myself with all the dire possibilities. I needed to turn my fear of Andrew into energy and decisive planning. I had my well-built boat, my two powerful engines, my hard-earned abilities. I decided I would keep running in the canal southwest toward Mexico until I found a river to head up.

Every mile I made running from Andrew was urgently undertaken. All my remaining time was valuable, every drop of fuel I had must be cherished. If the hurricane was to hit us and our piece of Texas, marinas and gas stations would close. I needed to stock up on supplies, too, make sure my radio continued to run. I felt like a fly buzzing round and round, trying to avoid a giant fly swatter. Forecasters were saying that this could be the most destructive hurricane in history.

Now the meteorologists were predicting that Andrew would strike between Mobile and the Texas coast. I wondered what Warren was doing with the *Zubenelgenubi*. A metal-hulled sailboat of that size couldn't be taken out of the water quickly; it had to be sailed somewhere to safety. He'd probably take her upriver. That was no longer an option for captains of ships like the *Stolt Surf.* They had now stopped letting the big ships into the Mississippi.

I stopped running from Andrew in the Intracoastal Waterway at Matagorda, Texas, right at the mouth of the Colorado River, about twenty miles south of Bay City. Ten Vietnamese-owned shrimp boats were lined up, waiting for the swing bridge to open and let them through. They were all going southwest toward Mexico.

I pulled in right before the swinging bridge and ducked into a dockside shop for supplies. The woman at the counter said some of the local shrimpers were going up the Colorado River. I decided I would follow them.

Up the river there were some stunted oaks I could tie onto. Would that be a good idea? What if one of the wide-around trees blew over and sank the boat? What if my anchor pulled loose and I was dragged by the pushing, smashing wind into the bank? I didn't want to get near any other boats. I'd seen on television what happens when they all get thrown together.

I finally anchored off the bank of a vast ranch. I was not far from Bay City now. The radio said that Andrew now appeared to be headed straight for New Orleans. Not long afterward the forecasters changed their minds and said no, maybe landfall would be closer to the center of coastal Louisiana and east Texas.

I hated the waiting. By the time the forecasters were sure with their predictions, Andrew would be hitting land.

Something on shore got the attention of my anxious eyes. There, not more than fifty yards from me, were three whitetail bucks with branching antlers. They were standing around a big, widespreading live oak tree, staring deep into the shadows made by the tree branches. The swelling muscles in their necks bunched with excitement.

The gray Spanish moss hung motionless from the branches; there was not a breath of breeze. Then the biggest of the bucks walked into the shadows, brushing the hanging veils. Out into the bright sunlight ran a doe, as elegant as the bucks were powerful. She ran to the next tree, a small one, about thirty yards closer to the riverbank.

In all the time I've spent in the woods, I'd never seen even one buck act like these three, so completely oblivious to me. Could the wildlife sense the devastation that was coming and be compelled to mate before the worst happened?

From the Texas coast I went up the Colorado River. On one ranch I saw this elegant whitetail doe. This part of Texas is well known for its superior deer.

I yelled out to the deer. Surely they saw me. But they were totally consumed. Two of the bucks ran at each other and locked horns and clashed. The third one, the smallest, took the opportunity to make a try for the doe. She ran away, and all three bucks followed. I could not see them anymore.

I found out a few days later that the three bucks and the doe had not lost their heads because of a coming hurricane. They were crazed like this every year at mating season. Last year, one buck in rut had killed an old man who was walking down a road picking up beer and soda cans. Apparently the hormone-crazed animal thought the old man was a threat.

Later that night Andrew came to the Gulf Coast and attacked the center of Cajun country. It roared into Atchafalaya Bay and ripped through Morgan City, a hundred or so miles east of Cameron Parish. I had once docked the *Cooper* there on the Atchafalaya River, right under the bridge.

The day after Andrew came to Louisiana, I got through to the Marker 7 Fish House and the Keys. Vicious Andrew had blown a tree through Red's houseboat and sunk it, along with two of their fishing boats, which had been tied to the houseboat. Billy and Red and their families were all fine.

Andrew had sent a storm surge of salty water up little Pear Street, sinking a couple more boats and coming within two inches of flooding Bob and Barb's classic Harleys. A few discarded parrot feathers were blown away when the screen and part of the porch were torn off, but the Fish House was in relatively good shape.

My friends in the northern Keys were stunned by what happened just a few miles north of them on the mainland. If Andrew had hit just a bit farther south, they would have nothing left. I could only get through to Kenny the lobsterman, one of Scott's neighbors. He sounded humbled, an attitude not easily attainable for him.

The Dream
of the
Weathered House

Τhe only reason I ever set eyes on Seadrift, Texas, was that I ran low on gas. That day I was in no mood to stop, look, or listen; I was hungry for the brawny speed and blow-back power of my boat. And it wasn't just the power and flash of fast movement that I yearned. It was the freedom of being alone, unencumbered by any stranger's life.

For the last few weeks I'd been feeling really dull, burned out. I was too easily annoyed by minor things. My dreams were occupied with Rita's arms, the sweetness and the sameness of home, the wind-dried sheets on my bed. It was getting time to end this journey. Right now, though, I was about to run out of gas. So I turned into the tiny port with the alluring name of Seadrift.

Seadrift is surrounded by two oceans—one of water, the other crops. But the citizens in this little town (population 1,277) definitely prefer the water. They draw their lives from the unpredictable sea and are repelled by the orderliness of the farmers' fields. The Seadrift people perch here on the edge of these Texas flatlands and don't go inland much; instead, they roam the waters of the many bays that branch out from their home port. Most return every evening in their modest bay boats to their unassuming homes. Few ever dare the open waters of the Gulf, not because they don't have the courage, but because they don't have the money to buy open-water boats.

Even though the land is very flat, the town of Seadrift at least is built on firm ground. There are no swamps nearby and few native trees. The town looks out upon Guadalupe Bay. It's 18 miles to the nearest Wal-Mart, in Port Lavaca, about 85 miles southwest to Corpus Christi, and about 350 miles straight north to Dallas. The condo and trailer-park people who come to the Texas coast to find a sun-warmed winter and bright blue skies are not wanted here by most of the natives. There is plenty of coastline for them elsewhere.

In Seadrift there are three restaurants, two laundromats (for the many locals who can't afford a washer or a dryer), an insurance agency, an auto parts store, a gas station, some churches, and a public school. A place that sells gas on the "main" road, Route 185, is basically a convenience store, open long hours. Seadrift recently received a new post office.

Depending on how good your eyes are, or how foggy it is, or how much you have drunk, you might look at downtown Seadrift and wonder if it's all a mirage. That's because you'll see a night scene where a shrimp boat has washed up on the beach in a wicked lightning storm. Down the street a bit, flocks of geese and ducks fly across a wall. Your eyes take in the boats, birds, fish, islands, the overwhelming skies and seas—all floating across the town with a magic reality. It is as if the locals cannot bear to be away from their boats and the natural world, so they bring the outside world into town with them. These haunting murals cover walls on the old drugstore, Elena's Restaurant, the insurance agency, and a few other unnamed buildings on the main street.

Before I ever saw downtown Seadrift, though, I set eyes on possibly the most exotic-looking woman I'd ever seen in a small town. As I pulled close to shore, I could not miss her sitting in the intense sun of a parking lot across from the fish house. She wore loose-fitting black cotton pants and a baggy black cotton T-shirt, all coated with shimmering white dust. She sat in the center of a sprawling green net, one deeply tanned bare foot propping up the net while she used a long needle to mend holes in it. Her black hair was windblown, thick and free. With her untamed appearance, crouched in the middle of the seventy-five-foot net, she looked like a big spider in its web.

I tied up across from the spider-woman and tried not to stare. I had to find out who she was. But first I went inside the small, white-painted office of the fish house. The woman in charge seemed tense, guarded around strangers.

Before I could say a word, the barefooted woman with the wild hair walked in. She looked to be in her late thirties or early forties.

"I need some fuel," I said to the fish house woman. The spider-woman stood in a corner, arms crossed on her chest.

"We only got diesel," the fish house woman answered.

The daughter of a shrimper, Diane grew up in a time when women did not shrimp, they stayed home, often barefoot and likely pregnant, but always expected to be cooking and cleaning.

"I can help you out," said the exotic one. She said her name was Diane Wilson. Her husband, a crewboat captain, had some big gas cans, and he could get some fuel in town, enough to get me down the bay to Rockport.

The only problem was that I'd have to wait until Leslie Wilson got home from work.

I asked if there was any place to get something to eat. Diane said that she would show me a place. I invited her to join me.

Once inside Elena's Restaurant, I understood why Diane was so instantly and obviously different from anyone I'd ever met. She was forty-four, part Native American, the mother of five children with ages ranging from six to twenty. She was also a shrimper, a net maker, and a reader of William Faulkner. And she was in a good mood because her best friend, Kathy, a local artist who had painted several of the downtown murals, had just interpreted a dream that Diane had been having for most of her life but never understood.

So far, Seadrift was shaping up like no other place I'd ever been.

We ordered burgers, which came wrapped in white paper. Diane's voice was rather loud, and our conversation held the other customers spellbound.

"In Texas, men are men and women are women. In the 1950s and '60s, I thought I knew what that meant. Men did the shrimpin', the travelin'; they sat and waited for dinner. The women did the cleanin', the cookin', the child raisin'."

A man in his seventies jerked his head up from his hamburger and stared a hole in the wall behind us.

"And especially in my family, a woman didn't speak, or at least she didn't speak much to or around men." When she was young, she explained, she had chafed against these expectations; she always wanted to be outside climbing trees or building things. And she very often felt an intense urge to talk, to express her opinions. She didn't. Instead, every once in a while she would lose her temper and express herself by breaking out windows in her family's house with her powerful fists. Diane said she had always had extraordinary physical strength. A gray-haired woman looked intently into her coffee cup, listening hard.

As a child, Diane used to dehead shrimp in the summer to earn a bit of spending money. She was always barefoot, tan, her thick black hair uncombed. She remembered when the people from the inland towns came to buy shrimp. The women stayed in their cars so their carefully controlled hair would not be messed by the wind. Diane felt so different from them, and she sensed these people looked down at her. She felt there was something wrong with her. Her hair should have been more under control, and her feet should not have been calloused, big, and dirty.

My bucket-sized iced tea glass was refilled by a waitress with an iron-red beehive hairdo. It stood stiffly above her ears.

"I wanted to shrimp, see," Diane was saying. "I wanted to go with Daddy. I wanted to say things that come on me, talk about stuff that bothered me." Instead she held it all in. Then one day she began to read Faulkner. Reading became her journey to understanding. Faulkner's people were just like her people; reading about them made Diane feel rare and extraordinary instead of terribly ordinary and insignificant.

"My father is considered very dignified. He's a quiet Indian type. He never struck us a day in his life, and he worked hard all his life, but he does not give any credit, does not value women at all. Whatever a woman has to say is stupid chatter. I can remember that's the most persistent thing he'd say, 'you stupid woman.'

"My brother, now, he's well educated. The males got the educations. He went to the University of Texas, was a jet pilot, all this good stuff. I felt that I had something to say and do just as important as my brother. It only took me twenty-five years to get the courage to do it."

We walked up to the cash register to pay our bill. All the people in Elena's had been still and silent since we'd been there. When we left the cafe, I walked the five blocks or so to the *Cooper,* and Diane went back to mending her net.

It wasn't half an hour before Leslie Wilson drove up in their old station wagon. Its air conditioning had long since given up, the paint on the top of the hood and roof was faded to gray, the car was dusty inside and out. Leslie was the father of four of Diane's children. His hair was streaked blond by the sun, and his face was lined and injured by the tough breaks of life. He was handsome, sort of a combination of a large Robert Redford and Steve McQueen, but he had a pained aura that diminished his forcefulness.

Leslie and I filled several gas cans and emptied them into my tanks. I should have been ready to leave then, but I couldn't. I asked Diane if I could speak with her some more, and she said we could do that in the morning at their house. Leslie said he'd come and get me around eight.

Diane and Leslie lived about seven miles east of Seadrift. The whooping cranes and sandhill cranes fly over their house late every fall on the way to the Aransas National Wildlife Refuge.

The thin sand road to Diane and Leslie's home cut through open fields, some of which were nothing but stubborn brush and mesquite. As we drove by, a Braford bull was pushing down a chunk of barbed-wire fence to take an in-heat cow for himself. We drove past a couple of old trailers, and I saw some unfinished boats resting in yards like dreams that have waited too long.

The Wilsons' house was a large two-story whose paint had weathered off. A net lay in the yard waiting to be dipped in preservative, which meant that part of the lawn could not be mowed. When we got there, Diane and Leslie's seven-year-old autistic son, David, was climbing barefoot up the slim columns on the porch.

There were no screens on many of the windows, no air conditioning either. And David, something of a mechanical genius, had taken apart everything he could—televisions, door locks, doorknobs, toasters. Diane told me they had trouble at Christmas because he tried to take off every Christmas light, everything shiny from the tree.

Diane and I sat on the porch swing to talk. David stared at me, then hit the screen door with a screwdriver several thousand times. Diane answered her children's questions and mine. David wanted me to ask him some questions. I asked him a few.

Diane spoke. "We found this house in Victoria. It wasn't painted, just stark weathered, and it had a For Sale sign on it. I never thought we could afford it, so I just passed it by. And then one time my mother-in-law dropped by on the spur of the moment and asked how much they wanted for it. They said two thousand dollars. She said two thousand dollars? And they said two thousand dollars. And so she came back and told us, and we bought it the next day.

"It was in the path of a major highway going through, and the land was worth more without the house. The house movers cut it right down the middle, and then they brought it out here. The fellow in charge was drunk, completely drunk. I had a place back farther on our land where I wanted the house, and I kept telling him to put it there, but he just parked it where he wanted to."

Talking about their old gray house caused Diane to remember a night not long ago. She was in downtown Seadrift, where she almost never went at night.

"It was raining hard," she began. "It was a dark and stormy week. My washing machine was totally broke down. It only breaks down when it's real stormy," Diane laughed. "I had about twenty loads of dirty clothes, and I spent about twenty dollars in quarters. My last twenty dollars, I might mention.

"I was real hard at work on the laundry when my best friend, Kathy, spotted my car and came in. She's from a very proper and well-off Nebraska family, and she married a guy from a rich Texas family. He became a shrimper, then they divorced.

"Luckily she didn't have her kids with her that night. That was probably the one time in our lives we didn't have a pile of kids around. No telling what we could accomplish if we had more nights like that one." She threw her head back as she said that, and her laughter spilled out like a six-foot wave.

"It felt isolated inside with the washers on spin cycle while outside it was stormin'. We just made it our domain in there. We were getting louder and louder. A few people came in and backed out of the place.

"Anyway, for as long as I can remember, since I was about ten, I had this recurring dream." Diane wove her story with passion. "It was driving me nuts, and it was a real simple dream.

"In the dream I was always on an isolated beach. On the beach there was a big, solid house . . . but there wasn't any paint on it. It had a weathered look to it, kind of plain. There were a lot of windows that were gleaming and glowing.

"Inside the windows I could see shining furniture, all interesting-looking pieces. Then I would be walking through the entire house, just being amazed at everything that was in the drawers and pulling them out

Diane at the helm of her boat, shrimping in Espiritu Santo Bay

and looking at them. All the precious things of value in those drawers! I still remember the gleam of the windows reflecting off the gleam of the furniture. It was just . . . it was just beautiful. It was beautiful inside.

In the laundromat that night I told Kathy the dream. "She just looked at me real gentle and said, 'Well, the house is yourself. And you're realizing that there are things of worth in the house, in you. You've always thought you were dull and weathered, insignificant, tired. That unpainted house is you, Diane.'

"It was so simple," Diane exclaimed. She told me how she'd suffered with low self-esteem all her life. She repeated that in her childhood home women were considered stupid. She told how happy she'd been that stormy night, after all those loads of dirty laundry were clean. She told Kathy she should put a shingle out in front of her house that said Dream Interpreter.

After that night, Diane's life changed. Understanding her dream gave her courage to speak out, to do what she felt was necessary. Now nothing shuts her up; no one can stop her. Today she is making up for decades of imposed silence.

Diane tells people, for instance, that she hears the bays crying. The waters from which four generations of her family have drawn their living are calling out to her for help. And she will not be quiet about it, no matter if some think she's a nut or a foolish, emotional woman. She now speaks up not just to her husband or to her fellow Texans, but also to the multinational lawyers and politicians and power dealers who are bringing more and more chemical plants to her stretch of the Texas coastline.

Diane knows that Lavaca Bay, Espiritu Santo Bay, Matagorda Bay, and San Antonio Bay—the bays of her youth and her father's youth—are hurting. She has fought against the muscular corporations and politicians whom she thinks "hold jobs above our water." She has spoken out when even the local men stay silent because they want the jobs the plants bring. She has even gone on hunger strikes in far-off cities like Dallas to call attention to what she feels is being dumped into her bays. Diane no longer retreats, shuts up, represses her feelings and opinions. She no longer has to punch out window panes.

Recently Diane was invited to go to India to an international conference. The purpose of the conference was to call attention to the pollution pouring from industrial plants in countries with few environmental regulations. They remembered industrial accidents in India and spoke of what might be happening in Mexico. Diane is sometimes called upon by Greenpeace to speak at environmental meetings. This year she was named Environmental Hell Raiser of the Month by *Mother Jones* magazine. These crusaders know she loves her waters, that she and her family have drawn their living from the bays. She is a voice of realism. Relatively few environmentalists come from her particular kind of life experience, her working-class roots.

The heart of Diane's message is that something is dreadfully wrong in her world of saltwater bays. In the past couple of years, black buzzards have begun to stand on the beaches, waiting for death to wash up. The largest dolphin kill in American history from "unknown" causes occurred in these waters, which once enriched Seadrift and filled the nets of its people.

Diane is convinced that the chemical plants on this lonely Texas coast are discharging toxic substances. They say they are not. Yet the dolphin die, dead fish wash ashore, and still the vultures wait on the beaches. Diane repeats over and over that she hears her bays crying. She thinks she can hear them when others can't because she's been on them all her life, and also because she is part Blackfoot Indian.

Her great-grandfather was pure Blackfoot; he made his living catching redfish. When people asked him what kind of Indian he was, he'd put his huge dark foot in their face and say fiercely, "Blackfoot."

Diane doesn't ever need to be asked what she is or what she believes. She is in your face whether you like it or not. She inspired me to speak my mind, not to hold back any longer. She changed me.

Diane and I talked for hours that day and the next. I stayed several days. Then it was time to move on. Her kids were starting school soon, and she needed to go up to Port Lavaca to do some school-clothes shopping. On their way to Port Lavaca, Diane and Leslie dropped me off at the place where the *Cooper* was docked.

I left early the next morning, but not before Diane and Leslie. They had left at sunup to go shrimping in Espiritu Santo Bay.

You Hit Him
with
What?

When I'm home and listening to Lyle Lovett sing about Texas, I get lonesome for the place. Being in Texas has always made me feel free, potent, aggressive, and optimistic. I wondered what my reaction would be listening to Lyle now that I was actually here in his home state.

I was having problems finding the cassette. I stood up and was feeling around in the fiberglass box above my captain's chair, where the VHF radio and cassette deck were, trying to grab the cassette I knew was there. Of course, a lot of times I *know* something's somewhere, and it might be in another state. Anyone in my family can attest to that.

Aransas Bay was gentle. The Texas coast was so unlike any of the Gulf Coast I'd explored yet, because it was almost totally protected by long, long barrier islands that created hundreds and hundreds of miles of mostly secluded bays. I could be in one bay or another till I got to Mexico.

The superheated September air moved around my body as I stood up, reaching, all the way back into the box, feeling for the Lovett tape. There it was!

At that moment I noticed someone waving from a boat. He was waving with both hands and seemed to be directing his signals to me. Did he need help?

Last month I'd heard the frantic calls for help of a teenager who'd come upon a huge man fishing alone in a boat. The man had apparently suffered a heart attack. The teenager was yelling into the radio, obviously hyperventilating, talking to the Coast Guard, screaming that the man was blue—screaming that the man had fallen into the water as he was trying to drag him into his boat. "HELP ME!" he finally yelled.

The Coast Guard dispatcher did a fine job calming the panicked teenager, talking him through the ordeal. The boy finally did get the man in his boat and to shore, where a helicopter was waiting. But I never did find out if the man lived or died. When emergencies happen out here there is no 911. There are no ambulances, no tow trucks, and no police. The Coast Guard is often hours away, as they probably were now.

I needed to get over to that man. Anything could have happened. Another crew member on the shrimp boat could have cut his finger off in the winch, or the chains could have snared someone's leg. I veered to the left. They were 300 yards away . . . now about 150 yards . . . now about 100 feet.

The waving man looked to be in his mid-twenties; he had long, wispy hair lying on his bare shoulders. I pulled back my throttles and slowed up. He had that malnourished look that some young shrimpers have, who are all lean muscle. His skin was so tanned he should have allowed himself to be a test case for skin-cancer research.

"Hey, we got an electrical short here. You got any wire cutters?"

That was a relief. They had a major hassle, but no emergency. Older, worn-out boats like theirs often leaked, and saltwater could play havoc with wires and electrical systems. I ejected Lyle's tape.

"Yeah, sure, I got some," I answered. Warren had advised me to get a certain kind of wire cutter that had different-sized holes for cutting different-sized wires.

Another young, long-haired man glanced at me from the wheelhouse. It was lucky for them I'd come along; I did not see another boat within a couple of miles.

I pulled out and away from them and circled back so that I could pull up side to side, my bow facing toward their stern. The sun-bleached, sinewy man who had waved me over grabbed hold of my railing. I put the *Coops* in neutral and said, "I've got my toolbox down below. I'll be right back." I was glad I could be of help.

My cheap plastic toolbox didn't keep the salt air out very effectively, and the wire cutters were somewhat rusted together. I pulled out a large can of WD-40, a spray-on lubricant, about the size of a can of hair spray. Oddly, the can made me think of Luke's bright red hair. It has two crowns and sometimes is so unruly that I have to wet it with hair spray to keep it from sticking straight up.

When I came back up the four stairs and into my cabin, the sun-bleached, scrawny man was standing on my back deck. He'd tied one of my ropes to his broken-down shrimp boat. He looked to be about five-foot-ten. I sprayed the wire cutters with the WD-40 to loosen them, then said, "Here they are. They should—" He interrupted me.

"We don't want them stupid wire cutters, man. We're taking your boat." Now he looked vicious. The other man was still lurking in the shadows of their wheelhouse.

My mind grew instantly still and rational. All right. Give them what they want. Don't argue. Don't provoke them in any way. There is no place easier in this country to get killed than out at sea, even if it's in a bay. Just do what they say. Don't even think of fighting back. There are two of them, only one of you.

"All right," I responded, not moving my hands at all. "What are you going to do with me?"

"See over that way?" he pointed south toward the Gulf, to the back side of the barrier island that formed one side of the bay.

"Yeah," I said, purposefully breathing slowly, never moving my eyes from his.

"We'll be dropping you off there. Someone will find you."

He now looked like one of those people who kills a whole family after he rapes everyone. My mind was feeding me too much information. I was trying not to panic.

"OK. You want me to drive the boat?" I asked.

"I'm gonna run this boat, idiot." He looked over at his comrade and motioned for him to come aboard.

A picture I carried in my wallet of Luke and Julianne, both hugging each other, their faces mashed together, came to me with incredible power. A rage overpowered my decision to give them what they wanted.

No, Peter, don't even think about it. It's guaranteed they've got a gun.

I thought of the rest of my family. I changed my mind again. This punk wasn't going to take my boat.

I jerked back my right hand, the one that held the metal can of WD-40, and brought it down on the top of his mangy head with all the power in me. At that moment, I didn't care if the blow killed him.

The skinny man slumped, lifted his head back up, and slumped farther, grabbing the railing. I grabbed his body and flipped him into the water. Then I untied my rope from their boat, expecting to get shot any second now. I didn't care.

I leaped up by the steering wheel, staying on my knees in case the other one started shooting. If the knocked-out one in the water got tangled in my propellers, so be it.

I looked back to see the other thief leaning over the rail, either helping his partner or trying to find him. At least he was not shooting. They surely had a handgun or two, and they probably also had a rifle. Almost all shrimpers carried a rifle in case they caught one of the huge sharks that roam these bays.

I blasted away until I had gone at least four or five miles. My hands shook—not from fear, but from anger; rage filled me. Those slimebags could have killed me. They had come very close to stealing my boat.

I needed to get on channel 16 and call the Coast Guard. I did not know where their closest station was, probably in Corpus Christi, quite a way off. I was not worried about the boat hijackers coming to get me; their boat moved slow.

"This is AL 2684 HR (my boat registration number), the *Cooper*. The pleasure craft the *Cooper* calling the U.S. Coast Guard. Do you read?"

There was no reply.

"This is AL 2684 HR, the *Cooper*, the *Cooper*, calling the U.S. Coast Guard, can you read?"

No reply.

I had backtracked now. What would I do if I could not reach the Coast Guard? I didn't want to go all the way back to Seadrift. I didn't have enough fuel.

"This is blah, blah, blah U.S. Coast Guard Group, come back, *Cooper*," I thought I heard.

"Yes, Coast Guard, this is the *Cooper*. Can we switch to channel 22?" Normally people wanting to have some kind of privacy switched to any channel other than 16.

"This is the U.S. Coast Guard switching to 22, *Cooper*." I did not have good reception.

"Yes, U.S. Coast Guard, this is the *Cooper*. I just had someone try to steal my boat."

"OK, *Cooper*. Can you give us your location?" the dispatcher asked.

"This is the *Cooper*. I'm in the east end of Aransas Bay, but the attempted hijacking took place four or five miles back to the west."

"Are there any injuries?"

"No, there aren't. I'm the only one on my boat," I answered. Then I remembered the thief in the water, his head bashed with my metal can. "Coast Guard, one of the men who tried to steal my boat may be injured. I hit him on the head with a can of WD-40, might have knocked him out, then dumped him in the bay."

"You what, *Cooper*? You hit him with what?" the dispatcher said. His voice became louder and more breathy. I couldn't tell, but he seemed to be losing his professional tone.

"Yes, Coast Guard," I said, "I hit him as hard as I could on top of the head with a can of WD-40." I thought I heard muffled laughing. Surely not.

"Yes, *Cooper.*" It was a different voice. Someone else had taken over for the dispatcher. "Are you all right? Over."

"Yes, sir, I'm fine," I responded. "I just want you people to go get these guys who just tried to steal my boat!"

He asked me to be more precise about my present location. I told him I was right at the east end of Aransas Bay in the Intracoastal Waterway. I told them I could see the sign for the Aransas National Wildlife Refuge.

He asked me to describe the attempted hijackers' boat. I did. I told him it looked like most of the other bay shrimp boats I'd seen in Texas. He asked me if I'd seen the name of the boat. I told him no, I hadn't; I didn't know if it even had one. He asked me to describe the men. I did. He asked me how they could reach me if they caught anyone. I gave him my phone number back in Tennessee. I explained to him that I was traveling; I was not from around here. He said he was glad that I was all right, that I had foiled their attempt. He said it would take them at least an hour to get one of their boats to the location. I figured the thief would have escaped by then.

"Listen, *Cooper,* tell me one more time, what did you hit the guy in the head with?" He must have gathered some people around him to hear this one more time.

"Yes, Coast Guard. I hit him *just as hard as I could* with a can of WD-40."

"OK, *Cooper.* You be careful now. If we find any good suspects, we'll get in touch with you. Have a safe trip wherever you're going, sir."

"Thank you, I will." I felt like telling him what I was doing and how far I had come and how little of the Gulf Coast I had left in my journey, but I didn't.

I never heard anything from the Coast Guard. I didn't really expect to. I did learn from other sources that there had been a lot of boat hijacking in the Gulf. (The Coast Guard does not publicize crime on the high seas, and the media do not scan their communications like they do those of land-based police.) That incident was the first time in my twenty years of traveling that I'd ever had to revert to violence to protect myself. I was just glad I had a suitable weapon on hand.

I wouldn't change a thing I did.

CHAPTER 48

Like
Flying

The bays along the Texas coast seem to go on forever. When the bays end, you've come to Mexico. And I was about to come to the southern end of the narrow bays I'd been traveling since I left Louisiana. The late September air lifted me with its warm, salty heaviness, and I felt like I was flying.

I only had about thirty-five miles more to go in the *Cooper* before my boat trip would be over. It had taken me almost two years to get here. By the time I'd gone up and down all the rivers I'd traveled and covered all the Gulf coastline from the Florida Keys to the Texas-Mexican border, I'd gone over twenty-five hundred miles in this boat.

I'd come a lot further on my inner journey. Of course, it was not miles that I'd covered in this way.

Looking back, my personal journey had been more like climbing a spiral staircase than traveling a road or a coastline. In the years since my walk across America I had climbed a bit, taken some steps downward, and had some pretty nasty falls. I'd stepped down instead of up when I'd become polluted with the easy come and go of my success. I'd fallen further when I became infected by anger and rage from the hellish skirmishes of divorce. Guilt from seeing our family unit blow apart had pushed me nearly to the bottom.

Over the past two years, though, I had felt myself rising out of that dark stairwell. And it wasn't just the magic of the sea at work.

Yes, the clean saltwater, warm and soothing, had helped to heal me. Yes, the heavy salt air that felt like a hundred caressing hands as it blew by me had done its part. Being rocked to sleep so many good nights by the

Gulf had been part of my prescription for returning to the best of me. After watching the sea worms mate and the tarpon leap and the manatees graze, I knew I could not stay away very long anymore from the waters and the creatures that dwelled in them.

And discovering that I was still up to the challenge of learning new skills, new ways of thinking had helped as well. I had begun with a beach-comber's knowledge of the sea. Now I had gone a long way toward being a proficient mariner. I understood something about the sea and its moods, and that understanding had renewed me.

But mostly it was the people whose lives I came to share that had changed me for the better.

Billy and Red's love for each other, their taking on of each other's demons and knowing what to do with them, gave me great hope. They showed me that no matter what happened in each other's lives, no matter how crazy Billy became because of all the horror of Vietnam and the worse nightmare of the way he was treated once he returned—his brother Red was there. Everyone else could desert Billy, but not Red.

I would try to be like them. I wanted to be there for my loved ones. Rita had that same love for me; she had proven that. She had somehow known that I had to go on this voyage, not because it was my job, but because my life depended on it. She had encouraged me, supported me. And then she had shown more faith in me than I had in myself.

Sweet Daisy Durante had become a huge inspiration for me. She was born into a time and place and situation where injustice was a given. She had suffered her share, or more than her share, of loneliness and pain. And Daisy had lived through it all without becoming embittered. She learned to see what was good, she sought out the good; she sang and smiled instead of blamed and cried. She loved and found that it really was what was in a person's heart that mattered. She should be a textbook; her example was worth telling. I knew I would remember Daisy's life and her example. She had definitely changed me for the better.

My Cajun friends, who for generations had endured the blasts of hurricanes and countless other misfortunes, had changed me, too. I loved the way they handled their lives when devastation overcame them. They first surged with energy, cleaned up the mess, rebuilt even better what had been blown away, then went back to their lives. They would not dwell on the bad. The same thing, maybe worse, could come again next year. Instead they worked harder, laughed louder, danced more, and cooked and cooked and cooked. There was no time for life-draining self-pity.

Diane Wilson amazed and inspired me with her courage and strength in speaking up for the health of the bays where she grew up. She spoke up in a place where a woman's voice was usually unheeded, even ignored. She had to speak out even though her family opposed her. But she followed what she thought to be valid and right. Diane overcame the oppression of being a woman in the man's world of Seadrift, Texas, and she has made a difference. If she could face those kinds of odds and still speak from her convictions, I could too. I vowed not to sit at the side of the world I lived in and let someone else take the lead, let things happen I did not agree with. Like Diane, I would stand my ground. I would fight for what I believe in.

Looking back over the miles I had traveled, I could think of so many other people who had touched me and changed me. There was Scott Bannerot, who inspired me with his scholar's mind, reggae soul, and adventurer's spirit, and the Furmans in Wilcox County who made me part of their family. I loved the gentle determination of the Gorilla Woman in New Orleans and the subtle, yet penetrating wit with which Judge Jackson responded to the KKK couple. These were the lives of so many uncommon, yet mostly unknown people. My memories of them would inspire me for the rest of my life.

I remembered the oystering couple whose boat was adrift, heading for the violent sea. Their faith in God seemed unshakable in their time of great need. Their example encouraged me.

And then there was Warren. Although he certainly would laugh at the comparison, he was like an angel delivered right to me—to teach me and train me with what I would never have imagined I would need to know.

In about an hour I would be at the mouth of the Rio Grande, the border between my country and Mexico. There would be no more stopping, although I'm sure that along this part of Texas there were enough fascinating people and places to keep me another year.

It didn't matter now, I was ready to finish.

Knowing when to end a stimulating adventure is an art. A great journey, a brilliant conversation, a superb meal can grow tiresome, irritating, and dull when they go on too long. And this journey was right on the verge of going on too long. I found I was tiring of people, of new places, of sand and sun. I no longer paused for sunsets normally potent enough to silence me for an hour.

Ahead of me, gliding a couple inches above the jade-green bay water, was a single adult pelican. I slowed only slightly so we could glide together at the same speed. Its long wings curved up at the ends and did not flap; occasionally a wingtip brushed the top of the water that undulated like silk.

The pelican could see me keeping pace with it, yet it did not swerve away or land in the water. We shared the easy freedom of this warm afternoon. Sometimes the Gulf gave out this kind of day as a gift, a kind of reward for sticking with it through the brutal storms and the steaming heat. It was just the day I deserved to finish this long journey, this adventure that I could not have done without the *Cooper.*

I'd observed hundreds of pelicans on this journey, and I had begun to feel like we had a lot in common. They are far from the most graceful sea bird. When they are young, in fact, they can be amazingly clumsy. Many young pelicans break their necks when they are first learning to dive into the water to catch fish. But if those first headlong dives don't kill them, they gradually learn grace along with survival. Eventually they learn to glide the way this pelican seemed to be gliding, the way my boat and I were dancing over the water now—just for the joy of it.

I came to where the Rio Grande River spilled its waters into the Gulf. I even flew into Mexican waters a short ways. It occurred to me that it would have been nice to continue on down the Mexican coast. I imagined secluded, black-sand bays, tropical waters, spicy foods.

But no, not this time. Part of me would always be singing a traveling song. Lately, though, my heart had been singing the blues. And it was singing loudest and hardest about missing home.

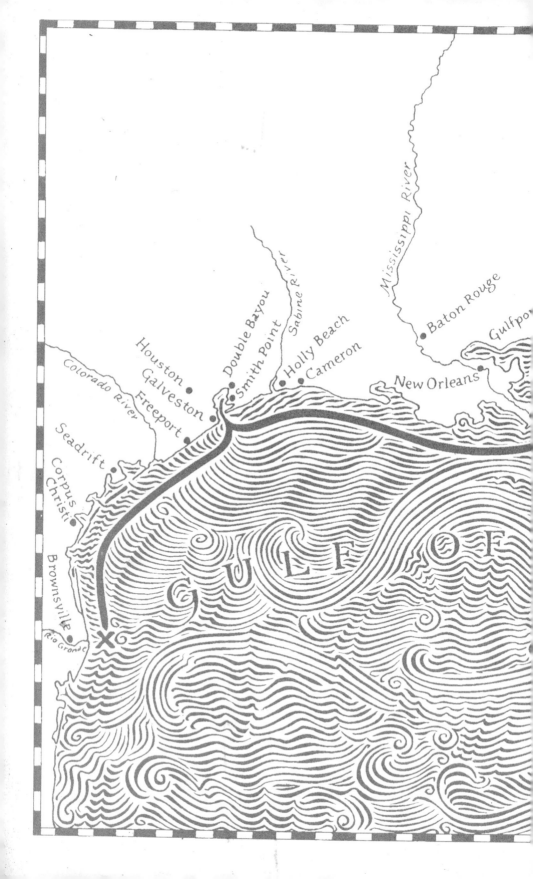

Houston
Galveston
Freeport
Double Bayou
Smith Point
Sabine River
Holly Beach
Cameron
Mississippi River
Baton Rouge
Gulfpo...
New Orleans
Colorado River
Seadrift
Corpus Christi
Brownsville
Rio Grande

G U L F   O F